J Y W N

#LIFE

THE WISDOM OF PHILOSOPHY, PSYCHOLOGY AND POP-CULTURE FOR LIVING A BETTER LIFE

Jym Brown – Peterborough, UK
info@jymbrown.co.uk

First published in 2020

Unless otherwise indicated, all illustrations in this book are by Jym Brown and Vanessa Mendozzi.
Edited by: Ameesha Green (The Book Shelf Ltd)
Cover design and typesetting by: Vanessa Mendozzi
Proofread by:Alex Horton

#Life: The Wisdom of Philosophy, Psychology and Pop-Culture for Living a Better Life.

978-1-8381151-0-4 Paperback
978-1-8381151-1-1 Ebook

www.jymbrown.co.uk

To my family, for making me feel like I am something and to my boys for making me feel like I have something to offer.

"Do not seek after the sages of the past.
Seek what they sought"[1]

Basho

CONTENTS

PART 3: THE JOURNEY

PART 4: CULTIVATING VIRTUE

INTRODUCTION

Living your 'best life', as the younger generation would say, is a social media craze that has swept the Earth. A movement largely predicated upon displays of picturesque settings, loving relationships, and emphatic experiences (or so the pictures would have you believe - #Life). Yet, whatever the motive, the premise is very real. Who would not want to be living their best life? Living a version of their existence not just superior to an alternative, but the most optimal one possible.

Sure, the validity of some of these social media claims could be questioned. The quest for 'likes' and 'followers' in order to validate or even prove our happiness is rather concerning. The use of sayings such as 'it isn't real until it's on Facebook' casts a rather bleak shadow over what is essentially the wonder of human emotion and experience. Questionable motives aside, the essence remains clear. People genuinely want something better for themselves than they currently have and will even resort to pure external gratification alone in order to achieve it, or worse, create its illusion.

The prevailing mindset is a far cry from the vision of wise old philosophers, or contemporary European psychologists. They sought, in their own language and form, to live or help others live out their days as beneficially as they could. There were no media platforms, no subscriptions, no selfies, nor statuses. There was only growing, learning, and if you were lucky, living 'rightly'. But the world of philosophy can feel as daunting as the intrepid cyber façade. Who do we listen to? Who should we like? Which philosopher is currently trending online? How do I make sense of something from 2,000 years ago? What does this outwardly inspiring meme actually mean? These are difficult questions and ones that I hope to answer in the coming chapters.

BACKGROUND

As a lecturer in coaching, development, and education, I spend a great deal of time reading and researching in order to help people improve themselves. Both academically and personally, all of my students are trying to advance themselves from where they are to where they want to go. After a decade of lecturing I have found a few consistent themes in this regard—the most important being that we each have our bespoke challenges, demons, and negative assumptions that hold us back, not just from growing, but from truly living.

My own particular brand of helping people to embark on this journey is by asking tough questions and using an array of often unexpected examples to illustrate the point. From Nietzsche, Confucius, and Aristotle to Homer Simpson, to 80s' movies and public figures, I regularly link the connections that seem so apparent to me, for other people. Sometimes it is not until we see things in the ridiculous that they really hit home. This book is my attempt to share this approach with you. It is my attempt to show you some of the connections that I have made between the scholars of old and the characters of new who have not only helped me, but have also helped those I have worked with.

My own journey through the world of philosophy and psychology began through my own search for explanation. Having struggled with many a health problem, both physically and psychologically, I sought direction, clarity, and insight. I wanted to know why life seemed so easy for everyone else, yet so difficult for me. I wanted to find the things that would magically change my circumstances and make everything 'better'. In some respects, this new learning hasn't changed me; not in a physical sense, anyway. I do indeed still experience many of the issues associated with 'being me'. But the knowledge I have gained from embarking on this journey has helped me to change my 'self' beyond that of my physical condition. Instead, I changed 'me' on a deeper level, a transcendent level.

This book is about helping you to do the same. It is about understanding your existence, what it means to live bravely and with an inquisitive nature. It is about venturing into the unknown in order to find that which you seek. However, what you seek is always just out of grasp. My intention is that by the end of this book, you will have the desire and the tools to help you grab it. You do not need to have a degree in psychology in order to appreciate the content, nor a library full of dusty old books. You just need a willingness to try. I have mixed the different genres of standalone quotations so that they work with each other in order to paint the right picture. If nothing else, you could always follow those quotations alone and you'll grasp the concept of the chapter.

CONTENT

To say there's a long list of potential topics for a book about life is an obvious understatement. There's a reason that the bible, Qu'ran, and Torah are as large as they are. Add to that the copious works of learned scholars, philosophers, and psychologists and you have a near infinite supply of prose to decipher. I am also an avid movie, music, and TV binger, often speaking in the lingo of numerous on-screen characters. Combine all of that together and I am not sure I've had an original thought for some years. However, there are many common themes that occur within philosophy and psychology that are just too hard to ignore.

The subjects that seemed to capture the minds of Socrates, Lao Tzu, Nietzsche, and Russell still populate the memes we so commonly absorb through our phones today. I have brought together a collection of these to try to shed some light on the proverbial mysteries of life and what these visionary people can teach us. But in doing so, I want to show the parallels that exist with modern culture and entertainment. You may be surprised to see the similarities between Homer Simpson and Aristotle, or the candid brilliance of Adam Sandler and the calculated and cool exterior of Bruce Lee.

"I always have a quotation for everything – it saves original thinking."
***Dorothy L. Sayers*[2]**

I have attempted to present a collection of these common themes as something manageable. At times I have had to restrict myself to just a few of the key elements so that this didn't become a Game of Thrones-length piece of work. I have also broken up the content into four parts to make the content more digestible.

Part 1 focuses on the self. This is a loose description in that the entire book is about the self. However, Part 1 concentrates on some core principles that help you to navigate the rest, starting with 'you' at the heart. The book's anchor is one of chaos and order. I use this throughout in order to help bring the content into perspective. The content also leads on from one to the next, building from the power of confronting chaos to investigating who you really are, how we can live in the moment, and how we can take charge of our existence.

Part 2 is about how we learn and develop. It is about how we move forward with greater knowledge and perspective. 'Learning to learn' might sound like a strange idea, but it helps us to accelerate the process of acquiring new knowledge and ability. What have you ever wanted to learn about and know? Do you think it is beyond your reach? Maybe you should think again. Part 2 is also about changing the way you think about life in general, your outlook, and your philosophy (yes, you do already have one). It is about challenging what you believe and why; what you look at and what you really see.

Part 3 is about crafting a journey that takes you closer to human flourishing. From changing the way you look at hardship and threats to identifying and valuing that which invigorates your soul. You'll hear what the great philosophers had to say about being creative and following your passion, combined with the scientific evidence that supports it. We'll discuss what it means to take risks and how they can change your life for the better. Particularly when this is portrayed so aptly by the confessions of the old and dying.

The fourth part explores the ways in which we can cultivate a more virtuous approach to life and how we treat each other. We begin with the removal of petty desires and attachments to objects and status that do not actually improve our lives. You'll also find out how it is possible to buy happiness, or at least how to improve your relationship with acquiring things. Virtues that we genuinely foster and nurture can also help us break the cycle of negative reciprocation, not only improving the lives of others, but ours also. You'll hear the new science around dealing with anger and frustration and what the healthier alternatives appear to be.

Lastly, there are some final words to help summarise the key messages from the book, along with a few things to consider for further thought.

A FINAL WORD BEFORE WE BEGIN

Being a big sports fan, I am often bowled over by the wisdom of John Wooden, arguably the most successful American basketball coach in history. He once remarked that "If you don't have the time to do it right, when will you have the time to do it over?"[3] You may be able to tell here that it wasn't exactly just basketball to which Wooden was referring. It may indeed remind you of such clichés as 'you only get one crack at life'. However, regardless of how you package it, it is no less true. When will you have time to have another go? How long are you going to wait until you learn that language you've always wanted to learn, go on that holiday, start that new career, stop falling for the 'wrong' kind of partner, or figure out why you react the way you do in certain situations, over and over again?

Please also bear in mind that the 'internal enquiry' which you are about to embark upon is neither easy, nor swift. I may be attempting in my own modest way to help make sense of this 'life knowledge' and expedite the process, but applying it is the real challenge. You may even find that the journey along this arduous learning curve is frustrating and abhorrent at times. Indeed, a change in perspective and knowledge can empower you to see not only the best in both yourself and the world, but also the less attractive sides.

"For in much wisdom is much grief; and he that increaseth knowledge increaseth sorrow."
Ecclesiastes 1:18.[4]

Though poignant, it is a rather melancholy perspective for the pursuit of knowledge, but one to which I can personally relate. The clarity of mind that can come as a result of improved insight can be rather overwhelming. But forgoing the 'ignorance is bliss' alternative, we can at least hope that being equipped with the tools for building our own house is a whole lot more liberating than waiting for it to appear on its own.

The famous psychologist Carl Jung once said that "Paradoxical views that are not made conscious (realised and dealt with) will be played out as fate".[5] In other words, you need to look deeply at who you are and identify the contradictions in your actions and thoughts. You may say you are this kind of person who wants these sorts of things, yet often your actions or inner desires may spell out the opposite. What will then happen is that the occurrences and outcomes of your life will appear as if out of your control and even fated for you. Now of course a major thing to acknowledge is that we do not and never will have control over everything that happens in our lives. But the sooner we realise our contradictions, the sooner we can rise above our inner obscurity and at least try to take hold of the reins.

If deep down you want to be living your best life and not just as an Instagram highlight reel, then this book will help you find the wisdom to do so. Through complex and sometimes flamboyant texts, to simpler forms and from very unexpected places, this book will dissect the major messages of wisdom and virtue in a way with which you can relate. The likes of Aristotle proposed a couple of thousand years ago that the pursuit of happiness was the pinnacle of human achievements or desires. Nothing has changed. Ultimately, if this book can help even one person get an inch closer to realising happiness or living their best life, then it has been a worthwhile venture.

Finally, please forgive the male-dominated 'subject' of some of the older quotations used. This is indicative of the period in which it was written and not a reflection of any sort of intended target market or underlying motive. I merely chose to preserve the authenticity and originality of the material, rather than address any gender-specific language. The overarching message of the book is that wisdom can come in any form and from any person. With any luck, you will remember that sentiment and realise the same.

"Happiness is the meaning and the purpose of life, the whole aim and end of human existence."

Aristotle[6]

"Mens sana in corpore sano."
(A sound mind in a healthy body.)
Juvenal[7]

"A sound mind in a sound body, is a short but full description of a happy state in this world."
John Locke[8]

PART 1: THE SELF

CHAPTER 1

IN A WORLD OF CHAOS, CREATE A LITTLE ORDER

"There was no such thing as absolute control, not in a fully functioning universe. There was just a variable amount of lack of control."

Terry Pratchett[1]

The way in which we perceive the world and the events of our lives is predicated on our understanding of the universe and its workings. For many, the knowledge of existence is limited to what we are taught in school and what we pick up from the odd compelling movie. Yet, the fundamental principles discussed in ancient philosophy and religion have the power to shed light on an otherwise gloomy landscape. From the darkness comes the light and from the disordered comes the ordered. Virtually every belief system of any note has advocated this notion, providing incredible narratives to illustrate the process. However, these are more than just fairy tales. These stories hold the key to the appreciation of so many facets of human existence and provide a metaphorical guide to the interpretation of life. If we forgo our judgements and take the time to explore, we can see that the myths and legends of old, regardless of their scientific authenticity, are more powerful that we could have ever imagined.

THE PHILOSOPHY OF 'BEGINNING'

Our universe, existence, and how we came to be has been described in many ways. However, the prevailing thread throughout this delicately woven narrative is one of darkness and chaos in the beginning. Chaos, though not necessarily in the form of its common usage nowadays. The ancient Greeks spoke of chaos arising from the darkness as an unformed state, or a void, if you will. They also believed that chaos and all other things are made of *apeiron*, a divine and infinite element. Everything is made from it and everything will return to it at some point down the line. Development of this concept saw chaos as the disordered state from which the ordered universe as we know it was made. The disordered, the unknown, the mess before structure and form became a reality. Virtually every civilisation sees this notion as a recurring theme. Biblical iterations of creation from nothingness and darkness, Mesopotamian myths of gods controlling the universe to prevent chaos ensuing, and the Norse belief of the initial gaping abyss—*ginnungagap*, before the first creations emerged—all appear to concur. In other words, everything comes from the disordered, the unstructured and chaotic chasm of being. The majority of mythologies and religions appear to also agree that to chaos everything will inevitably return.

*"**Bastian**: Why is it so dark?*
***Empress Moonchild**: In the beginning, it is always dark."*
From the movie 'The NeverEnding Story'[2]

ENTROPY

Interestingly, the mythological ideas also marry with that of the scientific world. In physics, the term 'entropy' refers to the level of randomness and disorder of something and an eventual decline thereafter. The idea is that everything around us—our possessions, the things we can see, feel, and touch—have been brought into existence from no form (or a less ordered state), with entropy being the process that will return it once again.

Imagine creating a wooden toy box. Created from raw wood matter that made little sense until fashioned into a box, this functional and ordered entity subsequently performs the tasks for which it was designed. But leave it long enough (thousands or millions of years) and it will degrade into something no longer resembling a toy box. Hence, entropy. In Stephen Hawking's illustrious work *A Brief History of Time*, Hawking also discusses the concept of disordered states always outnumbering ordered ones.[3] He cites a great example of a jigsaw puzzle having thousands of disordered combinations (that would not create the right image), but only one ordered state (the correct image).

Think about other examples in life. How many different arrangements of the thousands of pieces that make up your car would actually get you to work? If any of the engine pieces were missing or in a different order, the incredible act of combustion and propulsion would not occur and you would be stranded on your driveway. As humans, we tend to ignore how difficult it is to actually make something as we desire it to be. Any portrait artist will tell you that get the facial proportions wrong and you immediately make Scarlett Johansson look like something from the ape family. But our own cognitive biases (see chapter 6 and 7) are such that we ignore the miracle that is something coming to order. We see a relatively ordered world where the design has come to fruition as desired. Through training, measurement, and accurate production, what would be a one-in-a-billion chance of those atoms coming together in this successful form becomes an almost certain occurrence. However, given the laws of entropy, even the most robust of objects will eventually decay. Wood rots, paper disintegrates—and order turns to chaos.

Given the unlikely odds and inevitable regression, you can see that the dice are somewhat loaded in favour of chaos. It may also do a good job of illustrating why order should stand out more to people, as it is that uncommon an event in the grand scheme of things. Yes, our world is full of things brought to order, but universally, anything coming to order is a feat to behold.

Why is this rather bleak view of the world important, you may ask? Well, my intention is not to depress you, but to help illustrate the premise that things are not naturally set to order by default. If anything, you could argue that the natural state of all things is to be chaotic and crazy, and that the rare occasions it is not should be savoured and savoured well. When we think about life this way, it provides new context. Rather than expecting things to work out as a matter of course, we could instead not exactly assume the opposite, but at least appreciate that everything is regressing towards the disordered and therefore we shouldn't be surprised.

At this point I might sound like a poster child for pessimism, but that is not the goal. In reality, the mindset of success, completion, and the logical structure of things requires a psychological shift of expectations. Every day that we enjoy the former, we are enjoying a temporary hiatus from the natural order of things and as such, should appreciate both how great and how fleeting it may be. Rather than pessimism, think appreciation, perspective, and acceptance.

"Normal is an illusion.
What is normal for the spider is chaos for the fly."
Charles Addams[4]

"Chaos was the law of nature.
Order was the dream of man."
Henry B. Adams[5]

"Man plans, God Laughs."
Yiddish proverb [6]

THE BALANCE OF CHAOS AND ORDER

Importantly, there is nothing to say that the aforementioned conclusion is definitively the case. A slightly more proactive interpretation could be that of the Eastern persuasion. Daoism highlights a different strand of thinking in relation to chaos and order that might seem a little more palatable. You may have seen the Yin and Yang symbol, but may not appreciate the nature or origin of its meaning. The two segments depict chaos and order as balanced entities that co-exist. The mirrored image reflects both the need for one and the other, as well as the interplay between the two. We cannot have order without chaos. The Daoists believe that chaos and order also represented the known and unknown, the controllable and uncontrollable, and so forth. Understanding this paradox was to understand the balance of life and existence.

"Thus Something and Nothing produce each other;
The difficult and the easy complement each other;
The long and the short off-set each other;
The high and the low incline towards each other;
Note and sound harmonize with each other;
Before and after follow each other."
Lao Tzu [7]

"It is the way of heaven to take from what has in excess in order to make good what is deficient."
Lao Tzu [8]

The parallels with science's entropy are described more in the form of the *Tao Te Ching*, where 'Tao' is said to be the process of 'turning back'. Turning back, referring to the inevitable dynamism of the universe, but more cyclical in nature and ever so slightly more optimistic than that of entropy. It further demonstrates the need for opposites to complement one another in a harmonious dance and interplay of push and pull, where nothing (apart from the process of Tao itself, of course) remains the same.

Figure 1. Yin and Yang – the balance of chaos and order

The Daoists believed that the best way to live was to walk the line of chaos and order, intentionally maintaining the balance of life however you can. The sentiment here is extremely deep. Consider learning, for example. If you are to be entrenched on the side of order, you are, for want of a better phrase, 'in your comfort zone'. You are safe in the knowledge of what you 'know' to be right. You do not allow yourself to question that which you hold to be true. You have no reason to venture into the unknown, for the unknown is scary and full of embarrassing possibilities, poor assumptions, and naïve opinions. We may all know someone (possibly ourselves) who fits this bill. Perhaps you may throw my way that 'ignorance is bliss'. However ignorance is still, well, ignorance. Especially when it causes unfathomable atrocities, unhealthy prejudices, or just simple obliviousness.

The alternative is to venture into the unknown, into the chaos, and into the void. The Daoists would argue that this is where real truth, growth, and learning are obtained. Walking the line of chaos and order is to have one foot in either camp. Measuring your assumed knowledge with that of the new, questioning your actions, and testing alternative strategies. The hugely influential philosopher, Immanuel Kant, described enlightenment as a process of 'daring to know', which can easily be likened to that of exploring chaos, in whatever form that need take. Couple this with the biblical commands of God to Abraham:

"Go from your country, your people and your father's household to the land I will show you."
Genesis 12:1[9]

Simply, leave what you know and venture forth into the unknown. Let go of what is safe for what is new and uncharted. It is the proverbial 'red pill versus blue pill' option faced by Neo in the existential action movie, *The Matrix*. Where the 'blue' option sees life unchanged, unchallenged, and predictable. Whereas the 'red pill' explores a territory and reality unbeknown to the iconic hero.

"After this, there is no turning back. You take the blue pill—the story ends, you wake up in your bed and believe whatever you want to believe. You take the red pill—you stay in Wonderland, and I show you how deep the rabbit hole goes. Remember: all I'm offering is the truth. Nothing more."
From 'The Matrix'[10]

Now this may sound a little irresponsible. You may be thinking that this all smacks of drama and self-indulgence. However, please take this with a pinch of salt. I am not talking about uncalculated or unmitigated risks that put you or others in danger (we will discuss 'risk-taking' in chapter 9). It may be as simple as taking up a new hobby, learning a new skill, understanding a new perspective, and so on. Regardless, it is an exploration into something you are not familiar with.

FLOW

So, if chaos is to be explored to challenge our own 'order' and create a better self, should we just dive right in? Surely, if I am to learn and grow more rapidly, all I need do is charge headfirst into whatever I do not know? Much like the balanced view of Yin and Yang, there are other perspectives that take a measured approach. Csikszentmihalyi's seminal work *Flow* illustrates this point very well.[11] Briefly, 'flow' is 'optimal experience' and a heightened state of consciousness that makes us feel content, happy, and totally immersed in what we are doing. To illustrate this, Figure 2 shows a graph where 'challenges faced' and 'skills possessed' to meet those challenges are plotted as y and x axes respectively on a graph. If we draw a line from where the two axes meet at a 45-degree angle (otherwise known as a positive correlation), we find what Csikszentmihalyi calls the 'optimum flow state'.

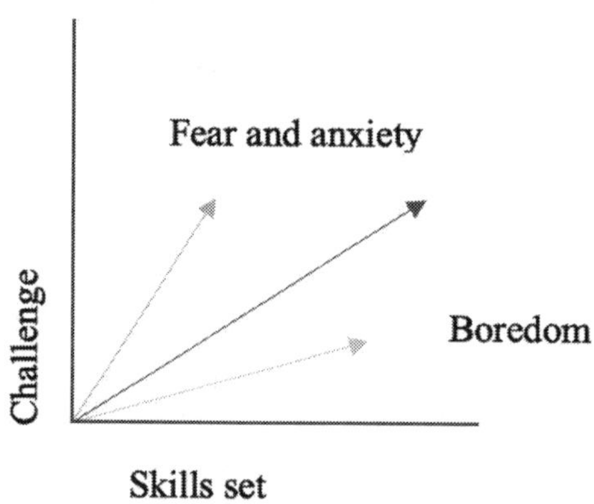

Figure 2. Adapted from Csikszentmihalyi's *Flow*[11]

However, if we were to draw a line at a steeper angle toward challenge, the increased demand leads to anxiety in the individual, due to the perception of being ill-equipped to deal with the scenario (see Figure 3). On the other hand, draw the line at a shallower angle towards skill and the capability of the individual is too strong in comparison to the challenge, and boredom arises. In essence, Csikszentmihalyi tries to illustrate that we all have a point at which we obtain flow, or our peak state of learning and operation. You might be familiar with terms such as the 'zone', where athletes, musicians, and professionals from a multitude of disciplines find themselves completely immersed in what they are doing. They are in a state of flow and have found their balance, so to speak.

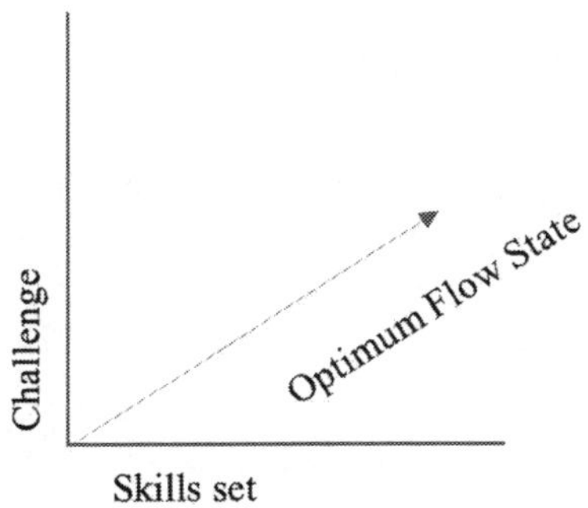

Figure 3. Indicating what causes anxiety and boredom[11]

Sport psychologists have explored this concept in a similar guise, that of 'Challenge and Threat States'.[12] Along with 'Catastrophe Theory', these are the dominant explanations for what is commonly known as 'choking' in sport.[13] The build-up of anxiety when our perceived abilities are viewed to be less than required for the task at hand, and the subsequent crash in performance when that anxiety is too high. This strikes a chord with the popular movie *A Knight's Tale*. Imagine your internal monologue telling itself:

"You have been weighed, you have been measured and you have been found wanting."
***A Knight's Tale (paraphrased from the book of Daniel 5:27)*[14]**

Consider, then, that the 'flow' state is essentially likened to that of the divide between Yin and Yang. The optimum balance between what you are comfortable doing and what you are not comfortable doing, what you can cope with and what you cannot. The threshold at which the greatest amount of learning and development occurs. Walk the line to find your flow state.

"The important thing in life is not triumph, but the struggle."
***Pierre De Coubertin (Founder of the Modern Olympic Games)*[15]**

"It is open to every man to choose the direction of his striving; And also every man may draw comfort from Lessing's fine saying, that the search for truth is more precious than its possession."
***Albert Einstein*[16]**

"You must do the thing you cannot do."
***Eleanor Roosevelt*[17]**

CONVERTING CHAOS TO FIND FULFILMENT

We have established a theoretical baseline for existence, that of disorder, and have talked about the relationship between that and the known. We have also highlighted the balance struck that provides the greatest opportunity for growth; grasping just beyond your reach, so to speak. Yet you may not feel sufficiently inspired. It is all well and good walking the line, but to what end? What direction do I take and what aspects of life do I apply this to? Fulfilment may well be the answer. Fulfilment, written so easily and yet obtained with such difficultly. Fulfilment, in my humble opinion, is a more apt concept for optimum human endeavour than that of happiness. But how is one to be fulfilled? This is a huge question in itself and one that we will address throughout the book, but for the sake of this small chapter, let's focus on the aforementioned theories. Daoist, biblical, and Greek philosophies would suggest that the movement towards a higher plane is a good start. Much like Heath Ledger earlier in A Knight's Tale, it is aligning yourself towards your north star, your big dreams or the best version of yourself. It is identifying where that star is and then utilising the theories of flow and balance in order to get there. As Jordan Peterson, the charismatic clinical psychiatrist, would say, "What better do you have to do with your time than that?" Rightly so…

The direction you take in life is therefore plotted against your graph of flow, your Yin and Yang. I actually like to think of fulfilment itself as being the process of 'converting chaos to order'. Turning the unknown into the known, the untravelled into the well-trodden. The objective is not having everything exactly the way you want it, for that would lead to the boredom discussed earlier. Instead, it is seeking out the chaos and turning it into the opposite. However, trying to marry this with the concepts of entropy leaves me pondering—if disorder is our base line and chaos our default setting, what good is it trying to bend it to our will? I think of it like the majority of goal-setting strategies (which we will come to soon), with our big goals broken up into smaller goals. Take, for example, trying to climb a mountain (our major goal). The entire journey is fraught with disorder. We stumble, trip, and fall. Yet with every step, in at least some small measure, we convert a little piece of chaos to order. Every mound overcome, every new peak reached, are all small conversions taking place. All the while accepting that we may indeed fall, and that is okay. After all, that is the nature of things (entropy). But to climb is to succeed in the conversion and the conversion creates the sense of fulfilment.

"Two roads diverged in a wood and I –
I took the one less travelled by,
and that has made all the difference."
***Robert Frost*[18]**

"The ultimate purpose of life, mind, and human striving: to deploy energy and information to fight back the tide of entropy and carve out refuges of beneficial order. An underappreciation of the inherent tendency toward disorder, and a failure to appreciate the precious niches of order we carve out, are a major source of human folly."
***Steven Pinker*[19]**

Similar to my own conclusions, Pinker explains fighting back the tide of entropy as the ultimate purpose of life. He talks of precious niches or small elements of order that provide the required refuge for a fulfilling life. This idea of working from the small to the big as a method of obtaining order is echoed by many other prominent thinkers and philosophers. Notably, the retired United States Admiral, William McRaven, who once said:

"If you want to change the world, start off by making your bed... If you make your bed every morning, you will have accomplished the first task of the day. It will give you a small sense of pride, and it will encourage you to do another task and another and another...
... And if by chance you have a miserable day, you will come

home to a bed that is made, that you made. And a made bed gives you encouragement that tomorrow will be better."
William H. McRaven[20]

In what has become a hugely popular meme of today, Jordan Peterson has commented:

"Your room (Bedroom), part of the cosmos that you can get to grips with...
If you want to organise your psyche... start by cleaning your room."
Jordan B. Peterson[21]

Both McRaven and Peterson do a fantastic job of making the complex extremely simple. They provide the proverbial paddle boat to help you defeat the tide. Take on the simple task of ordering the chaos of your bedroom and watch it spread, not just into your world, but into everyone else's as well. The escalation of this motivation will then be such that more and more, larger and larger tasks will be both attempted and achieved. A domino effect, if you will, where each domino is another progressive and beneficial step towards fulfilment. Peterson has also remarked on 'doing what you know you should do, but are avoiding', where avoidance is following the flow of entropy, but making a conscious choice to do what you know you should is to resist the tyranny of chaos.

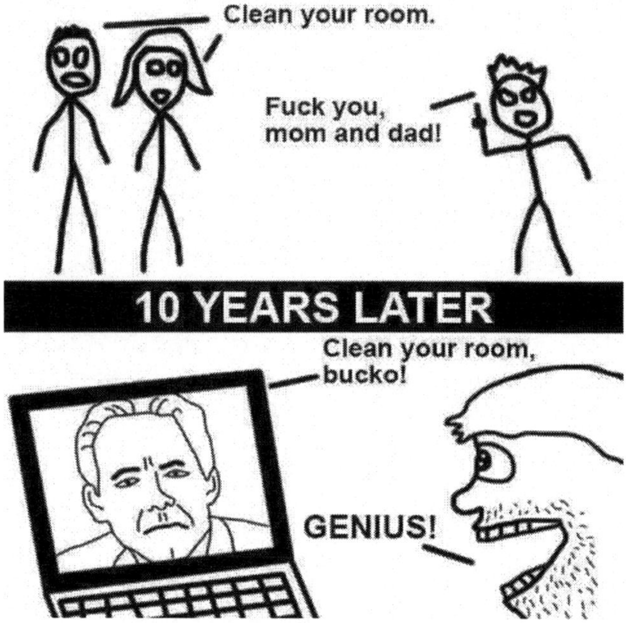

Figure 4. 'Clean your room, Bucko'

Jordan B. Peterson[21]

The meme in Figure 4 comically shows the scepticism of such a remark. Whilst very funny, it does help to show a key difference in the message being conveyed. On the one hand, the often-dictated axiom of 'clean your room' is impressed upon the youth from the ever-caring parents. In later chapters, we will discuss the value of autonomy, but for now let's just highlight this as 'an external demand placed upon the individual'. If we consider the natural urge for rebellion indicative of many an adolescent, it becomes easy to see why this 'wisdom' is somewhat lost on the target. Conversely, the realisation of creating structure where it does not exist is an entirely different revelation. The inference being 'realisation', rather than being told to do something. Being told is not venturing into your own personal unknown or Yin. On the contrary, it may just be the anchor for your Yang, the safe harbour for your ship. Or indeed it could be an ever-too-strong bearer of chaos, insurmountable for someone that young. One could also comment on the need to have lived through a certain amount of chaos first, in order to really appreciate the value in bending it to your will, that perhaps evades the majority of children. Either way, the sentiment appears clear.

To pull on this thread some more, the concepts of starting small, doing what you normally want to avoid and cleaning your room, have striking similarities with well-known ‘home help’ movements such as Hygge, Feng Shui and KonMari.[22] All of which stress the importance in one way or another of removing clutter, tidying, and organising your place of being. Mere coincidence or not? Scandinavian and Eastern cultures concur on having a tidy home and a tidy mind.[23] I am sure we have all felt this feeling after a big deep clean and tidy of our home or room. The sense of relief, tranquillity, and of being cleansed. But why is this? Well, the likes of Dr Joseph Ferrari and colleagues have found connections between cluttered and unorganised areas with a lack of focus, inability to process information, increased stress, and even depression.[24] It is as if the build-up of chaos around you creates a barrier to normal function.

The process of tidying and cleaning is thought to provide an ordered base from which to tackle life. Imagine spreading the order, rather than just fighting back the chaos, and growing your base from the epicentre of that which is your room/home until you can properly align other aspects of your life. We’re not talking about Obsessive Compulsive Disorder[25] here, rather a healthy and pragmatic view of organisation that is beneficial for your state of mind. Stoic philosophers also comment on the purity of simplicity in the home and what that does for the individual. Marcus Aurelius once wrote that “Very little is needed to make a happy life”.[26] Putting aside the conundrum of attachment to belongings, the removal of distractions, organising the clutter, and cleaning house can provide that motivating spark towards getting your life on track.

HOPE AND A BETTER ALTERNATIVE?

The idea that chaos can be converted may be the necessary fuel for hope itself. Hope is a belief in a different and better alternative or outcome. It is the internal psychological manifestation of previous victories against chaos. Without hope then, we have very little in our arsenal with which to battle entropy. This point is made well in the movie *The NeverEnding Story*,[9] where the concepts of hope and entropy (or nothingness in this instance) are discussed:

"***Atreyu:*** *But why is Fantasia dying, then?*

G'mork: *Because people have begun to lose their hopes and forget their dreams.*
So the Nothing grows stronger.

Atreyu: *What is the Nothing?*

G'mork: *It's the emptiness that's left. It's like a despair, destroying this world. And*
I have been trying to help it.

Atreyu: *But why?*

G'mork: *Because people who have no hopes are easy to control. And whoever has control has the Power.*"

The more sinister character in this exchange is alluding to control and power being possessed by either ourselves or entropy itself. Whilst the belief in absolute 'control' is but an illusion, it would appear it does make a statement of intent and one that can either be constructive or destructive in nature. Believing that we have the power to try to convert chaos into order, at least to some extent, provides hope and thereby the spark for appropriate action. Conversely, there are many philosophical perspectives that would question this, but these will be discussed at length in chapter 7.

Suffice to say that for now, life provides more than enough opportunity for conversion, as long as we are prepared to see it that way.

"Hope springs eternal in the human breast:
Man never Is, but always To be blest."
Alexander Pope[27]

GOAL-SETTING FOR A BETTER EXISTENCE

If we are to bring about a better existence in our lives, the points discussed would suggest that the following are required:

- A willingness to engage in the unknown
- Awareness of your current skill set/order
- A north star with which to align yourself (larger goals)
- Manageable pieces of chaos that you can convert (smaller goals)

Remembering that goals are achieved through the conversion of some form of chaos to that of order, the degree of effort required to do so will be greater for larger goals than for smaller goals. The larger the goal or the more complex the system, the greater the tide of entropy. As such, our large goals can be broken up into a *matryoshka* (Russian nesting dolls) of smaller and smaller goals. The larger the doll, the greater the effort or indeed maintenance of the effort required in order to achieve them. Fortunately for us, the effort/goal relationship is mutual in nature. The more entropy we overcome, the more it will seem like the effort was worth it all along.

"Goals justify the effort they demand at the outset but
later it is the effort that justifies the goal."
Mihalyi Csikszentmihalyi[28]

The setting of our goals is then the last thing to consider. One way to help construct these is to consider the balance of outcome versus process goals. Briefly, outcome goals are a desired end result or the attainment of things sometimes out of our control. 'To be the most successful computer software manufacturer of 2020' or to 'win the league next year' might be an overarching goal that fits this bill. Much like the Russian doll analogy, outcome goals can be made up of smaller outcome goals to aid the process of chaos conversion. However, due to the fact that outcome goals are dependent on external conditions (entropy, economics, other players, injuries etc.) and not just our own actions, complete reliance on them is not advised.

Outcome goals may provide the most common 'north stars' for people, however the utilisation of process goals (strong influencers of outcome goals) is advised. Process goals are strategies and habits that make the desired outcomes more likely. Take, for example, the goal of 'maintain a healthy mind'. What processes could we target in order to make this more likely? An obvious one would be 'consistently keep your room tidy'. Another might be 'write in your journal each day'. These sorts of adjustments, often small in nature, are the basis of huge changes. Making constructive process or habitual goal changes is what James Clear refers to as 'Atomic Habits'.[29]

Whatever the goals or the *processes* you choose, they are dependent on your actions. They are pieces of chaos that you can directly influence. Importantly, everyone's chaos is particular to them and therefore so are their goals. From outcomes to processes, small goals to large goals, it is up to you to march forward into the unknown and discover them for yourself.

FINAL THOUGHTS

Whether your view is of a Doaist perspective (cyclical in nature) or a scientific one (entropy-based), the idea seems consistent; from chaos comes order and from the unknown comes the known. The former viewpoint tells us that there is a requirement of chaos to upset the order, so that we have something with which to work. If we were to have everything perfect and just the way we want it, we would really have nothing. Nothing with which to engage, to do battle with, or to convert. As a result, we would never experience flow or obtain optimal experience that brings about true happiness or fulfilment. Our abilities need to be pitted against a worthy opponent, challenging us just beyond our reach if we are to grow and succeed in achieving our goals.

Our goals provide the direction of our efforts, which in turn validate one another. The greater the goal, the greater the effort required; the greater the effort, the greater the goal that can be achieved. But to stare straight into the darkness where our abilities appear substandard in comparison to the challenge is to evoke a potentially paralysing outcome in itself. Instead, the use of small and process-oriented goals to grow our basis of order helps us fight back the tide of entropy and bring light to the darkest of corners. By walking the line towards our north star, we find that the battle with chaos is not just necessary, but thrilling. We can indeed achieve more than just a simple act of conversion. We can reorder our universe and we can liberate our soul.

"Civilization exists by geological consent, subject to change without notice."

Will Durant[30]

CHAPTER 2

KNOW THYSELF—OVERCOME THYSELF

"Man know thyself; Then though shalt know the universe and God."
***Pythagoras*[1]**

"I never apologize... I'm sorry, but that's the way I am."
***Homer Simpson*[2]**

If our chaos is the place in which flow and real human growth is obtained, without an in-depth knowledge of who we are, can we ever really be equipped with the insight required to move forward? If you don't know yourself – you don't know where your own order ends and your chaos begins. Without this information, you cannot begin to meaningfully interact with the world or begin to make a better you. To 'know thyself' then, is the deconstruction of who you are as an individual and an investigation into not only what makes you 'you', but also into the 'what can I be?' In a world of instant gratification and interpersonal comparison, many often neglect to look inward rather than outward. But it is during this inward gaze that we explore things that often elude us. Am I quite what I portray to the world? And if I am, should I want to be? What could I be if I attended to all that which requires it? Who would I be if I did not?

In discovering who we are, we journey along a difficult path that, if poorly managed, can ultimately lead as much to ambiguity and torture as it can clarity and improvement. Yet, if we heed the advice of philosophers and psychologists, and genuinely acknowledge who and what we are, it can empower us to accept, nurture, and grow our 'self' into what it can be. We can highlight the contradictions that plague our personality (see the Homer Simpson quote!), battle our demons, and gain greater perspective on the faults and virtues of others. Thus, to truly 'know thyself' may be a reflection like no other, requiring more than just a mirror in order to see.

HISTORY

To 'know thyself' is one of the most commonly discussed phrases within philosophy and a maxim advocated by many cultures. It also forms the basis of the modern 'reflective practice', where individuals seek to explore their own minds and think introspectively of their behaviour, ways of thinking, and further actions. The first quote in this chapter was said to have been inscribed on the famous Temple of Apollo in Greece (circa 400–500BC) and is considered one of the 'Delphic maxims'. The phrase was attributed to virtually every Greek philosopher thereafter, appearing both in plays and other forms of scripture and teachings. The tradition has been continued even after the Roman destruction of Greek cultures in the mid-first century AD. The works of literary giants throughout millennia has seen the concept of 'knowing thyself' reinforced again and again. We might conclude, therefore, that there may be something to this axiom. So much so that the ancient Greeks do not seem to be alone in reporting its importance. A similar inscription was also said to be found in ancient Egypt:

"Man, know thyself, and you are going to know the gods."
***Inscription from Luxor Temple, Egypt*[3]**

"Self-knowledge – an ancient remedy so old that its value is easily forgotten... the reason the advice is so often repeated is that it works."
***Mihalyi Csikzentmihalyi*[4]**

The temple inscription suggests a movement towards the divine. The message is suggesting that to know yourself, absolutely, means bringing you closer to the loftiest of positions. The thought that being more in tune with yourself elicits a better quality of human being, perhaps? That knowing exactly who and what you are means a life more in accordance with our highest aspirations? Funnily enough, this sentiment is echoed in other parts or the world and in other times. Marcus Aurelius of the Roman Empire discussed (when talking about the self) that:

"It is in my control to do nothing contrary to my god and the divinity within me – no one can force me to this offence."
***Marcus Aurelius*[5]**

The mindset of Aurelius is shared across a multitude of religions and beliefs, that internal divinity is bestowed upon us all and that to act in accordance with this (our 'self') is the primary objective. The self, as described by the renowned psychologist Carl Jung, is:

"The archetype of wholeness and the regulating centre of the psyche ... a transpersonal power that transcends the ego."
***Carl Jung*[6]**

Interestingly here, is the suggestion of transcending the ego or essentially separating the sense of self from that of the ego or of going further. This, as we'll see, is a vital part of 'knowing thyself' and something we will discuss shortly. Jung goes on to say:

"The 'self' might equally be called the 'God within us'."
Carl Jung[7]

Again, we see the suggestion of the divine or holy within us. If we combine this sentiment with that of the earlier maxims in the chapter, we can arrive at the conclusion of 'knowing thyself' as a means of bringing us closer to the epitome of human experience, existence, and thus becoming more divine. But what does all this mean? Well, to put it mildly, we all have the capability and requirement to expend effort to get to know ourselves more intimately, if we are to live a better life. This is not the job of the holy or divine, but of us as individuals. For if the divine resides within us, we have all we need to get the job done. Alexander Pope said it well:

"Know then thyself, presume not God to scan; The proper study of mankind is man."
Alexander Pope[8]

SELF-REFLECTION VERSUS SELF-DESTRUCTION

Before we go any further, it is worth making a few clarifications as to what is meant by knowing ourselves. The journey of finding out who we are is as much to do with identifying 'what' we are rather than 'why' we are. The difference between the two might seem incidental at first, however research has shown that a simple shift in phrasing of the question can make a big impact. The work of organisational psychologists like Tasha Eurich has shown that people who ask 'why' in regard to aspects of themselves are actually less intuitive and knowledgeable about themselves than 'what' thinkers.[9] The reason appears to be that in asking 'why', we tend to dwell on supposed and often inaccurate reasons for certain eventualities (we'll discuss some of those reasons in chapter 6). Whereas asking 'what' questions allows us to investigate ourselves from an open-minded and information-seeking perspective, without the associated negativity and blame. So asking 'why am I the way I am?' is not as effective as asking 'what type of person am I?'

Interestingly, 'what' questions also help to articulate our emotions. In doing so, we disrupt the more negatively charged responses that originate in the amygdala and thus remain calmer and more objective.[10] But 'why' questions are still valuable when combined with a self-distanced or 'detached' perspective attained through a third-person view and achieved through aspects of mindfulness and meditation (see chapter 3).[11] This is where we see a further distinction between what we'll call self-reflection (careful consideration of 'what' we are and what we have done)[13] and rumination (negatively dwelling on why we are the way we are etc.).[12] For the purposes of the rest of the chapter, we'll continue under the assumption of facilitating self-reflection, asking 'what' questions. In the times that we do ask 'why', we will be doing so whilst urging a third-person perspective and thus not ruminating.

"Detached reflection upon experience, a realistic weighing of options and their consequences, have long been held to be the best approach to a good life."
Mihalyi Csikszentmihalyi[14]

Even in using 'what' questions to elicit this valuable introspective knowledge, there will likely be some potential negativity associated with doing so. We may not actually like what we find. But in order to move forward, we must first find out what we are dealing with (reflect). We have to peer into the chaos of our self in order to bring about the Yang of self-development.

UNDERSTANDING OURSELVES

To know ourselves is to understand ourselves. It is something that requires cognitive effort in order to glean from our minds that which is available. Actively seeking, rather than inactively perceiving, if you will. It means to strip away everything else and ask pertinent questions. What are you really like? Are you honest, virtuous, insecure, arrogant, fearful, or combative? Are you beneficial to those around you, or are you draining? Are you fulfilled, happy, or depressed? What makes you tick, what ignites the flame inside of you, and what makes you retreat into yourself? This 'active seeking' initiation of cognitive effort and deep introspection does come at a cost, however. It requires us to see past the illusion of appearance, the image we create for ourselves and others, in order to observe what is really there.

> *"If you seek the kernel then you must break the shell. And likewise, if you would know the reality of Nature, you must destroy the appearance, and the further you go beyond the appearance, the nearer you will be to the Essence."*
> ***Meister Eckhart***[15]

To look inward is therefore to 'break the shell' of yourself, to get closer to the essence of you. As you can no doubt imagine, breaking your own shell is not always easy or pleasant, but as the quote illustrates, it is an essential step along the journey to 'knowing thyself'. Fortunately, this inward-facing exploration in order to educate yourself on who you are is empowering and actually mirrors the process of education itself. The term 'education' is derived from the Latin words *educare* (to nourish or bring up), *educere* (to bring forth), and *educatum* (training and teaching). The emphasis being placed upon helping people to look within to find the answers and bringing forth both the true self and true knowledge. Galileo once wrote that "you cannot teach a man anything, you can only help him to find it within himself", further suggesting the need for self-exploration, rather than external dictation as a means of proper education.

*"**Neytiri**: You have a strong heart. No fear. But stupid! Ignorant like a child!*
***Jake Sully**: Well, if I'm like a child, then look, maybe you should teach me.*
***Neytiri**: Sky People cannot learn, you do not See.*
***Jake Sully**: Then teach me how to See.*
***Neytiri**: No one can teach you to See"."*
***From the movie 'Avatar'**[16]*

A sense of ownership is required to take up the challenge of internal investigation. Ownership that lets us come out of ourselves with newly acquired self-knowledge and self-awareness, which is extremely powerful for life.

"Knowing yourself is the beginning of all wisdom."
***Aristotle**[17]*

If the answers are said to reside within us, then all we need do is look inside to find them, right? This may seem pretty simple at first, however, as we have already found, our true self is often protected with the images we portray, the barriers we build, and the egos we protect. What results is often a reticence to engage with an honest assessment of who you are, stifling knowledge acquisition before it has even begun. It is much easier and safer to remain shrouded in falsity, naivety and indecision than face up to what is really going on. Especially given human beings' proclivity for deception at many levels.

"Man is least himself when he talks in his own person.
But if you give him a mask, he will tell you the truth."
Oscar Wilde[18]

Indeed, the difficulty with introspection of this kind can also come in the form of sheer reflective ability. In the world of Reflective Practice, there is an abundance of evidence to suggest that we all face barriers to how well we can reflect on certain things, especially ourselves. Examples such as reflective ability, emotional content, education, cultural implications, awareness of appropriate techniques etc., all contribute to our difficulty to reflect. Compound this with the difficulty in truly seeing ourselves and all our flaws/glory and we have a torrid task on our hands.

"Don't forget that I cannot see myself, that my role is
limited to being the one who looks in the mirror."
Jacques Rigaut[19]

The issue of perspective illustrated in this quote highlights the difficulty we all face. This may be a reason for the apparent discrepancy between our incredible ability to find both fault and good in others, and our decidedly underwhelming tendency to do the same in ourselves. Yet this is thought to be exactly the imbalance we should seek to address. Turning the microscope around for a change, seeing what we have otherwise been missing.

A great example of how we can easily turn the camera is to use an 'ideal' upon which to compare and contrast our actions. In the ancient Mesopotamia of 3,000 BC, for example, the king would be taken through a ritual once a year that stripped him of all his regalia. This process reduced him to that of any other community member or peasant, removing one of his obvious barriers to reflection. He would be asked to discuss all the ways in which he had not been virtuous or a worthy representative of Marduk, their favoured deity. This may serve as a great example to some of us who may feel beyond this level of introspection; for if a king were happy to look into the chasm of his being and bare his soul for the benefit of himself and others, then I am pretty sure we all can.

The use of some sort of ideal or predetermined set of values can be a great help, however it can be a little detrimental if we choose the wrong model. Paralysis of action, self-deprecation, and negativity can easily be derived if we are to take an all-too-stringent approach and 'marry' ourselves to our ideal. As was suggested earlier in this chapter, a healthy and balanced approach towards our questioning is what is required. Targeting the virtues of Mother Teresa or Gandhi may seem like an inspiring idea, yet in reality it may not be conducive to modern living, or sanity for that matter. Instead, 'knowing thyself' could centre around key tenets of your personality, such as acknowledging what your major faults are and the accentuation of your major strengths for personal development. For many of us, this could be as simple as addressing an 'argumentative nature' and trying to be less combative when interacting with people.

"It's silly to try to escape other people's faults. They are inescapable. Just try to escape your own."

Marcus Aurelius[20]

"Learn to ask of all actions, 'Why are they doing that?' Starting with your own."

Marcus Aurelius[21]

Aurelius made his thoughts on the matter quite clear. You are not only the beginning, but also the most important aspect of analysis. Philosophers agree that the ownership of these faults, and the generation of the tendency to look at yourself long before casting aspersions at others, is a beautiful and cathartic quality. It helps to overcome the ego and break down the walls of your self-perception that may otherwise be clouding your judgement. Often, we have bought into our level of self-importance assumptions of ability and grandiose judgements of who 'I' really am. Whilst recent research suggests that we are in general more accurate at assessing ourselves than someone else would be, that doesn't mean that we are addressing these aspects of our personalities appropriately, or indeed reguarly.[22]

The detached self-reflection mentioned earlier is a great starting tool to combat this issue. Some of the deeper insights that we can glean from within come from 'meta-perspectives', or seeing yourself through someone else's eyes. This is a great way of avoiding our proclivity for only noticing evidence that supports our current idea of ourselves.

"Know yourself. Don't accept your dog's admiration as conclusive evidence that you are wonderful."
Ann Landers[23]

"Self-awareness is not self-centeredness, and spirituality is not narcissism. 'Know thyself' is not a narcissistic pursuit."
Marianne Williamson[24]

This last quote also makes an excellent point. Whilst I may have highlighted the 'accentuation of positives' as a key element of reflection, it does not mean that we fall into the trap of constant self-praising or self-justification. Even the most obvious narcissist might extol the value of 'knowing thyself', a tool that has incidentally helped them to develop this inflated sense of self-worth. Instead, the analysis of who you are is about putting on your most objective pair of spectacles, not to perpetuate your ego, but to highlight necessary information in spite of how potentially embarrassing it may be.

BEING YOURSELF

There is a tendency nowadays for people to not only hold the belief but to praise the value in 'being yourself'. Whilst this is to some extent psychologically healthy, a more detrimental aspect can arise with people convincing themselves that their otherwise negative or harmful attributes and actions are 'just the way they are'. This 'acceptance' of faults, behaviours, and beliefs is often wrapped up in a person's identity, meaning that they take on the persona of 'themselves' as an easier alternative to interrogating what their actions really mean.

We can see this in many guises: the grumpy old men who won't change their ways, even though we can all see that they are aware of the often negative or stifling repercussions; the young 'goth' dressed all in black and hanging out in cemeteries; and the overtly extravagant or flamboyant individual who appears to be trying to make up for their insecurities, may all be examples of such acceptance. All would likely say that this is 'who they are', yet those close to them may be able to say otherwise. Being true to yourself and accepting the current version of yourself are two entirely different things. The conundrum is living in accordance with the best version of yourself, rather than accepting a lesser, more convenient, or disguised one. Just as Aurelius said earlier, ask yourself, "Why are you doing that?" "What drives you to act/dress/respond this way?" "Is this really 'you' or just the façade you put up in order to achieve a particular reaction?" Philosophy and psychology are all for living true to thyself and being comfortable in one's own skin, but only if it is honestly you. Honesty, therefore, is a prized entity and crucial to this journey of self-discovery.

"The single most powerful thing I can be is to be myself."
Dwayne Johnson[25]

With regard to an honest pursuit of inner wisdom, one must delve into the aforementioned motives for action. I have often found that when discussing the above, I regularly receive the justification of 'that's just who I am' or 'that's just what I like' etc. Indeed, neuroscientists are still baffled by something as simple as 'why do we like something'. So, you could argue that simply gravitating towards a sense of dress, for example, is purely an innate and (currently) indecipherable phenomenon. However, these tendencies to like something can also be more complex. As is often the case, group-based identity can play a role in this 'innate' preference.

Consider the 'goth' boy or girl dressed in black (or the appropriate colour of choice), behaving in a certain way, and listening to certain types of music. Is it not odd that numerous examples of these unexplained likes happen to coincide so neatly? In identity-based social psychology, we see a different explanation. People obtain a sense of self-worth and happiness based upon their sense of belonging to different groups. We each belong to a multitude of different social groups, from male/female, mothers, brothers, teachers, Labour voters, pet owners, and football fans. In some regard, the list of social identities is endless. Research suggests that the more social groups we belong to, the happier we are[26]. What's more is that the more strongly we identify with those groups, the more we feel we belong. Hence wearing the same clothes and football shirts, chanting the same slogans and reading the same books. We therefore act a certain way yet again to receive acceptance both from other people and ourselves. Even the supposed 'individual', who tries so hard to be so that they then join the group of other 'individuals' who are also trying to stand out from the crowd. Thus obtaining a sense of belonging to yet another, though less obvious, social group.

"Above all, review in your mind those you have seen in empty struggles, refusing to act in accord with their own natural constitution, to hold tight to it and find it sufficient."
Marcus Aurelius[27]

Aurelius speaks of the 'empty struggles' embarked upon by those who do not truly know themselves, yet cling to this ill-informed idea as sufficient for life. So, ask yourself again. What is my motivation? Am I really like that, or am I pursuing a need for some type of external identification or gratification? If you can answer these questions honestly and you still genuinely come to the same answer, then maybe The Rock is right, the most powerful thing you can be is you. However, those behaviours and choices may not all be as genuinely warranted as we may like to believe. The desire for group acceptance, the acquisition of social status, or even to avoid tedious arguments with spouses, immediately come to mind. Perhaps the appropriate question might be to ask 'what actions would be truly honest?'

"Honestly expressing yourself...it is very difficult to do. I mean it is easy for me to put on a show and be cocky and be flooded with a cocky feeling and then feel like pretty cool... or I can make all kind of phony things, you see what I mean, blinded by it or I can show you some really fancy movement. But to express oneself honestly, not lying to oneself...now that, my friend, is very hard to do."
Bruce Lee[28]

What is honest expression and what is a metaphorical show? What are you covering up for? Are your actions being dictated by ego, insecurity, fear of failure, the seeking of attention? The secret here is 'not lying to oneself', requiring once again an honest answer. Once we obtain these honest answers, what then? Well, perhaps this is where the real work begins. You have found your starting point. You have identified your virtues or lack thereof, you have wrestled with your motivations, weighed up your weaknesses and strengths, considered your identity and potential self-told lies. You have established ground zero for self-development. Now that you have acknowledged this, you have the resultant challenges to face and overcome. Like: what could I do to become less selfish? What risks could I afford to take? What actions can I take in order to let go of insecurities that drive my behaviour in large groups? What can I do to become less defensive at work? (Insert the relevant questions that apply to you, of course.)

IMPROVING YOURSELF

The Chinese phrase *xiu-yang* refers to self-cultivation through correction of both the mind and the character.[29] Daoists refer to this process as a movement towards the 'authentic self' and one that is in accordance with the nature of human beings. One might argue that this is the process you are now undertaking, moving yourself closer to your natural state. This cultivation is, however, not an easy task, nor is it a quick one. Seneca said it well:

"As long as you live, keep learning how to live."

Seneca[30]

Knowing yourself is an ongoing process, much like anything else in life. You can't magically overcome your issues by battling your demons in one week. Battling your demons is exactly that, a battle. The fight may at times and for certain factors be shorter, but for others we may continually be striving to better ourselves until the end of our days. Another important thing to consider is how much you are to let this battle rule your life. In a very famous and somewhat overused quote from Nietzsche (which I am knowingly compounding), he said:

"He who fights with monsters might take care lest he thereby become a monster. And if you gaze for long into an abyss, the abyss gazes also into you."
Nietzsche[31]

In other words, you can take on or become that which you are battling with. Or in this instance, you can become rather obsessed with introspection, thereby creating a new demon with which to duel (as per the issue of ruminating). The abyss is endless, after all. Aurelius offers a more opportunistic outlook than that of the bleak abyss, describing the active engagement with your own self as being the 'directing mind'. He states:

"The directing mind is that which wakes itself, adapts itself, makes itself of whatever nature it wishes, and makes all that happens to it appear in the way it wants."
Marcus Aurelius[32]

Rather, your journey is one that you choose to embark upon, orienting yourself accordingly. Aurelius also stressed the need to see this as a safe endeavour. He iterated that the 'internal retreat' was the most recreational and cathartic experience that we can ever have. That this facility was a way of replenishing, invigorating, and building the consciousness you both want and need.

"Retreat into your own little territory within yourself... Be your own master... look at things as a man, as a human being, as a citizen, as a moral creature."
Marcus Aurelius[32]

So instead, treat your journey of self-discovery with the attention and commitment it deserves, but be proactive about it. Enjoy the solace that comes from engaging in the battle, for you are one of the brave ones. Remembering all the while that this inner retreat is yours and only yours.

OVERCOMING THYSELF—IT IS YOU AGAINST YOU AND NO ONE ELSE

Bettering ourselves may often come at the sacrifice of our current image. After all, being better implies that what you are is not as 'good' as what you might become. In certain ways, you may be all too happy to let go of your current habits, seeing how beneficial new ones might be for the attainment of your life goals. Alternatively, some aspects of your current self might be a little more difficult to let go.

Battling demons is in premise quite simple. Overcoming them is much like the Yin and Yang analogy from the last chapter. A demon, from a mythological sense, is a manifest representation of the unknown. It is the thing we must do battle with, often requiring the sacrifice of something in return, in order to secure victory. The sacrifice of time and effort are obvious ones, for obtaining anything of value is likely to incur both. But the really difficult ones, the ones we struggle to defeat, may require the sacrifice of a part of yourself that you may not be ready to give up, or are at least unaware that you must.

These are the key aspects of self-discovery that the great philosophers have tried to illuminate. The struggle, the battle, and the courage are often synonymous with the search for inner wisdom, which appears no coincidence. The power over arms, or over others, is regularly seen as secondary to that of power over thyself. Possibly due to the degree of self-sacrifice required to obtain them. The Chinese philosophers commented on this idea well.

"He who overcomes others has force, he who overcomes himself is strong."
Lao Tzu[33]

"To know thyself is to not see defeat in a thousand battles."
Sun Tzu[34]

Again, this sentiment is simultaneously echoed among the Greek scholars, adding even more impetus to the claim.

"I count him braver who overcomes his desires than him who conquers his enemies, for the hardest victory is over self."
Aristotle[35]

"The first and greatest victory is to conquer yourself; to be conquered by yourself is of all things most shameful and vile."
Plato[36]

The emerging theme is that no amount of external hardship will amount to more than can be found within you. Perhaps suggesting that the pinnacle of all chaos to be overcome is again done so internally. 'Defeating yourself' or 'overcoming yourself' is what provides advantage (if you are so inclined) over others that have failed, or have chosen not to face their inner struggles. Of course, I would suggest that the healthiest approach might be to think only of your own development here, so perhaps this quote might help:

"Today is victory over yourself of yesterday; tomorrow is your victory over lesser men."
Musashi[29]

Musashi is speaking of the 'lesser men' as being the previous examples of yourself, before your daily triumphs. With each day you defeat the most recent example of 'you', and so on. The perpetual war of attrition with only one eventual winner or loser; you.

POSITIVE REFLECTIVE PRACTICE

Knowing thyself is also thought to be a goal surpassing that of just demon thwarting. Many philosophers and educational psychologists suggest that the introspection required to discover who you really are brings with it a more critical mind, and one that is more able to deconstruct issues and provide solutions. It provides greater clarity of thought now that you can separate yourself from what is happening in the world.

"Only as you do know yourself can your brain serve you as a sharp and efficient tool. Know your own failings, passions, and prejudices so you can separate them from what you see."
Bernard Baruch[37]

This ability to see things for what they are is a key aspect of reflective practice that was discussed earlier. General reflective practice is essentially giving deep, often systematic thought to a particular topic or issue in order to obtain new information. It is often described as the process of turning experience into knowledge and plays a major role in a multitude of professional development programmes and practices.[31] The art of reflective practice was popularised by the psychologist Schon in the 80s, but has been developed significantly thereafter. Many theorists have developed their own cycles and models to help guide the process of reflection and alleviate the issues found in initiating deep, critical thought. The famous 'Gibbs' Reflective Cycle' is shown below.

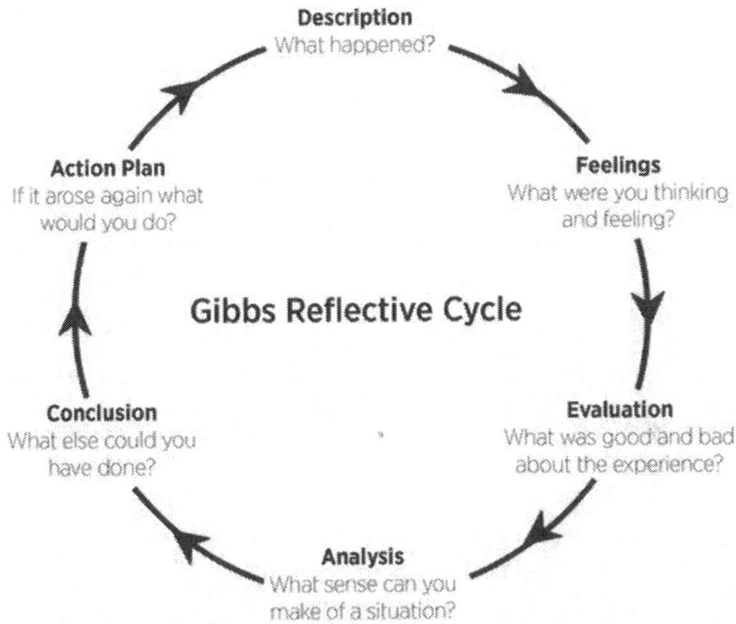

Figure 5. 'Gibbs Reflective Cycle'[38]

However, much like the introspection induced by attempting to know thyself (a form of reflecting upon oneself anyway), reflection can often lead to what is known as a deficit-based experience. In other words, we gravitate to what we do poorly, how we behave incorrectly, and what is bad about something, rather than to a more positive approach. Indeed, the preceding paragraphs may have felt like exactly that. Whilst there is a great deal of value in 'fixing' our faults if we can, reflection and self-reflection should be more than just itinerary listings of observed weaknesses. Some theorists are now taking a more proactive approach that limits the negativity generated by such endeavours. The 'Strengths Based Approach' by sports coaching specialists Ghaye and colleagues does just that. Four simple questions.[39]

- What do I want to start doing?
- What do I want to stop doing?
- What do I want to do less of?
- What do I want to do more of to capitalise on my strengths?

Notice again the 'what'-based questions, helping to prevent rumination on negative situations or things. This model can be applied to almost anything and is a great vehicle for self-appraisal or self-reflection. Consider something about yourself or something in your life and apply the model. Take parenting, for example—you might decide that you want to start doing more arts and crafts with your children. You may also decide that you want to stop having dinner separately or on trays in front of the TV. You may want to shout at your children less and work together with your partner more in order to improve your relationship as a family.

ALTERNATIVE CONNOTATIONS?

So far, we have considered the idea of 'knowing thyself' as a major movement towards enlightenment. However, not everyone shares this notion.

"Know thyself? If I knew myself I would run away."

Johann Von Goethe[40]

*"**Engywook:** Next is the Magic Mirror Gate. Atreyu will have to look his true self in the face.*
***Falcor:** So? That shouldn't be so hard.*
***Engywook:** Oh, that's what everyone thinks! But kind people find out that they are cruel. Brave men find out that they are really cowards! Confronted by their true selves, most men run away, screaming!"*
From the movie 'The NeverEnding Story'[41]

Whilst there may be merit to these comments, it may again reflect aspects of self-reflective technique and a tendency toward the negative. The idea that if we knew ourselves we would want to run away is a suggestion that once again 'ignorance is bliss'. If the real 'we' that is inside is that scary, is it not better to deal with it, rather than maintain a façade for the sake of appearance? Psychological well-being is somewhat contained within our ability to be at peace with both the events of the world and who we are inside. In that sense, facing the 'Magic Mirror Gate' is something terrifying but no less essential for our development. The fear associated with facing our true selves appears to be a representation of the inevitable chaos that follows and the contradictions that become apparent. But that is not a justifiable reason for avoiding looking in the first place.

On the other hand, perfectionism is not exactly the goal here either. Again, the issue of rumination comes to mind when we consider perfectionism. The sages of old are not suggesting that we tear ourselves to pieces, but rather objectively identify (using 'what' based questions) something we can do to improve ourselves and accentuate our existing strengths. That's it. Regardless of whether you are beginning your journey from a current place of happiness or unhappiness, the process is the same. As per chapter 1 pick something that you can calmly focus your attention upon. Identify a little piece of chaos that you can begin to convert to order. Then just like your room, let that new order spread to other parts of your psyche. It does require honest examination and you may indeed see a coward in the 'Magic Mirror Gate' rather than the hero you had imagined. So what should you do? Pick a small task with which to be brave and grow that into what you want it to be.

FINAL THOUGHTS

To 'know thyself' is as concrete a philosophical axiom as we are likely to get. From each corner of the globe we see its value espoused again and again. Yet the way in which we find out is just as important as the act of introspection itself. Asking ourselves questions designed to elicit information that we can action in a healthy way is paramount. When we ask ourselves 'what', we keep ourselves open to what we find. When we dwell on 'why', we can spiral into neuroticism and self-loathing.

Knowing thyself is about honestly examining who we are and moving forward appropriately. Yes, it may require a deconstruction of the image we have created for ourselves and for others. Whilst breaking the kernel can be difficult, it does not mean that it has to be painful. Just like any little problem or situation that we come across in life, we are all capable of coming up with ways to make something a little better. So why are *you* any different? Remember, there is a difference between accepting who you are so that you don't have to change, and understanding who you are so that you can change. Knowing yourself is to live true to your nature, but not at the sacrifice of cultivating the self into something better.

"...That is why you must know yourself – Immaturity lies only in total ignorance of self."

Jiddu Krishnamurti[42]

"What the superior man seeks is in himself; what the small man seeks is in others."

Confucius[43]

"You can't get away from yourself by moving from one place to another."

Hemingway[44]

CHAPTER 3

IN THE MOMENT

"If you are depressed you are living in the past. If you are anxious you are living in the future. If you are at peace you are living in the present."

***Anonymous*[1]**

"'What day is it?' asked Pooh.
'It's today,' squeaked Piglet.
'My favourite day,' said Pooh."

***A.A. Milne*[2]**

We have all heard the clichés. 'Live for the moment', 'seize the day' and 'what if you were to die tomorrow?' etc. But how many of us go further than just hearing? How many of us attempt to truly understand these ideas, where they came from, or how to apply them to life? Deep and meaningful messages can easily get lost in frequent usage or their apparently trivial nature. Whatever has become common about these sayings, no less detracts from their power or relevance in today's world. Interestingly, these sorts of messages have sprung up in different parts of the world, unbeknown to one another. Not only that, but the greatest thinkers of old have seemed to share the viewpoint that to live for now is possibly the most important part of living.

HISTORY

The Greek/Roman philosophers that founded the Stoic movement maintained this very aphorism. They believed that the key to profound and justly existence was to live out our days with as much quality and compassion as possible, living each day as if we were not to expect another.

"Begin at once to live, and count each separate day as a separate life."
Seneca[3]

"Live each day as if it were your last."
Marcus Aurelius[4]

The Stoics believed that the acceptance of life's events and each current moment as it happens, along with an appreciation for what we have, were key aspects to achieving happiness (*eudaimonia*). Accepting life as it happens also creates an emotional buffer of sorts, reducing our susceptibility to being controlled by desire or discomfort. The slightly morbid conclusion of living each day as if it were your last also highlights the potential benefits of recognising one's own mortality. Seneca goes on to say:

"We are always complaining that our days are few, and acting as though there would be no end of them."
Seneca[5]

If we can appreciate that our days are numbered, we may be better placed to appreciate today. Not just that, but the stoic philosophy of 'premeditation' or considering our death/terrible outcomes can create a sense of much-needed perspective when dealing with hardships. We see the same philosophy at work in medieval Japan and the samurai culture. They too believed that maintaining thoughts of death was actually a key aspect of living well.

"One who is supposed to be a warrior considers it his foremost concern to keep death in mind at all times, every day and every night, from the morning of New Year's Day through the night of New Year's Eve."
From the 'Bushido Shoshinso'[6]

Again, this may sound extremely depressing as well as irrelevant in modern-day society. "I am not a warrior", I hear you say. True, but that is not exactly what the samurai were suggesting. Take the following quote:

"One who is a samurai must before all things keep constantly in mind...the fact that he has to die. If he is always mindful of this, he will be able to live in accordance with the paths of loyalty and filial duty, will avoid myriads of evils and adversities, keep himself free of disease and calamity and moreover enjoy a long life. He will also be a fine personality with many admirable qualities. For existence is impermanent as the dew of evening..."
Daidoji Yuzan[7]

The emphasis here is on the freedom from normal existence that comes from a reminder of your own mortality. It is the ability to see past the trivial and live in the now, because you understand the impermanence of life. This does not mean that you give up planning for the future. Not at all. Rather, it means planning, preparing, and executing a good life, whilst accepting that at any moment it could all be taken away. Think about that for a moment. How would you conduct yourself if you were not to see another sunrise? Would you be dwelling on past mistakes, agonising over future circumstances that are yet to come, or would you be soaking up every second that was happening right now?

As it happens, the psychological community concurs with this sentiment. Eminent researcher Kenneth Vail has conducted studies into the rather therapeutic effects of just that.

> *"We should turn attention and research efforts toward a better understanding of how the motivations triggered by death awareness can actually improve people's lives, rather than how it can cause malady and social strife... The dance with death can be a delicate but potentially elegant stride toward living the good life..."*
>
> ***Kenneth Vail et al (2012)***[8]

MINDFULNESS

Premeditation, negative visualisation, and death consideration appear to be beneficial for living each day. Then what of living in the moment? Well, the further east we go, the more we seem to find on this front. For it is in the East that we see the birth of mindfulness and Zen practice. These two terms now seem to be rather 'in vogue' following the support from TV shows and celebrity endorsements. However, mindfulness and Zen are key parts of Buddhism and as such have been practised for a very long time. The fact that they are becoming so popular at present is possibly more indicative of our previous ignorance than our current wisdom. There are now copious amounts of books, TED talks, and podcasts extolling the benefits of the art that have only been created in the last decade. Yet, the roots of mindfulness have been evident all around us for as long as we can remember.

Take for example the topic of flow in the last chapter. Amidst the aura of flow, one feels as if all attention is on that one activity. The level of captivation is equalled only by the quickness of passing time. Remember that puzzle you once worked on where you suddenly realised the time and were shocked at how long you had been there? (Replace 'puzzle' with an activity that had you fully immersed.) Or how anyone in the close vicinity would have had trouble trying to communicate with you? When all you could see, hear, or interact with was the task at hand? This is the experience of mindfulness.

Mindfulness is the practice of being completely captivated by the present moment. Whatever may be happening, you are there, experiencing it. For with mindfulness, there is no future or past, there is only now. Whatever has come before or lies ahead does not exist. The only thing that exists is right now. Once a moment has gone, it is no longer 'now'. The highly influential book *The Power of Now* highlights:

"Realize deeply that the present moment is all you have. Make the NOW the primary focus of your life."
Eckhart Tolle[9]

"The basketball court for me, during a game, is the most peaceful place I can imagine. On the basketball court, I worry about nothing. When I'm out there, no one can bother me..."
Michael Jordan[10]

"Happiness is a state of activity."
Aristotle[11]

This may seem a little confusing at first and wholeheartedly deserves far more than a small chapter in order to explain. However, mindfulness is more than just a wishy-washy theory or fancy-sounding mantra. If we refer back to the scientific view of the universe, we can also see yet more philosophical alignment. Given that the universe is an expanding one that causes our concept of 'time' to even exist, physicists hypothesise that expansion rather than contraction signifies the direction in which time is moving.[12] Emphasis here on moving. It is never static because the universe is always expanding. Thus, what has gone before (in time) is no longer the same as when it was 'now', and the 'future' will only ever be played out as individual occurrences of 'now'. Until the eventual collapse of the universe, that is. This may be an oversimplified view of highly complex astrophysics, but it serves to demonstrate Tolle's expression. 'Now' is all we have. So, we need to pay attention to that rather than anything else. This seems rather simple. You may even believe that you are always conscious of the moment and living in the now. But before proclaiming your eternal and naturally acquired wisdom, I would urge you to reconsider. Take the words of Thich Nhat Hanh and the famous example of washing the dishes:

> *"Don't do any task in order to get it over with. Resolve to do each job in a relaxed way, with all your attention. Enjoy and be one with your work."*
>
> *"If while washing dishes, we think only of the cup of tea that awaits us, thus hurrying to get the dishes out of the way as if they were a nuisance, then we are not 'washing the dishes to wash the dishes' ... If we can't wash the dishes, the chances are we won't be able to drink our tea either. While drinking the cup of tea, we will only be thinking of other things, barely aware of the cup in our hands. Thus, we are sucked away into the future –and we are incapable of actually living one minute of life."*
>
> ***Thich Nhat Hanh***[13]

I would recommend thinking about this a bit longer. 'Wash the dishes to wash the dishes', not for any other reason. This is surprisingly difficult. How many other thoughts are running through your head whilst doing a particular activity? Driving to work, having dinner, being in the shower—all are likely to be accompanied by 'extra thought'. What meeting do you have later? What should you have for dinner? Why hasn't he called me back? What should I have said in that argument earlier? These extra thoughts anchor us to another action and another time, tearing us away from the here and now. Even whilst reading this passage, consider what thoughts you have just had away from those that are on the page. For a modern-day twist, observe the people around you on their phones rather than actually being present with the people that are right in front of them. Boyfriends, wives, children, friends, colleagues are all being ignored by the distractions in someone's head or hands. Shunryu Suzuki says:

> *"When you do something, you should do it with your whole body and mind; you should be concentrated on what you do. You should do it completely, like a good bonfire. You should not be a smoky fire. You should burn yourself completely. If you do not burn yourself completely, a trace of yourself will be left in what you do."*
>
> ***Shunryu Suzuki***[14]

> *"The present moment is the only time over which we have dominion. The most important person is always the person you are with, who is right before you, for who knows if you will have dealings with any other person in the future? The most important pursuit is making the person standing at your side happy, for that alone is the pursuit of life."*
>
> ***Thich Nhat Hanh***[15]

"When people talk, listen completely.
Most people never listen."
Hemingway[16]

The overarching message may be coming through now. Give all of yourself to whatever you are doing. For that is to be living in the now, in the present. In doing so, mindfulness practitioners say that you gain something in return. You gain that sense of immersion that you enjoy so much in other activities, but in every activity. This makes even the mundane seem so much more captivating. The idea is that you focus on things you would never normally see, if it were not for this extra attention.

"I clean this teapot with the kind of attention I would
have were I giving the baby Buddha or Jesus a bath."
Thich Nhat Hanh[15]

Mindfulness is not just about the mundane, either. The next time you are walking somewhere, try to be mindful. Try not to think about where you are going. Instead, feel the breeze on your skin, see the movement of the leaves on the tree. Observe the birds collecting food, the faint chatter of friends talking, or the passing of the clouds. This is mindful walking. Give it a try. You might be surprised at what you feel and see.

REAL-WORLD APPLICATIONS

But what of striving to fight back the tide of entropy, I hear you ask? How does this mindful approach work in the real world, especially when everything is set to chaos by default? Well, there is a distinction to be comprehended here. Let's look at these words from Thich Nhat Hanh and Shunryu Suzuki:

"All the elements for your happiness are already here. There is no need to run, strive, search, or struggle. Just be. Just being in the moment in this place is the deepest practice of meditation."

Thich Nhat Hanh[15]

"Calmness of mind does not mean you should stop your activity. Real calmness should be found in activity itself. We say, 'It is easy to have calmness in inactivity, it is hard to have calmness in activity, but calmness in activity is true calmness'."

Shunryu Suzuki[17]

The point here isn't that we shouldn't strive to better ourselves or work towards a goal (forgive the double negative). Rather, it is that in each moment we need to 'just be doing' whatever it is that we are doing and not with the future goal in mind at the time. If that is the case, we are not present, we are indeed in the future. Well, in our mind at least. With a sense of just 'being' comes a sense of calm. So, in other words, we can set up goals, tasks, and objectives that we want to complete, however when we are doing them, we are just doing them. Nothing else. This then provides us with satisfaction in the present, removing us from dependency on the future. It creates a sense of patience that is far too infrequent in modern life (if Zen practitioners are to be believed). 21st century living is full of instant gratification. So much so that actually having to wait for something is considered such an inconvenience that people are driven to distraction. A recent poll found that "Millennials experience 'Load Rage' after just one minute of waiting for downloads".[18] This might suggest that the need for a more mindful and thus patient life is a very important one. Interestingly, OnePlus have even gone as far as installing a 'Zen Mode', where phones will shut down for 20 minutes, allowing users to take a break from activity.[18]

"True happiness is to enjoy the present, without anxious dependence upon the future, not to amuse ourselves with either hopes or fears but to rest satisfied with what we have, which is sufficient, for he that is so, wants nothing."
Seneca[5]

"Forty seconds? But I want it now!"
Homer Simpson[19]

I often find that Homer Simpson provides the necessary 'counter wisdom' to really help hammer home a concept. Sometimes it isn't until we see the alternative that we really appreciate the brilliance and simplicity of the former.

A mindful approach to tasks is not just thought to be calming and patient, but also helps to improve concentration and work output. Mindful practitioners are thought to be more productive and accurate by removing distractions that would otherwise impact upon our attention and productivity.[20,21] There are strong links here with the world of performance psychology, whereby athletes and performers are taught to shut out distractions and remain focused on the only things they need focus on. Imagery and mental rehearsal are techniques that sports psychologists use regularly in order to help this process along.[22] Focusing on an internal image of ourselves helps to eradicate crowd influence, competitor rivalry, and other environmental conditions. The evidence behind these techniques suggests that the removal of these unnecessary thoughts is a great aid to performance and helps people connect their mind and body together.

*"**Nobutada**: Please forgive, too many mind.*
***Nathan Algren**: Too many mind?*
***Nobutada**: Hai. Mind the sword, mind the people watching, mind the enemy, too many mind... No mind."*
***From the movie 'The Last Samurai'**[23]*

PRACTISING MINDFULNESS

There is, of course, more to mindfulness and Zen practice than just the prevailing sense of 'being in the moment'. However, in essence, the techniques practised in meditation are tools to help you reach this aim. Briefly, the most important aspect of meditation practice is that of being aware of and in tune with our breathing. 'Belly breathing' in particular. This is where we breathe from lower down towards our abdomen, incurring an expansion of the belly, as opposed to higher up in the chest cavity. The same technique is also a staple diet of the breathing exercises used in Cognitive Behavioural Therapy or CBT, a very successful behaviour recognition and change therapy used to treat an array of mental health ailments.[24] Again, a modern practice utilising age-old techniques that until recently people may have viewed as somewhat 'hippy'.

"Breath is the bridge which connects life to consciousness, which unites your body to your thoughts. Whenever your mind becomes scattered, use your breath as the means to take hold of your mind again."

"In mindfulness one is not only restful and happy, but alert and awake. Meditation is not evasion; it is a serene encounter with reality."
***Thich Nhat Hanh**[15]*

Belly breathing helps to regulate blood pressure, reduce anxiety, and relax musculature. Combined with certain Zen practices, it becomes a power tool to help you stay more focused on the moment, or meditate. Meditation itself is essentially being mindful of your breath and that alone. Yes, this is often whilst sitting in a particular way and with a particular posture, however the essence is what is important. Depending on the Zen teacher, meditation is taught as being sat on the floor or in a chair, with a straight back, crossed legged (or lotus position), with your head held so that you could balance a book on top. The tongue also lightly pressing towards the front of the roof of your mouth, with a half-smile on your face. From there the process is simple, yet very hard to achieve. The task is to focus only on your breath. Belly breathe in and out, whilst seeing yourself only as a vessel that is taking in air and then letting it out.

Now this might sound simple, however for Zen practice there are many distractions. As you meditate, your mind will naturally wander to thoughts outside of just your breath. These could be positive, negative, constructive, or destructive. Ultimately, their nature is irrelevant. The objective here is to watch those thoughts appear in your mind, as if you were an objective bystander. Watch these unwanted thoughts (including the positive ones) arrive and then let them leave just as they came. Notice the emphasis on 'let them' leave. We are not trying to force anything at all. If you are truly seeing these thoughts arrive in a relaxed state, you will be able to watch them float by and leave. If you try to make them leave, wonder why they came, or anything else, they will stick around for a lot longer.

"To think in terms of either pessimism or optimism oversimplifies the truth. The problem is to see reality as it is."

Thich Nhat Hanh[15]

Hanh is showing that the focus is not on alleviating negativity or accentuating positivity, as that would be an 'effort' or 'striving to change' what is. The concept remains that experiencing the moment as it is, is the primary objective. With no attachment or opinion to what thoughts occur. Many Zen practitioners have additional techniques for generating the desired relaxed state. Counting your breaths is a great example. Every in and out breath counts as one. With the objective of counting for as long as is necessary. However, you may find this more difficult than you thought. Your mind will likely cloud with alternative thoughts and surprisingly lead you to lose count. Don't be put off, however. Just go back to one, two, three once again, without any stress or anxiety.

Another technique often used is that of asking yourself a Koan, or an important existential question. 'Who am I?' is a very popular choice and one that helps the user to achieve balance. Again, do not strive to 'solve the question'. Instead, let your relaxed mind just keep asking the question. In the end, what you may find in using these techniques is that you have not thought about that upcoming meeting, your overdraft, or the washing you still have left to do at all. What you have done is be more aware of your breath and its quality, and more in touch with the present moment than probably ever before. You may even feel slightly elated and refreshed, possessing a clarity of mind that you have seldom experienced. It can often be as if your proverbial turbulent sea has been flattened out into a serene, calm, and clear pool of water. If we revert back to the movie *The Last Samurai*, we see Katsumoto, the samurai general, states "To know life in every breath… That is Bushido."[23] The meaning is of recognising the existence of your life with every breath you take. Moment by moment, breath by breath. To understand that concept is to understand what it means to be living. Life, in every breath.

Regardless of techniques used, mindfulness and meditation do seem to be very beneficial. We are only just beginning to understand the power of breathing and being in the moment from a scientific perspective. However, initial evidence seems to be strong and we might all do well to learn more about it and start practising.[25]

"The true purpose [of Zen] is to see things as they are, to observe things as they are, and to let everything go as it goes... Zen practice is to open up our small mind."
Shunryu Suzuki[17]

MINDFULNESS AND SELF-REFLECTION—A CONTRADICTION IN TERMS?

Having talked at length in chapter 2 about the need to know ourselves, you could easily be forgiven for thinking that living in the now is diametrically opposed to knowing thyself. The art of reflection does essentially require thought both into the past and into the potential future. In order to be a functioning member of society, we need to be able to reflect upon our actions, the occurrences of our lives, and develop ourselves accordingly. As a result, we are putting at least some thought into the past and future. However, the same theory still applies (at least in a mindfulness sense).

Casting your mind in either direction would suggest that we are living in something other than the present moment. However, whilst we are reflecting, we are 'doing reflection'. We are objectively considering a specific moment, set of moments, or situations that have been deemed to require analysis. That is our job at that moment. Zen practice would have us contemplate this paradox as not being emotionally attached to the act of introspection itself (as mentioned in chapter 2 as to how asking 'why?' can sometimes be good). Think back to the example of meditation, where the idea is to let our thoughts go as easily and as quickly as they arrived. Not forcing, not reacting and not fighting. When tasked with reflecting, it requires us once again not to become attached to what we find, but rather enjoy the process. However, once we have finished 'doing reflection', we then transfer our consciousness to the present moment of whatever it is we should be doing thereafter. Perhaps even washing the dishes.

For those who embrace the present moment, the art lies in not worrying about past and future events. The fact that they are just that, past and future, means that they do not exist. If they do not exist, we should not be attached to them. Once you have finished your critique of actions, behaviours, and performance in that business meeting, parenting scenario, or argument, do not dwell on the implications of future action. Instead, extract what meaning and information you need in order to improve your behaviour and move on to the next task that requires your full attention. Anxiety, worry and depression come from lingering in either timeframe, rather than putting them to bed once you have processed the situation accordingly.

"I learned a long time ago that worrying is like a rocking chair. It gives you something to do but it doesn't get you anywhere."

From the movie 'Van Wilder'[26]

Buddhists even go one step further in ensuring that self-reflection is not taken personally (so to speak), encouraging the complete removal of attachment to the world and to the self. Their belief in the quest for 'nirvana' or enlightenment can only come as a result of this detachment (we will discuss this idea more in chapter 11). Whilst Zen is a key tenet of this practice, the practice of living in the moment and disassociating from ourselves and our lives in order to maintain our mental presence is a little different from complete detachment from life. The middle ground is perhaps an element of both Daoist authenticity and Zen disassociation in order to provide the premise for objective introspection, with less associated internal turmoil.

FINAL THOUGHTS

The concept of living for today and for the moment has seen a great deal of philosophic and anecdotal attention over millennia. From the sayings espoused by our parents, the stoic literary giants, and leading psychologists, the consensus appears formidable. Living in the knowledge that the succession of moments that make up life are not guaranteed, we can maintain a healthy perspective and conduct ourselves accordingly. For the profound existence of 'living each day as if it were our last' far outweighs the marred and paralysed existence of expectation, attachment, and suffered injustices.

If we can give our attention, our full attention, to whatever it is we are doing, we are likely to find innumerable benefits for relationships, productivity, and peace of mind. If we can stay fixed in the present and one true reality, we can let go of attachment to the non-existent past and future. Even when we choose to reflect upon our demons, mindfulness can help us do so in a healthy way—returning us back to the present moment and whatever it is that we are *now* doing. So when you are playing with your children, just be playing. When you are talking to someone, listen intently. Whatever you are doing, be immersed, captivated, and lost within it.

"They lose the day in expectation of the night, and the night in fear of the dawn."

Seneca[5]

"Happiness, not in another place but this place...not for another hour, but this hour."

Walt Whitman[27]

"If you aren't in the moment, you are either looking forward to uncertainty, or back to pain and regret."

Jim Carrey[28]

CHAPTER 4

BE THE DRIVER, NOT THE PASSENGER

"Sometimes, I feel the fear of uncertainty stinging clear
And I can't help but ask myself how much I'll let the fear
Take the wheel and steer
It's driven me before
And it seems to have a vague, haunting mass appeal
But lately I am beginning to find
That I should be the one behind the wheel."

'Drive' by Incubus[1]

"There is one path in the world that none can walk but you.
Where does it lead? Don't ask, walk!"

Nietzsche[2]

You are in control of your life, right? Constantly making decisions that shape a better life for you and those around you, based upon your personal motivations? Or are you going with the flow? Being 'behind the wheel' is a concept that may be generally assumed, but nevertheless rarely realised. Being the driver is to be in control of your journey, regardless of the direction ventured. It is the autonomy that removes the shackles of conformity, expectance, social influence, and also passivity. It is the manifestation of our realisation that living is steering, accelerating, and braking, not being unknowingly chauffeured through life. But 'taking the wheel' with conscious awareness, heartfelt and considered cognition, is anything but simple. The combination of our own minds, fears, and predispositions with that of the world's influence often makes us change seats; all the while subdued by the distracting or even alluring view outside of the window. Sometimes, we do not know we are being driven, until we arrive at an unwanted destination, unsure as to how we got there.

"Never confuse movement with action."
Hemingway[3]

WHO IS DRIVING?

What we are talking about is essentially autonomy. In a healthy and fortunate environment, we may all have some degree of autonomy in life (depending on your philosophical beliefs of free will, destiny and so on), or at least an illusion of autonomy. However, the question is to what extent we actually exercise this autonomy and to what end? There is a difference between possessing autonomy and being autonomous. The latter is the realisation of the former and the manifestation of observable personal control. This may take some level of introspection in order to identify which camp you fall into. We may possess autonomy but fail to use it and we may believe we do not have any, yet are piloting our own ship extremely well. The important thing here is to identify where you sit, so that you can do something about it. There is an old poker saying that was brought to life by Matt Damon in the movie *Rounders* that may provide a little insight.

"If you can't spot the sucker in your first half hour at the table, then you are the sucker."
From the movie 'Rounders'[4]

In other words, if upon a modest amount of reflection you still cannot identify which seat you're in, then you're probably the sucker (metaphorically speaking, of course). This may sound like an over-simplification of a difficult conundrum, especially if you believe such autonomy to be merely illusory. But regardless of whether the seat is illusory or not—we should be able to determine in which seat we are sitting. Identifying which seat you are in is a great first step to claiming some autonomy. From there, an understanding of the psychology that surrounds our motivation to engage with aspects of life in the first place is then a pressing matter. Why is this important, you ask? Well, when it comes to being the driver, you need some fuel in the tank.

MOTIVATIONAL PSYCHOLOGY

Motivational theory can essentially be broken up into a few schools of thought and logical order. If we consider motivation in the realms of achieving an end product (which does not always need to be positive, by the way), we can more easily comprehend the idea. For all life is somewhat driven by the need to achieve something for our efforts. Whether that be a cup of tea from a minute or two's worth of preparation and waiting, the attainment of drunkenness through the hard slog of alcoholic beverage consumption, or the chiselled frame of a devout weightlifter, all are the exchange of effort (or lack thereof) for an end result.

The early works on motivational theory came in the predominant form of 'drive theories' in the early to mid-20th century. Psychologists like Freud and Hull suggested that people are motivated by innate drives to satisfy urges, or as it were, reduce inner tensions upsetting homeostasis (the internal balance of the body and mind). This biologically minded theory garnered further attention in other forms like Maslow's hierarchy of needs, where the most basic of needs or urges need to be met first, before any further action can take place. The world of psychology then sought to develop a further understanding of what motivates people beyond what may have been regarded as more primal or instinctive action. The mindset was that 'drive theories' were somewhat simple and didn't aptly characterise the more complex dynamic of human motivation.

In 1959, Robert White suggested that human beings derived motivation from the desire to affect their environment, suggesting that this desire was predicated upon the demonstration of competence in a given task or field. Interacting with our environment whilst engaging in successful attempts at displaying competence would therefore increase feelings of efficacy and thus, increase motivation. In 1978, Harter further developed White's concept and posited what is known as the Competence Motivation Theory.[5] She suggested that motivation is both developmental and multidimensional, meaning that it changes over time and depends on which domain it occurs in. The interplay between cognitive, physical, and social domains, along with potential biological factors, was suggested to account for the individual differences between people's motivations in life. In addition, she suggested that people gravitate toward activities in which they feel competent, or indeed, have experienced some form of success. Conversely, people will also actively avoid, or disassociate from tasks or environments where they do not experience or even expect a feeling of competence.

Taking this viewpoint, life can be perceived as a series of opportunities in which we are biologically driven to try to display competence and essentially feel good about ourselves for doing so. Yet, human desire and activity is so diverse that this may be a tad too simple to encompass all motivation. So, psychologists eventually started branching out from drive theories in order to include other aspects of motivation, namely intrinsic/extrinsic motivation and task/ego orientation. In short, intrinsic motivation is being motivated by pleasure, enjoyment, and mastery of a task. Whereas extrinsic is being motivated by external pressures, rewards, or constraints. Interestingly, there is an obvious similarity between these two types of motivation and the distinctions between task and ego orientation.

Task orientation comes from the belief that the primary source of achievement comes from learning, development, and improvement purely for the sake of the task. Task-oriented people self-reference their development, comparing their current situation against that of their past. They link effort with increases in mastery, whilst linking mastery with competence. So essentially, they are saying "if I try harder, I'll be more successful". What's more is that task-oriented people rationalise failure with applying the wrong strategy for improvement, highlighting that they simply need to 'find the right strategy'. As a result of all this, task-oriented people are found to exert more sustained effort, even in the face of failure. I am sure you are already seeing the similarities between task orientation and intrinsic motivation. Doing something for the sheer benefit of being able to do it, immediately removes the external focus of requiring a pat on the back, a medal, or a sense of superiority over others. What's more is that in order to achieve this feat, what better approach is there than one that is driven by a self-referenced, trial-and-error-based strategy that runs on self-sustaining energy?

> *"Yes, I've made a great deal of dough from my fiction, but I never set a single word down on paper with the thought of being paid for it... I have written because it fulfilled me. Maybe it paid off the mortgage on the house and got the kids through college, but those things were on the side – I did it for the buzz. I did it for the pure joy of the thing. And if you can do it for the joy, you can do it forever."*
>
> **Stephen King**[6]

Ego orientation is primarily the opposite, where someone's situation or ability is referenced against that of other people. Ego-oriented people see a different relationship between effort and ability, in that high effort must mean less ability in the first place and that low effort that results in success means high ability. As a result, the ego-driven individual with low perceptions of ability will likely undertake easier tasks requiring less effort, thus 'showing off their ability'. Alternatively, they may disengage from the tasks completely in fear of the potential failure coming their way. Conversely, if they perceive their ability to be high, they are still likely to sustain effort accordingly.

"You do yourself a great injustice when you look to outside of yourself for validation."
Considered to be from LaTisha Cotto[7]

"I'm not popular enough to be different!"
Homer Simpson[8]

At this stage, consider yourself and what kind of motivation or orientation you possess. You will have probably sensed the emphasis already, but intrinsic motivation and task orientation are viewed as the healthier and more sustainable of the two. Whilst ego orientation and extrinsic motivation have their place, they are less advantageous. A famous sports psychologist said it well in that extrinsic motivation is like a thirsty car engine; the more you use it, the more you'll need to keep filling it up or find an even larger stimulus. Whereas intrinsic motivation is more like a muscle in that the more you use it, the stronger it will become.[9] We have probably all seen this in reality. We need only see a parent battling with a child, using treats in an effort to bend them to their will. However, with each utilisation of this extrinsic tool, the parent needs better, bigger, or tastier bribes to have the same effect. This is what is known as a behaviourist strategy of change and encouragement (think 'Pavlov's salivating dogs').

Self-Determination Theory (SDT) rounds off the motivational content.[10] Deci and Ryan surmised that greater perceived competence led to greater levels of intrinsic motivation. Later, they developed their theory to encompass a more well-rounded concept as to why people choose to do something and how those choices and subsequent efforts are driven by themselves, rather than by external influences. SDT is therefore about fostering positive and beneficial life choices based upon the need to fulfil innate desires of competency, autonomy, and relatedness.

This is where we see the return of autonomy. Being autonomous, or rather consciously responsible for the choice and initiation of behaviour, is a core aspect of SDT. Relatedness however, is a sense of belonging to others and their environment, which provides a bit of a different lens to just being the driver. SDT suggests that if the three components of the theory are nurtured, the individual will experience greater psychological health, self-actualisation, and prosperity.[11] If detrimentally effected, the opposite will occur. Someone may have greater feelings of competence and relatedness in certain facets of their life, experiencing greater intrinsic motivation as a result. Conversely, the same person may feel forced into something (pushed into the passenger seat) within another facet, resulting in a reduced perception of autonomy and thus, reduced motivation and psychological well-being.

STANDING STRAIGHT

The concept of what we choose to do and what we are forced to do is an interesting conundrum. If the need for autonomy is exactly that—a need—then should we not consider the other needs that are also important for the individual? The aforementioned 'hierarchy of needs' from Abraham Maslow illustrates this very well.

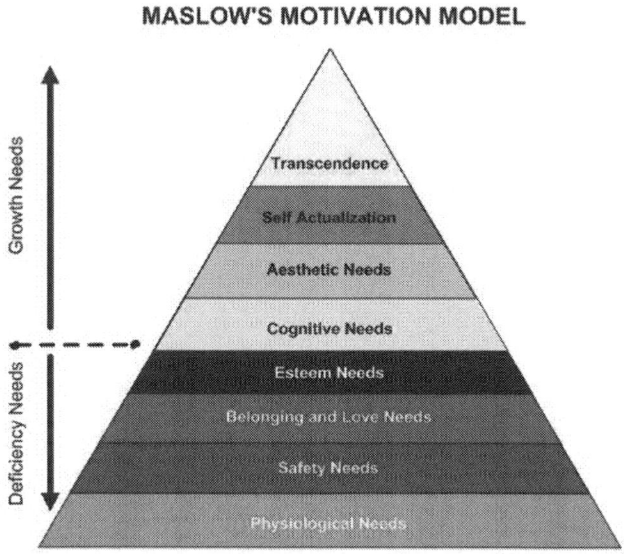

Figure 6. Maslow's updated hierarchy of needs[12]

Maslow originally developed a 5-tiered model that was updated to include the one pictured above. The premise is that no learning or development of learning can occur in life without the most basic of needs being met. These 'physiological and safety needs' include things such as food and water, shelter and warmth, protection and so on. Once these are met, the individual requires the inclusion of belonging, trust, and friendship in order to be able to progress in life. It is thereafter we see the tier of esteem needs, including achievement and independence. The pyramid ultimately sets the individual on a journey toward self-actualisation, where fulfilment and realisation of potential are obtained. Importantly for this chapter, the hierarchy reinforces the need for the individual to be the main driver in their life, sacrificing their opportunity for self-actualisation if not. The same sentiment appeared to be realised many moons ago, suggesting the above needs to be a prerequisite foothold for sustaining a fulfilling existence:

"The body cries out not to be hungry, not be thirsty, not be cold. Anyone who has these things, and is confident of continuing to have them, can rival the gods for happiness."
Epicurus[13]

So, if our level of autonomy is that important, we should surely be wise to protect and organically grow our own? Marcus Aurelius was also a great exponent of developing autonomy and independence. He believed that it was everyone's duty to navigate themselves and be their own strength, rather than relying on others.

"You should take no action unwillingly, selfishly, uncritically, or with conflicting motives... Your duty is to stand straight – not held straight."
Marcus Aurelius[14]

This rather resilient aphorism is one that shows the solidarity of autonomy. Taking action without choosing to do so is to be firmly placed in the passenger seat. Consider yourself and what actions you take. How much of these are 'going with the flow' or are as a result of influence from others? This does not mean that we need to be ignorant and immoveable beings, resistant to the needs or wills of others. Rather, it means that behaviour either begins or ceases through your conscious initiation. Notice as well the emphasis placed upon criticality, suggesting again that we should scrutinise our options in order to make sure our actions are considered and balanced. As a result, our actions will be without conflicting motives and thus honest. If we are able to do this, then we are indeed standing straight. To be held straight is to experience the reverse. The dependence on others, or indeed the ignorance to realise that we are the slaves of our environments, is to be held straight. Interestingly, Shunryu Suzuki echoes a similar thought with regard to autonomy and self-dependence:

"The most important thing is to accept yourself and stand on your own two feet."
Shunryu Suzuki[15]

"Your time is limited, so don't waste it living someone else's life."
Steve Jobs[16]

However, this does not mean a reluctance to ask for help or seek guidance. To act of your own volition to do so would still be an example of autonomy, especially given the critical and considered thought stressed by Aurelius. Consulting someone wiser, or more experienced would definitely aid you in being critical as to your options, whilst helping you to identify and quash any conflicting motives. You may even consider this to be the mark of a centred and empowered individual, taking the guidance of a chosen person in order to help *you* make a decision.

The 'self-sufficiency' described above is a key component of the ancient Greek moral philosophers' views on happiness in life, or *eudaimonia*. To be more specific, these wise men used the term *autarkeia* to represent what we might know as self-sufficiency and that this notion provided inner tranquillity or *ataraxia* (freedom from mental strife). *Ataraxia* was actually seen as the 'ultimate human good', something upon which the Stoics agreed.

"It is foolish to ask of the gods that which we can supply for ourselves."
Epicurus[17]

"Autarkeia – 'that state in which the ego depends only upon itself'... we find in all philosophical schools the same awareness of the power of the human self to free itself from everything which is alien to it."
***Pierre Hadot, modern Stoic and philosopher*[18]**

"You must expect great things of yourself before you can do them."
***Michael Jordan*[19]**

EMPOWERMENT

Both self-sufficiency and autonomy help us arrive at the conclusion that a sense of empowerment is required in order to obtain *autarkeia*. The term 'a sense of' becomes very important here. You may argue that we do not have any sense of power or control and that any feeling we do have is but an illusion, especially when this is combined with the content of the first chapter and inevitable chaos. However, much like the conversion of chaos into order, a sense of empowerment is an understanding that we can take control of both our perceptions and actions in this world. The need to be autonomous is nothing without a sense of being 'able' to be autonomous and thus empowered. One might comprehend autonomy and its benefit, but feel utterly devoid of any. Therefore, to be empowered is to believe that you can actually affect yourself and your environment.

The importance of empowering people has grown significantly in recent years within educational, leadership, and sporting psychology. Carol Dweck's 'growth mindset' for education, new age entrepreneurial companies that give away responsibility to employees, and democratic coaches are all prime examples of the shift in approach toward empowerment.[20] We will discuss Dweck's work significantly in chapter 5 on learning, but the latter two examples deserve further mention here. Companies like Google, Apple, and Facebook adopt a very different business management strategy compared to the archetypal examples of the past. Rather than a company led by the dictatorial chain of command seen in most hierarchies, these companies give away power to others and see them grow into their roles. When leaders give power and trust to those working for them, they see a marked increase in work ethic, productivity, and creativity.[21] When employees can choose to work hard themselves, they often do. When employees feel that they can impact upon both their own and their company's destiny, they are more likely to make that impact.

"It doesn't make sense to hire smart people and tell them what to do; we hire smart people so they can tell us what to do."
Steve Jobs[22]

The world of sport psychology would refer to this as 'Autonomy Supportive Behaviour', most notably by Mageau and Vallerand in 2003.[23] Using SDT as somewhat of a fundamental basis, they created a motivational model for coaches that had autonomy supportive behaviour as a key element. In order to motivate people, we must first let them feel empowered, or rather have the opportunity to be autonomous, along with the belief that they are equipped to make their own decisions. Again, what we see is an increase in effort, communication, teamwork, and so on. People even become more invested in something they feel they can impact upon, especially when those impacts are given credit. This increase of investment is a large contributor to the love that people can feel for their individual pursuits and sometimes even their jobs. Actively pursuing something you love or feel invested in is the spark that has driven many a 'genius' to be recognised as just that.

"Working hard for something we don't care about is called stressed; working hard for something we love is called passion."
Simon Sinek[24]

"What really motivates people at Facebook is building stuff that they're proud of."
Mark Zuckerberg[25]

In some respects, autonomy is often a product of time. As we grow from infancy into adulthood, we are in the large given greater opportunities for autonomy. Our parents go from guiding or even dictating our every move to letting us make our own decisions—and often mistakes. If we plot this increase of autonomy against the perception of wisdom, we could assume that wisdom is not just the acquisition of knowledge, but rather a product of increased autonomy. This rings true with the opinion of Immanuel Kant, who talks about the alternative option of not seizing one's autonomy:

"Laziness and cowardice are the reasons why so great a portion of mankind, after nature has long since discharged them from external direction (naturaliter maiorennes), nevertheless remains under lifelong tutelage, and why it is so easy for others to set themselves up as their guardians. It is so easy not to be of age. If I have a book which understands for me, a pastor who has a conscience for me, a physician who decides my diet, and so forth, I need not trouble myself. I need not think, if I can only pay – others will easily undertake the irksome work for me. That the step to competence is held to be very dangerous by the far greater portion of mankind..."
Immanuel Kant[26]

This may go some way as to explain the breakdown of autonomy that comes from later age and increased reliance on grown children to be the responsible and effective adults in the family.[27] The reduction in autonomy seems to marry with the reduction in conviction exhibited by the once-powerful individuals, who now find themselves living sheltered and less dynamic lives. Once an individual loses a sense of autonomy, a sense of reliance is found. Reliance that leads to the ease of guardianship by others, so aptly highlighted by Kant.

If there is any merit to this train of thought, it may also explain the behaviour of the infamous 'millennials'. Take, for example, the world of computer games that the millennial generation, and younger generations since, gravitate towards so greatly.[28] These games allow the user to exert complete autonomy in a world of fantasy, without any of the associated real-life risks, embarrassments, and setbacks. Players can, as a result, reinvent themselves in a guise of their choosing, maintaining complete control. Even better is the idea that if things go wrong or at least not according to plan, you can always hit reset. Given that life presents no such opportunity (well, not with such ease of use), is it any wonder that young people gravitate towards this alternate and safer reality? When you provide autonomy at the click of a button and remove significant consequences for their actions, you provide a world of escape where people feel thoroughly empowered.

We can see a trend emerging here. Humans need autonomy and to feel empowered to exercise that autonomy. If you are in a position of facilitating that autonomy, then you should probably do it. Parenting could therefore be suggested to be best when it is autonomy supportive, encouraging considered expression and standing straight, rather than being held straight.

"As soon as you trust yourself, you will know how to live."
Goethe[29]

"The greatest fruit of self-reliance is freedom."
Epicurus[30]

"Your people must learn to be masters of their own fate."
Optimus Prime, from 'Transformers'[31]

FINAL THOUGHTS

With an increase in autonomy comes an increase in realisation of personal identity, purpose of life, and expression of will. As we have seen, if you are consciously and willingly choosing your path, you are more likely to be invested in that life choice and thus more engaged. As far as SDT and Kant are concerned, this also means the facilitation of competence and relatedness. The initiation of your journey rings true with Bruce Lee's 'honest expression' in chapter 2. Mix all this together and we have the recipe for a fulfilling life driven by our own steam. We are prepared and equipped to make our own individual mark on the world. Walt Whitman said it so eloquently when he described the opportunity that exists for those who are driving their own lives. In the midst of all the drama of life, the abundance of external influence, and the tendency towards apathy, lies an opportunity for us all to contribute something that is ours and ours alone. That contribution, like a canvas painted to your own design, can take any form. Whatever metaphor you choose to illustrate this sentiment, painting or driving, the important thing is that you are holding the brush or the wheel. You and no one else.

"The question, O me! so sad, recurring—What good amid these, O me, O life?
Answer.
That you are here—that life exists and identity,
That the powerful play goes on, and you may contribute a verse."
Walt Whitman[32]

"There is no one out there to tell us 'here is a goal worth spending your life on'. Because there is no absolute certainty to which to turn, each person must discover ultimate purpose on their own."
Mihalyi Csikszentmihalyi[33]

PART 2: KNOWLEDGE AND PERCEPTION

CHAPTER 5

LEARNING TO LEARN

PART A: WHY WE NEED TO FAIL

"He who would learn to fly one day must first learn to stand and walk and run and dance. One cannot fly into flying."
***Nietzsche*[1]**

"You tried your best and you failed miserably. The lesson is... never try."
***Homer Simpson*[2]**

Learning is a strange concept. On the one hand it is something that we all do and yet, in many circumstances, somehow still believe to be beyond our reach. We place limitations on our own capacity such that we convince ourselves we are inadequate. High levels of learning are often seen as a mystical entity, belonging only to those endowed with the even more magical 'talent', the key to which access is granted. We are taught this, conditioned towards this, and our brains even find their own evidence to support this. But the wisdom of old and the science of new can shed a different light on this unfortunate psychological indoctrination. The way in which we learn is so much more than just repetition, perceived natural 'gifts', and immediate success. Our abilities are in fact a product of processes, mindsets, and efforts, wrapped up in a long succession of failure. Here, learning is not 'bestowed upon', but acquired; learning is not winning, rather losing, over and over again. For in the failure lies opportunity, information, and new territory that we can explore within our own minds, taking us wherever we choose to go.

HOW DO WE LEARN?

How human beings learn is a very tricky question and one that many have sought to answer. Over the last century or so, educational psychologists have been trying to accurately determine how learning takes place and how we can improve the rate at which it occurs. Interestingly, the dominant theories of learning followed the general attitudes to behavioural sciences of that time. Initially, the behaviourism movement was thought to adequately explain learning. The behaviourist approach is one of stimulus and response (Pavlov and his salivating dogs again). The idea is that certain stimuli will incur certain reactions and that with continual reinforcement, this reaction can be conditioned. The terms classical and operant conditioning are used to explain this process, where in the case of Pavlov, the recurrent ringing of a bell at feeding time for dogs eventually caused the dogs to salivate even without the presence of food. In other words, the dogs became conditioned to associate the sound of the bell with food and thus salivated accordingly.

The behaviourist approaches subsequently caused a shift in how people were educated, leading to what we might refer to as your more archetypal and dictatorial teaching methods that we are probably all familiar with. Conditioning people to respond a certain way through certain stimuli does indeed work. The use of positive or negative reinforcement that encourages or dissuades people from certain behaviours has repeatedly been shown to have effect.[3] However, there are several limitations. Behaviourism is bound by its own laws, so to speak. Using that approach, we are not invoking original thought. We are merely conditioning people into or out of particular behaviours. The issue lies in whether or not the person doing the conditioning happens to actually know what is 'right' for them to do in the first place. Also, the idea that our behaviours and knowledge are being shaped by stimuli suggests that there is an appropriate stimuli for anything we need to assimilate into our being – which is not necessarily the case.

Behaviourism was effective in being able to condition large groups of people to obtain the same information. Given that it is an environmental theory based on observable behaviour, if you can alter the environment and thus the stimuli, you can control the behaviour. The emphasis here is on controlling behaviour, something that behaviourists like Skinner thought was the purpose of psychology. But the idea that literally everything we learn and do is based on stimulus and response negates any form of internal processes and cognition occurring. As a result, behaviourism was overtaken by alternative theories.

Cognitivism became the dominant discourse among psychologists in the 1960s, viewing the individual and their learning as more of a computer, processing information in order to learn. The theory placed the individual at the centre of the process, actively engaging with information, storing and processing it in order to inform future behaviour and knowledge recall. So rather than the passive, almost victim-like nature of the behaviourist subject, in the cognitivist world, the individual is in control. However, this idea was predicated on things like memory and recall, along with the philosophical idea of human internal computer programs, which in itself had limitations. In many people's minds, computers will never be able to reach the cognitive heights of humans, due to the fact that computers have to be programmed with 'laws' of processing.

The more flexible nature of human thinking and behaviour meant that cognitivism was thought to be a little limited.

Constructivism is the other dominant theory of learning. Some of you may have heard of such pioneers in this field as Piaget and Vygotsky. The constructionist approach is of building knowledge internally, rather than acquiring or processing new knowledge like a computer. The theory is based primarily on social interaction in order to facilitate the building of these internal structures. If people are in contact with the relevant facilitator of knowledge, they can develop understanding through discussion and observation etc., and continue to build their knowledge 'houses'. However, much like the others, constructivist theories are not without their critics. The social element and 'group thinking' is thought to potentially stifle the individual in terms of their own individualised cognition.[4] Couple this with the emergence of humanistic approaches, where individuals are thought to want to develop their personal potential requiring a mixture of approaches, and we have a bit of an impasse (think of Maslow's hierarchy in chapter 4).

Humanistic approaches are based on the individual nature of human experience and thus the belief that humans find the answers within themselves. We can almost view this concept as an extension of constructivism and cognitivism, whereby the processing and building of knowledge creates our understanding internally. Strangely, within educational psychology, humanism is a relatively modern trend (of the last 20 years or so), playing more of a role in current educational practice than ever before. Here we see the teacher act as facilitator adopting a 'person centred' approach.[5] Whilst this approach is not consistently delivered in schools, it does suggest a movement in that direction within educational practice. Yet from a philosophical perspective, it is well established and steeped in history. I have already mentioned the thoughts of Galileo, suggesting that 'you cannot teach a man anything, you can only help him to find it within himself'. So, the idea that internal exploration is the key to learning is nothing new. Humanism strives to create independent thinkers, capable of navigating the world themselves, whilst using available resources to do so. Interestingly, some of the greatest philosophers have sought to encourage the same mantra.

> *"When you want to teach children to think, you begin by treating them seriously when they are little, giving them responsibilities, talking to them candidly, providing privacy and solitude for them, and making them readers and thinkers of significant thoughts from the beginning. That's if you want to teach them to think."*
>
> ***Bertrand Russell***[6]

OUTSIDE OF THE BOX

Thinkers are what change the world. Thinkers are the ones that are not bound within the confines of stimulus and response, or by the limitations of those around them. Thinkers are the 'outside of the box' people that we hear so much about, where the box is the traditional behaviourist and socially constructed prison that prohibits original thought. Now this does not mean that education is therefore detrimental, but does suggest that it can be rather stifling if not facilitative toward original thinking. Consequently, this idea saw recent attention through the pioneering work of Sir Ken Robinson.[7] His annotated presentation on divergent thinking was a huge online hit, with millions of viewers on YouTube and TED. He discussed that education often conditions students out of original thinking by suggesting to them that there is a predetermined 'answer' for everything. If all the thinking has been done and therefore all of the answers have been found, why would I need to think for myself? (This sentiment is a basis for intellectual curiosity, which we will discuss later in this chapter.)

He also highlights previous studies into divergent thinking, where

98% of 5-year-olds were classified as divergent-thinking geniuses. Unfortunately, testing the same children 5 and 10 years later saw that number shrink drastically. In other words, education restricted divergent thinking and limited creativity. This does not exactly bode well when we consider that a large amount of jobs that will exist in 10 years, do not exist now. Creativity is exactly what young people need in order to prepare them for the future, rather than a narrow viewpoint of existing intellectual superiority. This idea that education actually restricts our views and limits our creativity is not a new concept, though:

"The only thing that interferes with my learning is my education."
Albert Einstein (paraphrase of Grant Allen)[8]

Einstein saw that his ideas came from his ability to think for himself, rather than rely on already discovered knowledge. If we only travel to the extent of our existing knowledge, we never learn anything new. Einstein was a master of the 'thought experiment', with which he created theories that we have only now been able to prove through developments in technology. Interestingly, it wasn't until Isaac Newton was forced to stay at his home during the plague years and contemplate his work creatively that he was able to develop some of his most startling ideas. Whilst the educational system was far from comparable to today, there is still synergy in that 'education', as it were, was nothing in comparison to freedom of thought. Removing the idea that we 'already know' what there is to know, is the very precept for emptying your proverbial cup, allowing for more knowledge to be received. We will discuss this in more detail in chapters 6 and 7, but the following quotes might help articulate the aforementioned for now. Observe the similarity between the 'educated' expert having a lack of divergent thinking, whereas the beginner's mind (like that of a child) is divergent to the core.

"Some of the most brilliant, creative people I know did not do well at school. Many of them didn't really discover what they could do—and who they really were—until they'd left school and recovered from their education."
Sir Ken Robinson[7]

*"**Moat**: It is hard to fill a cup that is already full."*
From the movie 'Avatar'[9]

"If your mind is empty, it is always ready for anything, it is open to everything. In the beginner's mind there are many possibilities, but in the expert's mind there are few."
Shunryu Suzuki[10]

THE MYTH OF LEARNING STYLES

The puzzle of how we learn has brought about many a development in educational practice. One notable inclusion is that of learning styles. Many of you will have been exposed to this, having been told that you fit into one camp or another. Visual, auditory, kinaesthetic etc. You will possibly even have been tested for this supposed learning style. However, despite being promoted in virtually every school, college, and university for many years, there isn't actually any evidence to support its use. Tesia Marshik in her TEDx presentation *Learning Styles and the Importance of Critical Self-reflection* discusses this point well.[11] She discusses how studies examining the matching of a supposed style of learning or style of teaching to match that learning style, has any impact of the learning that takes place. There are several videos on YouTube by notable researchers that illustrate this issue well, but suffice to say the 'myth of learning styles' is exactly that. Instead, what matters is meaning. Meaning derived from whatever resource and function is necessary. Whatever process that is required in order to help the individual create a sense of meaning internally, often corresponding with the individual being involved in the discovery of that information. This discovery is part of the 'doing' referred to by many a previous philosopher, once again illustrating that they may have had it right all along.

"I hear and I forget. I see and I remember. I do and I understand."
Chinese proverb[12]

"For the things we have to learn before we can do them, we learn by doing them."
Aristotle[13]

Rather than just preach to those who wish to learn, we need to involve those who wish to learn. By involving people, or indeed involving yourself, you are centrally placed in the knowledge acquisition process. You see, hear, feel, and smell your way through an experience that cements a greater understanding than you would have otherwise gained. Tesia Marshik uses a great example of teaching someone about flowers and their smells.[11] Are you supposed to tell someone how a flower smells, all because they are apparently an auditory learner? Or do you encourage them to go and smell them? When you put it that way, it seems obvious. Some of us may indeed have a preference for how we learn, however this does not make a difference when tested, much to the dismay of those who believe the opposite. It seems that with the right conditioning and conviction, we will argue strongly about something that does not exist, convincing ourselves of its reality. Perhaps the behaviourists were right after all!

If meaning is what is required for us to learn something and education needs to remove the ceiling on divergent thinking, then where do we go from here? The phenomenological approaches adopted in countries like Finland may be the answer.[14] With this approach, the experience of the individual is the main priority, rather than the experience of others. It lets the individual explore a situation and use their own perspectives to create meaning. It is a tool that elicits a much greater amount of self-teaching, reflection, and creativity for overcoming hurdles. Consider at this point that the most innovative people of the world have often taught themselves as they went along, immersed in a field that interested them, exploring the world through their own eyes.

MAKING MISTAKES

At the heart of the philosophy behind more meaningful learning is the approach to and processing of mistakes. More traditional and mainstream theories of education that we have discussed essentially sought to eradicate mistakes. Mistakes meant that you had not learned the 'answer'. Mistakes showed an unwillingness to react accordingly to the given stimuli or provide the right recitation of information dictated. However, mistakes are exactly the opposite. They are vital sources of information that help inform experience and nurture divergent and independent thinking. As Sir Ken Robinson puts it:

> *"We stigmatize mistakes. And we're now running national educational systems where mistakes are the worst thing you can make — and the result is that we are educating people out of their creative capacities.*
> *... If you're not prepared to be wrong, you'll never come up with anything original."*
>
> ***Sir Ken Robinson***[7]

Effective learning is littered with failure. How we perceive and deal with this failure is what makes the difference between what we can learn and what we end up learning. Failures are not to be avoided; they are to be actively sought. Much like the last chapter suggested, failures are not representative of who we are (well, unless you choose to see it that way). The 'pain' associated with failure is a core component of both the overcoming of chaos and therefore future success.

"We cannot learn without suffering."
Aeschlyus (attributed to Aristotle)[15]

"To err is human."
Alexander Pope[16]

"Failures are not your own self. See to it that you are free from them. Only when you can relinquish them can you really be free and no longer assailed by them."
Thích Nhất Hạnh[17]

If we are to assess the lives of the 'successful' people, we see a significant trend. Business leaders, sports people, musicians and the like, all have a story of failure upon failure. The failed businesses, the losses and struggles to learn techniques, the record label rejections, all led to the creation of the successful entity you admire on TV. J. K. Rowling was reportedly turned down 12 times by publishers before finally landing a deal with Bloomsbury.[18] Failure, it would seem, is not indicative of the product you have but rather your and the world's perception. If the opposite were true, Harry Potter would have been no more than a forgotten dream and a lost manuscript. The Japanese proverb of 'Nana korobi, ya oki', or 'fall down 7 times, stand up 8' is a great way of viewing failure and one that we are all glad Rowling adhered to (standing up 13 times, that is). Even though the maths is debatable (depending on your assumption of the original position), the sentiment is clear. Being knocked down is nothing but a change of position and one that you can right pretty easily.

"Our greatest glory is not in never falling, but in rising every time we fall."
Oliver Goldsmith (often attributed to Confucius)[19]

"I've missed more than 9000 shots in my career. I've lost almost 300 games. 26 times, I've been trusted to take the game winning shot and missed. I've failed over and over and over again in my life. And that is why I succeed."
Michael Jordan[20]

Unfortunately, the idea of failure is wrapped up in fear and loathing. The already discussed indoctrination of perfection has created a fear of failure that is often paralysing for many. It is this fear that attaches each outcome to our sense of self, preventing us from embarking on that quest that we so dearly want to pursue. The fear of failure is therefore a powerful thing. For what else could separate us from our dreams?

"We walk away from our dreams afraid we may fail, or worse yet, afraid we may succeed."
William Forrester from the movie 'Finding Forrester'[21]

"To conquer fear is the beginning of wisdom."
Bertrand Russell[22]

Fear of failure is a large concept to explain in itself. We will discuss this in more detail in the next chapter, though. So we will continue for now focusing on failure being not a necessary evil, but just necessary. The very essence of what Sir Ken Robinson is trying to convey is a change in the narrative of learning. If we change the assumptions and preconceptions as to what failure means, our resultant reactions will too be changed. So what then to think of failure? Let's start with the simple idea that you just haven't figured out the right strategy yet (emphasis on both 'strategy' and 'yet').

In a previous chapter looking at task orientation and intrinsic motivation, we first saw the notion of trying to come up with the most appropriate strategy in order to be successful in a given task. This is the basis of the mental shift required for revising our views on failure. Instead of a negative reaction and feeling that we have got it wrong, we can actually see failure as an indication that an alternative strategy is required. This becomes an unemotional response (much like chapter 2) that enables us to rationally consider the challenge at hand, rather than fretting about how we look after this momentary 'mistake'. The 'yet' refers to the belief that with the right investment of effort and the analysis of information provided by the 'failure', we can determine a more optimum strategy to benefit our end result. By taking this approach, we are turning the 'threat' of a failure into the 'challenge' to find the right strategy. Bearing in mind that we have already discussed the psychological benefits of viewing challenges where threats once stood, this idea only reinforces the need for change.

INTELLIGENCE AND NATURAL ABILITY

Is learning and therefore success just a case of finding the right strategy and information? Is it really that simple? What about intelligence, talent, and all the other things that some appear to be endowed with? Well, to the answer the first question simply, yes is the answer. Philosophically at least, any problem or challenge is just about taking the right strategy. From how to perform a difficult task like juggling, making a successful business, or even the creation of a universal theory to marry general relativity and quantum mechanics, the utilisation of the appropriate strategy is the answer. The issue that most people have is the belief that many things are beyond their potential.

Intelligence is a very tricky concept. IQ is a construct that involves aspects of fluid intelligence (cognitive reasoning, '*g*', '*Gf*' or the '*g factor*') and crystallised intelligence ('*Gc*', what we might normally consider as knowledge).[23] Also, IQ is a relative score, meaning that it is in comparison to normative scores across large populations. In other words, IQ is how you score against other people your age etc.[23] The latter is extremely important when it comes to the improvement of IQ, which we will discuss shortly. IQ has been shown to strongly correlate with many aspects of human life 'success' and is about as robust a method of measuring intelligence as you are ever likely to get in the world of psychology.[23] That being said, it is not without its issues of accuracy and reliability.

The problem with IQ arises when we consider our ability to change our IQ and the importance we place on it in terms of the impact it has on our learning and on our lives. One only needs to type 'can I change my IQ?' into a search engine to see that this debate is hotly disputed.[24] Even among professionals of the same field, the question as to whether we can improve our intelligence is still a sore subject. Whilst the average intelligence of Western communities seems to be increasing decade by decade, jumping on that finding to suggest that we can individually improve our IQ is possibly a mistake.[25] I mentioned earlier that IQ is relative. Combine this with evidence that nutrition seems to have an impact on IQ development across nations and we see that greater nourishment in large communities is having an impact on that rise.[26] In other words, if people are not struggling for food, their brains develop more efficiently and thus the average IQ score increases.

One of the things that people tend to jump onto is the fluctuation of IQ across ages. Research has shown that IQ fluctuates more so in adolescence than at any other time. Other than that, the variability of IQ is pretty small over our lives and flattens out after our 20s.[24] Some believe that 'brain training' can improve IQ, however the evidence of this shows the opposite. We just get better at the games, not more intelligent.[23] The semantics of intelligence seem to be argued as much as anything else. The evidence appears to lean towards a few key conclusions, including: IQ is largely constant, good nutrition and breast milk improve IQ in early development, knowledge can increase in spite of IQ, and that we can make ourselves appear 'smarter' by improving our cognitive functioning and strategies employed.[24]

FINAL THOUGHTS

It's important that we take the right things from this. No amount of breast milk is going to improve the IQ of a 45-year-old man and adolescent fluctuations of a girl's IQ is not exactly indicative of what she will end up with. I'll offer a significant takeaway from all this—your IQ is pretty much fixed, however that isn't necessarily what you should be focused on. Instead, your attitude towards learning and development, and your perception of intelligence *is* what you should focus on.

PART B: IT'S ALL IN THE MINDSET

"To get good, it's helpful to be willing, or even enthusiastic, about being bad. Baby steps are the royal road to skill."
Daniel Coyle[27]

Simply put, IQ is akin to the software or processing capabilities of a computer that will impact our speed of knowledge construction, for example. However, just because someone has slightly better software, doesn't mean that we cannot run that program. What most people are confusing with IQ is their level of knowledge. Knowledge is what we have learned and IQ is our level of fluid intelligence. They are not one and the same. When these two things are confused, we can begin to convince ourselves that we need to be 'intelligent' in order to learn something that probably does not require a huge amount of IQ to do so. We construct a narrative whereby we tell ourselves and others that we are not intelligent 'enough'. But who are we to accurately surmise as to the intelligence required in order to learn this information or perform that task? Ultimately, we do nothing more that create excuses and safety blankets that prevent us from challenging ourselves in tasks that are well within our intellectual capabilities.

MINDSET

The pioneering work of Carol Dweck and colleagues has been the catalyst for an educational breakthrough of late.[28] I would recommend that everyone read *Mindset*, both for the sake of yourself and your children, or your potential children to come. Essentially, Dweck found that the mindset taken by individuals is the single most important factor for fulfilling potential. She provides a distinction between 'fixed' and 'growth' mindsets, showing what impact they both have on our ability to learn and on our perception of what is possible, given our level of IQ. Consider reframing your perceptions of 'how intelligent you need to be to understand… (insert the relevant topic of choice)'. Unfortunately, many of us have incorrect assumptions about what is within our limits and therefore maintain fixed mindsets, permitting us not to put forth the effort. There is even evidence of a potential placebo effect on IQ tests, showing that attitude towards intelligence is very important.[29]

Roughly 70% of people fall within one standard deviation of the mean (average) IQ score (between 85 and 115).[30] These people encompass a huge array of professions, skills, languages, and knowledge bases. In that respect, the majority of us have the ability to learn about and get better at pretty much anything we desire. What it takes is the right mindset, effort, and strategy. Yes, there may be individuals with more of a head start genetically, but any skill is a learned behaviour. Knowledge and skill are thus a movable feast and not a stable component.

> *"In a growth mindset, people believe that their most basic abilities can be developed through dedication and hard work—brains and talent are just the starting point. This view creates a love of learning and a resilience that is essential for great accomplishment."*
>
> ***Carol Dweck***[28]

Now, the growth mindset is not a gimmick or a positive mantra designed to convince the individual of something that does not exist. The growth mindset is a genuine disposition from which we infer the correct assumption that knowledge and ability can be developed. This concept is supported by a wealth of empirical data that can be repeated over and over again.[31] People who adopt a growth concept ("With sustained effort and willingness, I can overcome") outperform those with a fixed mindset ("I can't change my intelligence/ability") over time.

Dweck gives many examples in her book *Mindset*, illustrating some core points. Maths is a regular theme within her work due to the evidence suggesting that fixed mindsets are more common in that subject.[31] Using a 6-point scale questionnaire to identify the mindset of students, their performance was tracked over time. Students with a growth mindset not only experienced significantly greater maths results, but displayed some interesting differences. Students with growth mindsets were more oriented towards goals, cared more about learning (rather than just test scores), valued effort much more highly than their fixed counterparts, and reacted to failure with more 'mastery oriented' behaviours (like in chapter 4).[31]

There are several reasons for these findings, but they largely centre around people with fixed mindsets wanting to validate their ability through results. In other words, they think that getting a good result or not is indicative of their ability and, as such, build an identity and belief system around that (either good or bad). Practically, this means that if they receive a bad grade, it hits them much harder than someone that does not need a grade to validate their maths-based self-worth. Receiving a bad grade therefore means 'I am bad at maths', rather than the growth mindset response of 'I haven't got the right strategy yet'.

Consider the value of this for a moment. Whilst you do, consider the danger of the fixed mindset as well. If we focus on the outcome and attach our self-worth to it, we restrict our development. Now apply that to everything in life. How many things do we all attach a fixed mindset toward? Bear in mind that you can have both a fixed or growth mindset to different aspects of life. For example, 'I'm not good at languages!' is something I often hear and subsequently question. The fixed mindset impairs and even prohibits an attempt at developing their ability. The fact that they have already successfully learned their own language and are using said language to convey their inability to 'learn a language' seems to evade their awareness. Perhaps I will write a book on life's contradictions somewhen in the future. If you can learn a language, you can surely learn another, right? Unfortunately, the same is said of many things in life. Many of us hold beliefs in our inability to change or develop our prowess in a given topic. A belief that is simply not true.

Many have a problem with the examples above. In the light of ultra-positive motivational slogans/psychology, self-appreciation, and mental health concerns, we are taught to tell people how wonderful they are. With regard to self-worth, appreciating themselves for who and what they are is of course a good thing. However, attaching that to the idea of an outcome is exactly what creates fixed mindsets. Praising a child for being 'so clever' or being 'so beautiful' reinforces that the child should identify with being clever or beautiful. So, when a situation arises that threatens that sense of intelligence or attractiveness, what do you think happens? On a small scale, they avoid the threat and continue to operate in a safe environment, unchallenged and therefore undeveloped. On a larger or more significant scale, they capitulate. If I am no longer beautiful, what am I?

You may be forgiven for thinking 'what do I say to my child/spouse/friend? Can I not ever praise them for being intelligent or beautiful?' In moderation, of course you can. However, think about what you are reinforcing. Think about what you reinforce to yourself or how you let the words of others reinforce a potentially fixed mindset in your own mind. Rather than outcomes, think about separating the individual from a fixed identity and praising learning, effort, and resilience instead. Dweck describes this issue well in a learning context:

"So what should we say when children complete a task—say, math problems—quickly and perfectly? Should we deny them the praise they have earned? Yes. When this happens, I say, 'Whoops. I guess that was too easy. I apologize for wasting your time. Let's do something you can really learn from!'"

Carol Dweck[28]

This may well seem harsh to parents' eyes. However, rather than dwell on the perceived travesty of not constantly telling your child how amazing they are, think more about what you want them to be. Do you want them to be confined within the prison of their perceived fixed abilities, scared to reach beyond them for fear of failure? Or do you want them to be free from insecure identity attachment and become robust and resilient individuals who make themselves better at everything? As mentioned earlier, many people have a mixture of fixed and growth mindsets attached to different aspects of themselves. This is in part down to what was reinforced to them by society. Likely, the things that were not suggested to us as being indicative of our self-worth are the things that we believe to be malleable components. Have you ever taught yourself something, just for the sake of it? If so, did you persevere until you could do it? You were exercising a growth mindset in order to do so. The motto of 'improvise, adapt and overcome', loosely attributed to the American Marines, is exactly what the growth mindset is all about. The key, though, is not believing that it only applies to certain parts of your life.

"Do not imagine that, if something is hard for you to achieve, it is therefore impossible for any man: but rather consider anything that is humanly possible and appropriate to lie within your own reach too."

Marcus Aurelius[32]

The idea of resilience is therefore a major part of growth mindsets. It is the enjoyment of the process that learning takes, as much as the outcome gained. Overcoming problems and achieving goals is inherently fulfilling. So is the process of learning. If we can enjoy the journey of learning, we will be invigorated and renewed with energy to help us overcome obstacles.

"Becoming is better than being."
Carol Dweck[28]

"Anything that is successful is a series of mistakes."
Billie Armstrong[33]

Enjoying the learning journey means embracing mistakes. In turn, this allows for a whole new outlook on what we are doing, what we want to achieve, and the process required to get there. Recent work of Mathew Syed in *Black Box Thinking* highlights this point well.[34] His work refers to changing the idea of mistakes as something to seek out and learn from, rather than avoid. Often, human beings are so concerned with failure that we end up setting vague or too easily obtainable goals, blaming others for poor outcomes or even covering up mistakes. The most dynamic and advanced industries in the world take exactly the opposite approach to failure. Syed discusses the world of aviation as a case in point (hence *Black Box Thinking*). Acknowledging exactly what went wrong and actively seeking alternative strategies is what has dramatically improved the aviation world in terms of safety and mortality rates. Alternatively, he discusses the blame culture inherent within the medical profession, which only maintains the existing unwarranted mortality rates due to mistakes in care and process.

"We cover up mistakes, not only to protect ourselves from others, but to protect us from ourselves."
Mathew Syed[34]

"Be not ashamed of mistakes and thus make them crimes."
Confucius[35]

"By seeking and blundering we learn."
Van Goethe[36]

Mistakes are not just errors we can learn from, they provide biological enhancements, too. Daniel Coyle, author of *Talent Code*, discusses this at length.[27] He brought the idea of talent and skill improvement in any discipline being the product of the development of neural pathways in the brain to the forefront of public awareness. Coyle highlights the laying down of myelin around neurons in order to strengthen the signals being sent. He describes it as something similar to insulation around copper wiring, strengthening the signals by removing wasted activity. Practising a particular pursuit at any level of current competence allows for these neurons to fire more frequently. The more they fire, the more myelin is laid down. With regards to challenge and problems, the signals are developed by firing 'sub-optimally' during practice, essentially requiring demands to exceed competence. In other words, we need to both practise something and create an environment where the performance that is targeted is beyond our current capability. Coyle also describes the 'sweet spot', where practice is at its most beneficial.

"Struggle is not an option: it's a biological requirement."

"The sweet spot: that productive, uncomfortable terrain located just beyond our current abilities, where our reach exceeds our grasp."

Daniel Coyle[27]

There is a striking similarity between Coyle's words and the content of chapter 1. Coyle is stating that our level of myelin creation is relative to how difficult the task is in relation to our ability. The 'uncomfortable terrain' that is 'just beyond our capability' is the proverbial division between chaos and order in the Tao, the optimum challenge point that provides the conditions for achieving flow and maximal growth. It would appear that the philosophical is more than just that, it's actually biological and physically quantifiable. Couple this with growth mindsets and challenging situations that help build new circuitry in the brain and we have a powerful weapon for self-development.

"Picture your brain forming new connections as you meet the challenge and learn. Keep on going."

Carol Dweck[28]

"What ignited the progress wasn't any innate skill or gene. It was a small, ephemeral, yet powerful idea: a vision of their ideal future selves, a vision that oriented, energized, and accelerated progress, and that originated in the outside world."

Daniel Coyle[27]

Consider the opposite for a moment. To practise or exist in a state of comfort is to reside too deeply in order. The high level of competence in relation to the task at hand creates the boredom that prevents flow. As a result, our neurons are not firing under a state of duress and thus no additional myelin is deposited. Our performance remains constant, if not even diminished, based on a reduction in enthusiasm. The key is practising at the right level with the right expectations, at the uncomfortable divide of chaos and order, where we can continue our pursuit of a better self.

"When what we have mastered becomes mundane, we feel pain. The antidote is pursuit."
Kelsey Ramsden[37]

"You must do something, but inasmuch as with your limited capacities it will be impossible to make anything easier that it has become, you must, with the same humanitarian enthusiasm as the others, undertake to make something harder."
Soren Kierkegaard[38]

Practice is more than just level of intensity or difficulty, though. Practice, when utilised to its maximum potential, is a targeted activity. Anders Ericsson is a pioneer of what is known as 'Deliberate Practice'.[39] His work has spawned an array of additional work on what is generally known as the '10,000 hours rule' (Malcolm Gladwell's 'Outliers'[40] and Matthew Syed's 'Bounce'[41]), though often slightly misunderstood. Ericsson's method is rooted in 'how' we practise, rather than just 'how much' we practise. The emphasis is on breaking things down into sections and working specifically on things that need attention, rather than just mindless repetition. This affords people more opportunity to utilise their time efficiently and focus on aspects that will provide a direct improvement. One drawback, however, is that deliberate practice can be viewed as a little boring (due to a misinterpretation of the diligence required for deliberate practice). People often avoid targeted and deliberate practice as it takes away the opportunity for more frivolous activity that sits within our zone of comfort. Motivation to practise deliberately is therefore a factor to be considered. But for that problem, we can revert to the growth mindset and task orientation/intrinsic motivation. If we develop a mindset that promotes attaining new information and improving our standards, we become less interested in just showing off our ability. As a result, enjoyment is found in the improvement, rather than the resultant execution of a skill, technique, or correct answer.

The theories and evidence appear to coalesce. Interestingly, not only does 10,000 hours of deliberate practice appear to be a golden figure (a lot of time, I know), but that deliberate practice seems to be optimal at approximately 3–5hours a day (as per Coyle's work).

"Deep practice is not simply about struggling; it's about seeking a particular struggle, which involves a cycle of distinct actions."

Daniel Coyle[27]

MARGINAL GAINS

This type of practice creates minute improvements on a daily basis that add up to huge improvements over time, or 'marginal gains' as the world now seems to know it. You may be familiar with the term from any number of industries. Famously, David Brailsford is a major exponent of marginal gains, which led to the incredible turnaround of British Cycling over the last 16 years. Brailsford adopted the '1%' approach, in that he addressed everything possible in attempting to gain this subtle improvement, from the bike, to living conditions, hygiene, recovery techniques etc.[42] Whilst his techniques were not exclusive to just the rider, it does show the value of these small and sometimes imperceptible changes. Much like our brains, focusing on 1% incremental changes can bring incredible results over time.

"Excellence is never an accident. It is always the result of high intention, sincere effort, and intelligent execution; it represents the wise choice of many alternatives – choice, not chance, determines your destiny."

Aristotle[43]

"Throughout your life advance daily, becoming more skilful than yesterday, more skilful than today. This is never-ending."

Yamemoto Tsunetomo[44]

"Marginal gains is not about making small changes and hoping they fly. Rather, it is about breaking down a big problem into small parts in order to rigorously establish what works and what doesn't."

Matthew Syed[34]

EFFORT, PERSISTENCE, AND INTELLECTUAL CURIOSITY

What we have seen in this chapter are the prevailing theories about how we learn. We have dealt with the psychology and biology of learning, as well as the preconceptions that surround this. However, the final elements that need mentioning are that of effort, persistence, and curiosity. Without effort, we have the tools with which to learn, but not the impetus to start, continue, or overcome. Angela Duckworth's research states that 'grit', or the 'combination of passion and persistence', is the most important predictor and indicator of achievement in any discipline. Grit actually appears to be wrapped up in conscientiousness and openness in terms of The Big Five personality traits, but regardless of its correct categorisation, effort seems to be the obvious but underappreciated component that unlocks our ability.

"Genius is one per cent inspiration and 99 per cent perspiration."
A paraphrase of Thomas Edison[45]

"Failure is acceptable. but not trying is a whole different ball park."
Michael Jordan[46]

"Development requires deliberate effort, while tempering desires and knowing contentment."
Lao Tzu[47]

Deliberate and focused effort seems to be a prerequisite for performance improvement. Though in order to obtain this development, our effort must be maintained for long enough that noticeable changes occur. This is a mark of the now ever-popular term resilience, or the ability to recover after setbacks. Consistently refocusing your intentions and learning strategies, making sure that the demand is just out of your skill set, and chipping away at your deliberate practice requires an unyielding effort. In a later chapter we will discuss what we can do to feed this effort and maintain the fire inside for continuous improvement.

Intellectual curiosity was alluded to earlier by Sir Ken Robinson's comments on how education effectively beats that out of us as children. Curiosity is essentially defined as the desire to know something. So it makes sense that curiosity in itself is a major part of our ability or inability to learn something. Indeed, research shows that heightened curiosity (by generating predictions) increases memory retention of correct answers and stimulates physiological processes associated with learning (increased pupil dilation etc.).[48] Curiosity increases 'the relevance of the knowledge gap' and is linked to intrinsic motivators rather than extrinsic motivators.[48] In other words, the more we have invested in finding something out, the more persistent and resilient we will be in the search for that knowledge.

"Curiosity is the wick in the candle of learning."
William Arthur Ward[48]

Improving and following our curiosity is something we will discuss more in chapter 10. For now though, the prevailing idea is one of 'interest' and a 'desire to bridge the knowledge gap'. This final ingredient is what keeps us going in those dark times when things seem too difficult. It is one of the qualities that made pioneers like Stephen Hawking so inspiring. The sheer vigour with which he followed his 'intellectual quest' powered him through a cornucopia of barriers—all in order to explore his ultimate goal of a "complete understanding of the universe, why it is as it is and why it exists at all".[49] Whilst this level of intellectual pursuit is beyond many of us, the sentiment and the drive behind it is not. Being curious about something is within us all. We just have to hold onto it.

"You're never going to learn something as profoundly as when it's purely out of curiosity."
Christopher Nolan[50]

FINAL THOUGHTS

The evidence suggests that learning is neither simple nor easily understood. However, what does appear clear is that there are some key elements to human learning development that are consistent. We *need* to fail. Failure brings vital information. It provides the necessary landscape for converting chaos, because if we can achieve it easily, then it is obviously already within our scope of ability and order. If perceived appropriately, failure creates a motivational climate that brings with it enjoyment and fulfilment. Attitudes are changed so that we do not just enjoy challenge, but actively seek it out. In turn, our neural pathways and signals are strengthened, constantly reinforcing a better pattern of action. Intentionally selecting activities that facilitate these conditions provides the marginal gains that add up to sizeable ones over time. Mix all of the above with effort and curiosity and we can learn anything. So what is it that you have always wanted to learn but have always thought impossible? What have you started learning that you later gave up on? In what ways have you convinced yourself that you've hit your ceiling? Answer these questions and then ask yourself again, how do we learn?

"Try again, fail again, fail better."
Samuel Beckett[51]

"Trying is the first step towards failure."
Homer Simpson[52]

CHAPTER 6

GET SOME PERSPECTIVE!

"We see things as we are, not as they are."
Anais Nin[1]

*"**Stuart:** Oh, Sheldon, I'm afraid you couldn't be more wrong.*
***Sheldon:** More wrong? Wrong is an absolute state and not subject to gradation.*
***Stuart:** Of course it is. It's a little wrong to say a tomato is a vegetable, it's very wrong to say it's a suspension bridge."*
The Big Bang Theory[2]

How do we view the world? Is our perspective fixed or can it change? How did we build this perspective in the first place? We human beings are steered by our view of the world and our beliefs, which impact how we interact with the world. We follow the narrative we tell ourselves, the directions we see for ourselves, and the future we imagine for ourselves. Our upbringing, personality, education, and our predisposition for bias (discussed in the next chapter), can lead our perspectives to be skewed. Instead, we mislead ourselves, getting lost both in our physical direction and our spiritual one. Importantly, our perspectives can change. We can not only see things differently, but can experience them differently, as long as we are motivated to do so. When we see how our perspective is created and how it affects our responses, we can begin to change both ourselves and our outcomes. With only a modicum of knowledge, we might just reveal that which we have always needed. If nothing else, by challenging yourself to address your perspective you may end up being a more enlightened, flexible, and all-around better person. Perspective is an amazing thing; depending on how you look at it, of course.

"Everyone knows nowadays that people 'have complexes'. What is not so well known, though far more important theoretically, is that complexes can have us."
Carl Jung[3]

THE PHILOSOPHY OF PERSPECTIVES

Our perspective begins with our embedded philosophy of life, which some people refer to as our 'worldview'. A worldview is the fundamental beliefs or presuppositions that we hold, which impact how we perceive all things. Whilst we may not know that we have a distinct worldview, we all do. Just because we have never thought or been required to articulate it before, does not mean that our decisions and views are not dictated by it. Artur Nilsson has researched the notion of worldviews extensively and has commented that "research has shown that we are prewired to construct meaning before our perceptions even reach consciousness".[4] In other words, when we are met with situations and stimuli, we both log and react to this information based upon our core beliefs, without necessarily knowing that we have done so.

Nilsson goes on to say that throughout human evolution, we have had to communicate and collaborate, requiring us to share our basic beliefs and systems of perception through story and narrative. As a result, we gravitate towards people who do indeed share those beliefs and perspectives, pulling away from those who do not. What's more is that we view new situations and material through the lens of our worldview, rather than through complete objectivity. Let's just consider that for a moment. Our worldview impacts our immediate response to virtually everything that happens in our lives, even without us knowing about it consciously. We construct and obtain meaning from our experiences and do not always actively engage with that conclusion or question it. Given that we also then use those conclusions to assess the world and those within it, the importance of our worldview is rather emphatic.

Nilsson also discusses the idea that our worldview is somewhat invisible to us. Without engaging in discussion and analysis about how we see the world, our worldview remains hidden but ever active. With that in mind, the self-awareness and introspection discussed in chapter 2 becomes even more prevalent. It is only through this investigation that we can begin to highlight the aspects of our worldview and challenge them accordingly. Again, ignorance is not bliss, for it is still ignorance nonetheless.

Worldviews are thought to essentially cover all major aspects of philosophy (even without knowing it). As a result, you may actually hold beliefs about the following (as broken down by Ken Funk), regardless of ever having questioned them:[5]

- **epistemology**: beliefs about the nature and sources of knowledge
- **metaphysics**: beliefs about the ultimate nature of reality
- **cosmology**: beliefs about the origins and nature of the universe, life, and especially Man
- **teleology**: beliefs about the meaning and purpose of the universe, its inanimate elements, and its inhabitants
- **theology**: beliefs about the existence and nature of God
- **anthropology**: beliefs about the nature and purpose of Man in general and oneself in particular

- **axiology**: beliefs about the nature of value, what is good and bad, what is right and wrong

Many of these categories may seem rather irrelevant to your everyday lives and something that you have never bothered to consider. However, you may be surprised as to just how often these more obscure categories affect your life. Take, for example, axiology and its potential impact on your political stance. Your beliefs of what is right and wrong will likely dictate your affiliation with some form of political leaning or ideology. Combine that with your anthropological beliefs and you have an interested backdrop on which to base your perceptions of taxes, benefit systems, and equality, for example. So again, whilst your worldview may be invisible or undiscovered, it is more than likely active and influential.

Your worldview creates an underlying premise for what you believe is and should be. It dictates your understanding of personal values and what you expect from others. It's what binds or separates you from people and is what you ultimately tell yourself to reinforce those beliefs. Your worldview dictates the direction of your confirmation biases (which we will discuss in the next chapter) and forms the perspective you have of the world and everything in it, including yourself.

> *"One of the biggest problems with the world today is that we have large groups of people who will accept whatever they hear on the grapevine, just because it suits their worldview—not because it is actually true or because they have evidence to support it. The really striking thing is that it would not take much effort to establish validity in most of these cases... but people prefer reassurance to research."*
>
> ***Neil deGrasse Tyson***[6]

BEING STUCK IN OUR EXISTING PERSPECTIVE

As the quote from Tyson suggests, it is easy to become entrenched in a worldview that impacts our perspective on life. That perspective is fed by our current belief system, which in turn is fed by our knowledge and interpretation thereof. Much as the quote from Anais Nin at the beginning of the chapter, "we see things as we are, not as they are". Our interpretations are a product of our personal beliefs, not the other way around. We do not all perceive something objectively, but rather uniquely in relation to our own makeup. In other words, if you and I were both to experience the same thing, we would likely have different interpretations and extract different meanings, not because the event was different for us both, but because we are different people with different beliefs (think about political differences on the same topics).

Thus, our everyday judgements could be seen as nothing more than manifestations of ourselves playing out in reality. What it does mean is that understanding another person's mindset becomes very difficult, as you are not them and, as such, do not see things the way they do. Ultimately, what remains is an ignorance towards other perspectives and a tendency to settle into our own. We'll discuss an answer to this conundrum shortly.

"That we can judge only with regard to our own system, being ignorant of the relations of systems and things."

Alexander Pope[7]

"Each person does see the world in a different way. There is not a single, unifying, objective truth. We're all limited by our perspective."

Siri Hustvedt[8]

CATEGORISING OUR PERSPECTIVES

There is an array of different philosophies of life that provide the basis for all manner of worldviews. Many of which have subtle differences, stemming from some core tenets or conceptualisations. From Socrates' Idealism (ideas are the most important thing, where reasoning should move us to the highest plane of beauty, love, and justice) to the depressingly popular Nihilism (there is no real meaning to life, so what the hell?) and everything in between. Like many things, the common philosophical discourse is often entwined with the prevailing cultural movements of the present time. One might argue that a postmodernist worldview (which we'll come to shortly) has become increasingly prevalent in recent years, motivated by perceptions of oppression in respect of genders, races and so on. Again though, whatever philosophy is followed, the point is that these are a perspective and one that frames what you see, rather than what you see framing your perspective.

It would take far more than just one chapter to describe every known philosophical viewpoint, so instead it is worth discussing the dominant philosophical categories, from which the remaining ones were likely born. It is also worth noting that the ones highlighted are less to do with practical techniques for fulfilling lives (like Stoicism mentioned previously, for example) and more to do with metaphysical and epistemological aspects. Simply put, we are looking more at how these philosophical perspectives explain the world, rather than just how we are supposed to live in it.

PHILOSOPHICAL PERSPECTIVES

Idealism, as alluded to earlier, is the belief that ideas are the only true reality and that those truths are to be held above all. The idealist therefore has lofty 'ideals' that they believe should be aimed towards. Many a famous philosopher would be described as an exponent of idealism, such as Descartes or Kant. Likewise, Socrates' disciple

Plato followed the same thought, however Plato's disciple Aristotle did not. Instead, Aristotle claimed that reality is the physical world we can observe, measure, and study. It's by this method of thinking that we find the term logic, as it refers to the study of forms and the reasoning that comes from studying them. As a result, we can construct a wealth of knowledge about the physical world through studying it. A realist, therefore, is someone who would not necessarily engage in thought-provoking and open-ended discussion, but would rather test a theory and obtain 'factual' information. The idealist deals with theory and opinion subjectively, whereas a realist seeks to find the 'real answer', assuming that there is one.

"Scratch the surface of most cynics and you find a frustrated idealist — someone who made the mistake of converting his ideals into expectations."
Peter Senge[9]

"What I've found in my research is that realism and self-honesty are the antidote to ego, hubris, and delusion."
Ryan Holiday[10]

Pragmatism is the concept of reality as an ever-changing entity. Reality changes based upon what we experience. As such, a pragmatist doesn't search for a fundamental truth, but seeks to develop knowledge through experience to help them navigate through life (hence a more 'pragmatic' method). A pragmatist is more malleable in terms of their opinions and level of inquiry, adopting an approach of 'whatever works' as the best solution to a problem. Existentialism places the individual at the centre of existence, with no meaning to the outside world without us. Reality is thus a product of the individual. As a result, existentialists value the pursuit of self-knowledge with careful consideration of their own decisions and decision-making processes.

"Pure pragmatism can't imagine a bold future. Pure idealism can't get anything done. It is the delicate blend of both that drives innovation."
Simon Sinek[11]

"With every increase in the degree of consciousness, and in proportion to that increase, the intensity of despair increases: the more consciousness the more intense the despair."
Søren Kierkegaard[12]

Postmodernism is the idea that objective and universal truth does not exist, but is merely one line sold to people in a controlling attempt from the powers that be. People are forced to learn or acknowledge 'the truth', which is nothing more than exploitation of marginalised sectors of society and the reinforcement of dominant hierarchies. Think of someone who sees everything in life through a lens of oppression. From class to race and gender, the postmodernist sees the world as being subjected to human lies and domination. Nihilism is an acknowledgement that life lacks meaning. It is often referred to as existential nihilism, where the belief is that concepts such as morality are culturally designed. Friedrich Nietzsche is often placed in this camp, due to his questioning of concepts such as good and evil and their relative existence. In the common form, a nihilist is someone who questions the point of something, in terms of its ultimately meaningless conclusion.

"I think you can get to a point where nihilism, if that's the right word, is overwhelming, and the basic laws that society has set up, either religious or social laws, become meaningless."
Bruce Springsteen[13]

There is a broad spectrum of philosophic perspectives (this is far from an exhaustive list). When considering life and everything within it, we can take myriad approaches and hence adopt myriad perspectives. A key thing to contemplate is which category you may slot into and what impact this may have on your life. I am not for a moment suggesting that any one of the above concepts is correct, but merely that they exist (or not, for the nihilist). So at this point, try to consider which of the above perspectives most aptly describes your views. Which were you drawn towards? What examples can you easily identify that illustrate this? Think about debates you've had, statements you've made, and reactions you've had to various circumstances of life.

CHANGING PERSPECTIVES AND THE PRACTICAL IMPLICATIONS

Identifying our otherwise invisible worldview provides the opportunity to start reassessing our perspectives and seeing how it may challenge our beliefs. Whilst we may be somewhat entrenched in a particular viewpoint, it does not mean that we need to stay that way. Our genetics, socialisation, and education may have led to a rather inevitable personal philosophy, compelling us to remain in our perceived state of known order. Yet, as we will find out in the next chapter, this is rarely a good thing. If you believe you 'know' what is right, you may need to think again. You may end up contemplating your position on something in particular and arriving back at the same place. However, the mere act of contemplating it is worth the effort. Challenging what we believe is part of our exploration into chaos, after all. As mentioned earlier, Aristotle suggested that it was a mark of intelligence to 'entertain a thought without accepting it', and no one is saying you need do so. But attempting to see something differently may well be worth the effort.

"Compulsion is a bad thing, but there is no compulsion to live under compulsion."
Epicurus[14]

One example of our need to exercise our ability to change perspective is for that of empathy. Empathy is essentially our ability to place ourselves in someone else's shoes, to see things through their eyes, and understand how they feel. In the more emotionally sensitive world of today, one might think that empathy would be a prerequisite for modern-day life. Yet, recent research by Sherry Turkle has shown a significant reduction in empathy levels over the last 20 years, possibly in line with the rise of technology.[15]

Turkle talks about this issue extensively in her excellent book called *Reclaiming Conversation*. She cites studies that have shown up to a 40% reduction in empathy over the last two decades in college-age youths. She suggests that the rise in technological communication is limiting the development of young people's ability to communicate face to face and thus reducing the ability to recognise emotional cues and build relationships. This alarmingly significant reduction in what is an essential life skill may call for even more importance of perspective challenge and management. How can we truly engage with others if we cannot empathise with them? Whilst that might fit nicely with existential philosophies from earlier, it may not be beneficial to our relationships, working environments, and social structures.

"You never really understand a person until you consider things from his point of view – Until you climb inside of his skin and walk around in it."
Harper Lee[16]

"Empathy begins with understanding life from another person's perspective. Nobody has an objective experience of reality. It's all through our own individual prisms."
Sterling K. Brown[17]

Our ability to shift our perspective is more than just imagining a stroll in their shoes. It is a cognitive transition away from our internal system for want of a different one. It is seeing something in a different light. In this instance, we are seeing a situation from someone else's perspective, rather than exactly looking through our own eyes in a different light. However, this experiment can inform our knowledge and beliefs about said situation, providing us with insight we did not previously have. If we do not develop this capacity, then we are to continue using the same proverbial goggles of old.

Our perspective is therefore one dimensional in as much as we can begin to view the world only in relation to that viewpoint. 'The law of the instrument' or the tendency of adapting 'jobs to fit tools, rather than tools to fit jobs' is an insightful thing to consider here. In as much as we adapt our realities to fit our views, so to speak. In other words, we can be blinded by how we normally think, what we have to hand, or what we are prepared to do, and consider nothing else outside of this. Consider those that have one process for everything they do, one strategy or solution for every problem, or one 'go to' response when challenged. For example, a parent who uses the same response towards their child's poor behaviour, negating any difference between the reasons for said behaviour. 'Go to your room' might then regularly prevail over a more reasoned response.

"I suppose it is tempting, if the only tool you have is a hammer, to treat everything as if it were a nail."
Abraham Maslow[18]

"All seems infected that th' infected spy,
As all looks yellow to the jaundiced eye."
Alexander Pope[19]

These people are stuck. More so because they are unaware that they are stuck. Much like Pope says, your predisposition dictates your perception and renders you powerless to see outside of this. Well, powerless until you challenge your views, that is. With this challenge comes the opportunity to view all manner of things differently.

CHANGING THE NARRATIVE

A change in perspective can alleviate many a mental struggle. Whilst we may all think of the 'glass half full or half empty' analogy as rather tired, it does a wonderful job of showing the flip side of our views on the same matter. In this case, a mere shift of worldview is found through the reassessment of liquid volume, or of semantic classification at least. Maybe there are many more things in life just waiting for a further reassessment? However, the metaphorical leap in perspective through a change of narrative is no real leap at all. It is nothing more than a simple adjustment that can remove a ceiling, open a door, or calm the storm.

"From the sublime to the ridiculous there is but one step."
Bernard Le Bovier de Fontanelle[20]

"Chemistry can be a good and bad thing. Chemistry is good when you make love with it. Chemistry is bad when you make crack with it."
***Adam Sandler*[21]**

As Adam Sandler demonstrates in usual comedic fashion, a change of narrative only need be subtle in order to be poignant and enlightening. Unfortunately, it often takes verbal wizardry or a particular well put together meme in order to help us see the hilarity or ignorance of our current mindset. When it refers to the positive or incidental, it seems that much easier to swallow or comprehend. But throw in some emotion, criticism, or chance of repercussion and the pill is almost inedible. Like the content of chapter 2, when things relate to *us*, they become harder to take. Imagine someone saying to you, "You're so pessimistic—it really depresses the people around you". How would you take that? Would you even gratify that with some genuine consideration? But really challenging your views might lead you to take a more positive or 'glass half full' approach, like Jordan's words and Nietzche's famous line:

"I've never lost a game. I just ran out of time."
***Michael Jordan*[22]**

"That which does not kill us makes us strong."
***Friedrich Nietzche*[23]**

Yet for the most part, our changes of perspective are often entwined with our ego, our need for superiority, or indeed reluctance to appear vulnerable. As a result, we may cast them aside or stamp our feet before accepting them. After all, these potential revelations reveal our shortcomings and a world of chaos untamed. Those of us who are inclined to tough it out may indeed realise that it was there to be seen all along, if it weren't for our eyes being closed, of course. Many of you will have had some form of experience that has hammered this point home, even though you were always secretly aware. Starting a new and 'better' romantic relationship after a painful one comes to mind. The depressing and defeated perspective that spawned the words 'I'll never find love again' eventually realises that indeed there are 'plenty more fish in the sea'. We can even shift our perspective surprisingly quickly, given the right motivation.

"All truth passes through three stages. First, it is ridiculed. Second, it is violently opposed. Third, it is accepted as being self-evident."

Artur Schopenhauer[24]

*"**Thor**: He may not be perfect but he is still my brother*
***Black Widow**: He's killed 80 people in two days*
***Thor**: He's adopted"*

From the movie, 'Avengers Assemble'[25]

COGNITIVE FLEXIBILITY—A PRECURSOR TO CHANGE

It would appear that our perspectives have the propensity to be stable, flexible, or in some cases even both. Just the mention of an enlightening quote and we may begin to see things differently. How well that changes the fabric of our being though is still in doubt, particularly when we consider more revelatory information. It is one thing to see, read or hear something that resonates with you and challenges your view momentarily. But actually taking something on board and making notable or valuable changes to your lifestyle or behaviour is not an easy thing to do. To really have this new perspective change your own, you have to feel it and live it. If your worldview or philosophy is based on your deep-rooted beliefs, then anecdotal evidence to the contrary will likely not be enough to alter one's reality. Hence the idea of epiphanies being realised long after the information was present, as it took genuine experience in order to cement them internally.

*"**Bart**: I am through with working. Working is for chumps.*
***Homer**: Son, I'm proud of you. I was twice your age before I figured that out."*
The Simpsons[26]

A core part of maintaining healthy approaches to life is what I refer to as 'cognitive flexibility'. Rather than maintaining our existing thoughts, the emphasis could be on maintaining flexible thought. The key is in not believing yourself to be a fixed entity, but instead a malleable property that can adapt both its physical and mental structure to suit its environment (much like the 'growth mindset').

*"**Messenger**: The thousand nations of the Persian Empire descend upon you. Our arrows will block out the sun!*
***Stelios**: Then we will fight in the shade."*
From the movie '300' (attributed to Dieneces, the Spartan warrior)[27]

Bruce Lee describes the essence of flexibility of both mind and body in his famous comparison to water:

"Don't get set into one form, adapt it and build your own, and let it grow, be like water. Empty your mind, be formless, shapeless — like water. Now you put water in a cup, it becomes the cup; You put water into a bottle it becomes the bottle; You put it in a teapot it becomes the teapot. Now water can flow or it can crash. Be water, my friend."

Bruce Lee[28]

Lee is describing the need to bend and move in accordance with life. If you consider this in regard to perspective, it is the need to maintain both the awareness of how fragile our existing one is and a preparedness for necessary change. Being formless is having the ability to form anything. It is a readiness for change based upon experience and knowledge, and a reluctance to just accept something outright. Not holding fast to a fixed perspective is like saying "I think this, but I may not be right—and if I'm not, I'll adapt accordingly".

This approach offers more than just a different way of considering opinion. It also offers greater objectivity when confronted with issues. We have all heard of 'keeping things in perspective', normally in reference to not making 'mountains out of molehills', exaggerating, or exacerbating something. With a flexible mind comes an objective one. One that is able to detach from emotion and amplitude, favouring rationality and calmness. Your last argument with a spouse or colleague may serve as a prime example. What were you really arguing about? What was the issue and how significant was it? Did it warrant the responses given? Were you concerned with solving the issue, or demonstrating that you were right? Was it an opinion-based argument and is there a chance that you may have been wrong? These questions can more easily be answered by a mind that is flexible enough to entertain them in the first place. In that way, Pope's 'mighty contests' appear not so formidable and what was once thought to be serious appears ever more trivial.

"What dire offence from am'rous causes springs,
What mighty contests rise from trivial things."
Alexander Pope[29]

FINAL THOUGHTS

Important as it is, our worldview is often unknown to us. It remains hidden until challenged, questioned, or until something provokes its response. Whilst we may have been led into our current perspective, we can indeed change. By investigating our philosophical views, we can begin to see how we have arrived at our conclusions and what impact they have on both ourselves and our neighbours. Importantly, we can even begin to see things from other people's perspectives.

By questioning your response to situations, you can identify what tools you have at your disposal and whether these are appropriate for the circumstances. With a little cognitive flexibility, you can begin to shed new light on otherwise darkened or possibly even too familiar territory. As Dweck would have us believe, you are not fixed, you can change, and you can 'be like water, my friend'.

"My soul is not contained within the limits of my body.
My body is contained within the limitlessness of my soul."
Jim Carrey[30]

"Mondays are fine. It's your life that sucks."
Ricky Gervais[31]

"You can put a cat in the oven, but that don't make it a biscuit."
Wesley Snipes, from the movie 'White Men Can't Jump'[32]

CHAPTER 7

A TENDENCY FOR NARROW-MINDEDNESS

PART A – ASSUMPTIONS, CONVICTION AND OPINIONS

"The fundamental cause of the trouble is that in the modern world the stupid are cocksure while the intelligent are full of doubt."
Bertrand Russell[1]

"I am so smart, I am so smart, S-M-R-T, I mean S-M-A-R-T."
Homer Simpson[2]

In what parts of your life do you rely on your assumptions? How many of your actions are steered by what you assume to be true or definitely to be the case? How often do you proclaim an assumption to other people without so much as an attempt to verify what you think you know? We've all heard that to assume makes an 'ass out of you and me' and yet we seem to continue nonetheless. In simple matters like assuming the bus will 'turn up on time and I therefore won't be late for work', it is rather inconsequential. However, our assumptions run much deeper than the more trivial in nature. We may all be victims and culprits of inaccurate assumptions. The issue is to what extent and about what in particular we fall victim to. Our ignorance towards alternative viewpoints, our acceptance of our assumed 'knowledge' as fact, and our willingness to push these ideas upon others are a major contributor to professional, personal, and social problems. Many of the disagreements we have, prejudices we hold, and potentials we fail to realise are caught up in our assumptions.

ASSUMPTIONS

Generally speaking, an assumption is something that is accepted as true, without proof or sufficient evidence (virtually the same as a 'belief'). Often that proof may not be readily available, requiring a search for greater information before reaching an unwarranted conclusion. For many, this is more than they are prepared to undertake. In order to appreciate a lack of proof, we must first appreciate that we don't know as much as we think we know.

The key then is to understand our predisposition for assumption and challenge our current thought processes. By doing so, we increase our capacity for new knowledge by lifting the ceiling on what we 'know' to be true. We broaden our horizons and become more flexible with our assumptions, or indeed remove the idea of assumptions entirely. Without strict assumptions, we are more inquisitive and flexible, thus liberated from the rigidity of ignorance and naivety. We all know someone to whom these negative observations apply: friends, colleagues, the stubborn uncle who never changes his narrow mind. But much like everything else in this book, perhaps they aren't the ones we should be looking at. A mirror will likely provide us with all the opportunity we need to see the danger of misguided assumptions and acceptance of what we 'know' to be true.

ONLY RIGHT UNTIL IT'S WRONG

Much like the old saying goes, 'you don't know what you had till it's gone', the same could be said for assumptions. Until your assumption around a particular topic has been let go, you are probably unaware that you held it in the first place. In other words, something is only 'right' in our minds, until we realise that it's 'wrong'. Take a scientific theory or rule, for example. Something can be shown to be accurate 99 times in a row, but as soon as it is shown to be false even just once, the theory is disproven. Much like the chapter on failure, from the perspective of knowledge or ability, an incorrect assumption or strategy essentially meant that our knowledge was naive to the new standards required for success.

Our previous knowledge may have sufficed for past tasks, but with a new stimulus or challenge we find that what we had is now subpar to what is needed. If we observe this similarly to the preceding paragraph, we might say that our ability was 'right' until it was 'wrong'. Our awareness of what is lacking is therefore a determining factor in our ability to either change our strategies, knowledge, or even just change our minds. Many a philosopher has articulated this as awareness of ignorance, or of learning being an exploration of our ignorance. You might consider this a rather harsh view, however the idea is clear. Our lack of understanding is the root of our cognitive and physiological limitation that we must break in order to move forward.

"Education is a progressive discovery of our own ignorance."
Will Durant[3]

"The farther you go, the less you know."
Lao Tzu[4]

The concept of being aware of our shortcomings is a difficult one. It is based on the premise of knowing what you don't know or actually *that* you don't know, which is inherently confusing. Philosophically at least, the beginnings of this idea were said to have originated with Socrates. Due to the fact that he left no writings, the words of Socrates are brought to life in the writings of Plato. In Plato's *Apology*, Socrates suggests that he is wiser than another due to 'not believing he knows that which he does not'. The belief that we *do* know that which we do not is a fundamental flaw in knowledge that leads to the incorrect assumptions of truth, ability, and righteousness that this chapter is all about. This dilemma is sometimes referred to as the Socratic Paradox, for which no easy solution is to be found. Importantly though, there are many ways in which we can investigate this and therefore arm ourselves with ideas to try to overcome the issue of incorrect assumptions, not least of all knowledge in the first place.

One of the ways we can illustrate the transition of ignorance to wisdom (for want of a better phrase) is through the 'Four stages model'.[5] Whilst the model was originally used more for teaching and the development of skill, it does a great job in this context (see Figure 5).

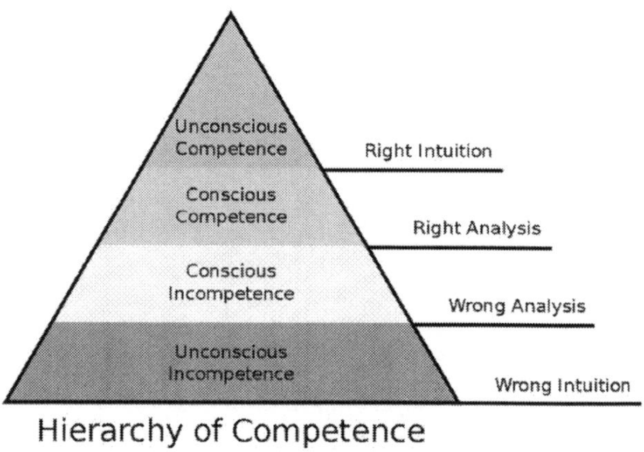

Figure 5. Four Stages of Learning Model[6]

Unconscious incompetence is the lack of awareness regarding our own limited understanding. We essentially 'don't know that we don't know' and 'don't know what we need to do or should do'. It is here that our deepest and most ignorant assumptions lie. Whilst this may not always be our fault initially, remaining in this zone through a lack of thought and sheer narrow-mindedness is what we aim to avoid. In this stage, we are blissfully unaware of what lies outside our own knowledge and beliefs, much like a newborn baby who knows nothing of what it means to pay their taxes. This notion of unconscious incompetence can be applied to anything in life and any type of idea or thought.

What is important is understanding that we are all susceptible to this level of ignorance, regardless of our intellect and education. Even the brightest of historical scientists eventually had to yield and accept ignorance of things like the birth of Newton's Laws and Einstein's Theory of Relativity, or the premise of a spherical earth and so on. They didn't know that they didn't know, until they knew they were wrong (if you know what I mean).

Conscious incompetence is the realisation of a gap in knowledge or ability. It is an awareness that other information, or other ways of doing things, exist. They may not understand this material, but they do know that they are yet to possess it and that it may bring them value if they did. Arguably, this is the birth of open-mindedness and the precursor to the pursuit of greater wisdom. By recognising the difference between our existing knowledge and the possible knowledge available, we have effectively unveiled a world of possibility. As a concept, if we can apply this to one thing in life, we can therefore apply it to all. This is not just a forward-thinking strategy, but one that can be applied in reverse. By thinking back to our previous beliefs, we can observe our own ignorance in full swing and laugh at the once unenlightened image of ourselves.

Conscious competence and unconscious competence refer more to the level of cognition required to execute the task in question. This is more prevalent with regard to skill development and therefore how much we have to concentrate on something in order to perform it. The third stage is the acquisition of this new knowledge and skill that we recognise we need. Finally, being able to draw upon that information with ease marks the fourth stage. Let's take driving, for example. From initially having no idea about cars, to then understanding that there is much to learn, to then performing actions under great concentration, to finally being able to drive for 20 minutes whilst singing to the radio and forgetting how you even arrived at your destination. That is essentially the four stages model in action.

Importantly, the model is cyclical in nature. What can often happen is that different levels of abstraction require their own cycles. If we continue the driving theme, we could assess the difference in knowledge and skill required for driving to the shops versus racing a Formula One car. We 'know' how to drive, but we don't 'know' anything about those types of cars—thus unconsciously incompetent. The assumption that we do is perhaps the more pernicious and perilous belief that restricts us from transitioning to the second stage. Without moving up, we are destined to forever believe that we could easily fill Lewis Hamilton's shoes, merely on the basis that we haven't had a car accident or that we can adequately pilot our Ford Focus.

We can also illustrate the issue of stagnating in the first stage, by comparing it to other models and theories. The transtheoretical model is another pertinent example.[6] Here we see the development of an individual's actions, beliefs, and behaviours represented in another cycle. The connection can be made with unconscious incompetence and the pre-contemplation stage (see Figure 6). In this stage, people are again unaware of what may need to change, or maybe don't even believe they need to if entrenched in what they 'know' to be right. At precontemplation, one is now identifying the deficits in their knowledge or actions, moving towards preparation and action in order to overcome these (conscious incompetence).

What is important is that each model reflects the ignorance that we human beings are prone to, as well as some of the reasons we may use to want to stay that way.

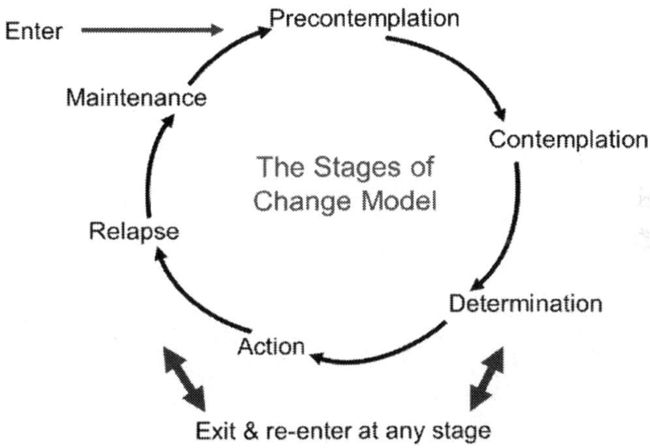

Figure 6. Transtheoretical model[7]

THE DANGER OF CONVICTIONS

Given that we may have a tendency for ignorance, it is important to discuss its associated dangers, signs, and repercussions. An assumption of knowledge over 'what is' can create strong convictions (a firmly held belief), whereby the individual removes the possibility of alternatives. The fact that they 'know' this is the answer, or that this is 'how it works' and this is 'what happened', creates a buffer between them and the next stage of awareness or competence. We often find that once some people make an assumption and generate a belief (which we will come to shortly), the strength of their conviction is so strong that no rational argument could ever convince them otherwise. This is especially true of emotive topics, or ones where people are 'required to have an opinion'. Unfortunately, convictions remove the necessary flexibility to further our knowledge and arrive at an evolved and enlightened conclusion. The individual is essentially saying that 'I know all the information and thus my judgement is correct'. Bearing in mind the scientific and religious views or practices that have fallen to greater knowledge through the ages and we have a recipe for disaster. It wasn't that long ago that women were burned at the stake, for they were 'known' to be witches.

"Convictions are more dangerous foes of truth than lies."
Friedrick Nietzsche[8]

"Light thinks it travels faster than anything but it is wrong. No matter how fast light travels, it finds the darkness has always got there first, and is waiting for it."
Terry Pratchett[9]

OPINIONS AND DEPTH OF KNOWLEDGE

Opinions are essentially a subjective view or judgement about something (not always based on facts or high-level knowledge). Some might argue that an opinion is slightly more informed than that of an assumption. Where an assumption might lack significant evidence, an opinion might be an interpretation of some evidence, rightly or wrongly. Opinions rely upon a degree of certainty grounded in some form of knowledge. Indeed, that knowledge can be subpar and thus lead the individual astray. Conversely, they may still have the 'right' opinion regardless. However, the important aspect is the removal of certainty from a viewpoint. As discussed earlier, one only need have their ideas shown to be incorrect once for all to fall apart (assuming they are willing to be proven wrong, that is). Whilst an opinion is made from some degree of knowledge, the variation of accuracy places the individual somewhere along the continuum between 'ignorance' and 'good knowledge', or rather some way along their journey to open-mindedness.

"Opinion is the medium between knowledge and ignorance."
Plato[10]

The degree and quality of knowledge used to formulate the opinion is therefore key. If poor, then it will most likely lead to poor opinions and viewpoints. If shallow, the opinions are proportionately deep. The old phrase of 'a little bit of knowledge is dangerous' strikes a chord here. Originally taken from Alexander Pope, the idea is that the confidence and strength of conviction obtained by a little bit of knowledge can often be dangerous, if firstly assumed true and secondly, if assumed to bestow that individual with the wisdom to exercise it. I am sure we can all think of people or situations where this 'little bit of knowledge' has done that.

"A little learning is a dang'rous Thing;
Drink deep, or taste the not the Pierian spring:
There shallow Draughts intoxicate the Brain,
And drinking largely sobers us again."
Alexander Pope[11]

The Pierian spring was the ancient Greek fountain of knowledge. Pope is talking about the need for a thirst for knowledge that goes far beyond that of a little learning, for a small level of understanding can cause all manner of inflated senses of wisdom and self-worth, curable only by diving deeper into the knowledge itself. His remarkable gift of poetry does a fantastic job of illustrating the need to desire more knowledge than is probably required to formulate an opinion. Without which we would do nothing other than warp our sense of what we know to be 'right'. Striving for more than the minimum is what removes certainty, strength of conviction, and the danger associated with knowledge acquisition.

"Inquiry is fatal to certainty."
Will Durant[12]

"The more you know, the more you know you don't know."
Aristotle[13]

Interestingly, Aristotle touches on the idea that with increased knowledge about a topic comes the realisation of how much more there is to learn. The more aware we are of what else there is to learn (consciously incompetent), the more our current knowledge can be proportioned and therefore rationalised. Consider that if I know 8 pieces of information about something out of a perceived 10 available pieces, my now 80% knowledge may contain a fair grasp of the situation. However, if with further inquiry I realise that actually there are 100 pieces of available information, the opinions generated by my now mere 8%, do not seem well founded at all. Thus, 'the more you know, the more you know you don't know'.

So, think about something on which you have an opinion. Say, the education system, politics, Premiership League football, or virology (the study of viruses). How much do you really know about that discipline or situation? Are you aware of what there is left to know? Importantly, is that *really* all?

FINAL THOUGHTS

We all likely make assumptions of some sort or another every day. For the most part, these may be nothing more than trivial cognitive leaps that require little attention. However, the problem arises when our actions and perceptions are driven by a multitude of assumptions and, more importantly, a reluctance to challenge them. This lack of willingness to investigate our assumptions can lead not only to our narrow-mindedness, misinformed actions, and firmly held beliefs, but can also affect other people's. What's more is than when we buy into our sense of competence within a particular topic, we place a barrier between ourselves and the remaining information that would see our perceived ability brought back into check. Perhaps the first stage of the prevention of poor assumptions and incorrect opinions is as much to do with being humble as it is with being knowledgeable?

PART B – HOW BIASED ARE YOU?

How much are your thoughts complete your own? How well can you see the *real* picture? "I have no biases", you might say. "I make sure to stay as objective as possible and don't allow myself to be swayed." Well, unfortunately for us all, we are subject to a multitude of biases that impact the way in which we interpret information and react to stimuli. For the most part, we are completely unaware of how we are being led or how our brains are fooling themselves. But with awareness of such biases comes the ability to identify situations where this may be happening and what we can do about it. But make no mistake, we are *all* biased in one way or another. We just don't know that we are.

COGNITIVE BIASES

Unfortunately, more issues exist with the formation of opinions than just a lack of awareness of volume of information. The human mind has an array of what are known as 'cognitive biases' that affect our actions and convictions. A cognitive bias is an issue with the thinking process that affects judgements and actions. What causes them is generally the initiation of cognitive bypasses or shortcuts, known as heuristics. Daniel Kahneman has studied heuristics extensively, with a detailed overview of his work found in *Thinking: Fast and Slow*.[14] Heuristics are actually facilitative in some respects in that they help us make sense of the world. Our evolutionary development has led to certain heuristics that are lifesaving. Cutting away the thinking time required for a reaction to a potential life-threatening stimuli could be the difference between waking up the next day or not. A rustle in the bushes that startles us, creating a sense of alertness and a release of adrenaline, is a heuristic for such dangerous situations.

Recognising the signs that might indicate a lurking tiger ready to grab a 'you'-shaped meal is obviously very helpful. The increased hormonal release that fuels your fight or flight response is an excellent example of a heuristic and its associated chain reactions within the body. But heuristics are not always so facilitative. Much as that tiger in the bushes could indeed be a squirrel or even just the wind, heuristics can lead us down the wrong path. Using previous experience and turning that into a heuristic means taking out the legwork involved in making simple decisions. Whilst beneficial for such conundrums as what to wear to work today, in more technical decision-making processes, utilising the same pattern or thinking might not be the best course of action for you. For one, it restricts you by definition, to 'inside the box' thinking. It can create behavioural patterns that mean you fail to change in response to new situations and circumstances. The old saying of 'doing what you've always done means getting what you've always got' comes to mind.

Unfortunately, human beings often gravitate toward a heuristic when actually a greater level of cognition is required. We essentially take the easy mental option. A common example might be the availability heuristic, or the process of making decisions based on what information is available, or what you can easily bring to mind. If we consider the issues that surround our ignorance, one might be able to see the potential problem with using this heuristic approach. Once again, the answer lies in greater investigation whereby we grow the available information to help us make a more informed decision.

"This is the essence of intuitive heuristics: when faced with a difficult question, we often answer an easier one instead, usually without noticing the substitution."

Daniel Kahneman[14]

The predisposition for employing a variety of different heuristics creates a multitude of potential cognitive biases. It is these biases that anchor us towards certain ways of thinking, preventing us from transitioning out of our current opinion or conviction. Some of the more significant or popular biases are: confirmation bias, attentional bias, anchoring bias, the Dunning-Kruger effect, and cognitive dissonance as a whole. This is by no means an exhaustive list, but needless to say there are many forms of bias to which we are all susceptible.

Confirmation bias is very common, particularly for those who wish to remain in their current state of thinking. In short, it is where an individual seeks information that confirms their current idea of what is correct or what is the appropriate course of action. Think about those who will ignore the wealth of circumstances that would disprove their theory, in the search for the one occasion that it holds true. I once had a friend who used to fall into this trap when visiting a casino. Thinking that he could predict a 'pattern' in red and black results at the roulette wheel, he failed to acknowledge all the times that his predictions were false. Instead, he recognised only the few spins in which he won as compelling evidence that 'I knew there was a pattern'.

Attentional bias is reliant on the premise of us having only a certain amount of attentional focus to go around. That results in us paying attention to some stimuli whilst ignoring others. Tunnel vision comes to mind. Anchoring bias is based upon how our opinions and decisions are impacted by the first piece of information we receive. Consider being shown an antique and being asked to guess whether its value is more or less than £1,000. You might consider this a 50/50 call and give your answer. If then asked to give an estimation as to the actual value of the piece, you are statistically now more likely to give a higher estimation, after having been primed with the initial number of £1,000, than you would have done if that original figure had been given as £100. The £1,000 sticks in your mind as an anchor from which to make your assessment, affecting your 'fair' judgement thereafter. Without any additional market information, your anchoring bias takes over and commits your decision.

The Dunning-Kruger effect is an interesting form of cognitive bias that pertains well to this chapter.[15] Similar to the illusory superiority discussed previously, this effect relates to the underestimation of ability in the skilled and the overestimation of ability in the unskilled. This is the essence of Bertrand Russell's quote at the beginning of the chapter, where the 'stupid' are full of conviction and the intelligent full of doubt. The Dunning-Kruger effect has been widely studied and is a potential reason for why incompetent people rise to positions of power. It is their inaccurate estimation of their ability that causes inflated confidence. That confidence is often an attractive trait that businesses look for and, as such, that person is promoted. Meanwhile the more competent but less confident individual remains doubtful and less dynamic as a result.

The Dunning-Kruger effect is a failure to aptly characterise our own ability. On the one hand, the less knowledgeable are ignorant of their incompetence (unconsciously incompetent), whereas the more competent suffer from perhaps the downfall of conscious incompetence. The former are often unaware of the complexity of the task, or the standards required or actually possible in that context. The latter are potentially more aware of this concept and as a result rate their competence accordingly. What results is a skewed analysis of where we really sit in this game of intelligence hierarchy.

"Do you see a man who is wise in his own eyes? There is more hope for a fool than for him."

Proverbs 26:12[16]

If the Dunning-Kruger effect impacts our views of our own ability, then cognitive dissonance affects our views once a new perspective has been provided. Cognitive dissonance is thought to be a state of psychological or mental stress caused by holding opposing beliefs about a particular thing or situation. This can be in the form of knowing something is bad, but doing it anyway, or believing something is a certain way and then being presented with evidence to the contrary. Cognitive dissonance is a stressful condition that we human beings try to alleviate quickly. Unfortunately for us, we generally do that in a few ways. We tend to change our behaviour, justify our behaviour, or ignore the other belief/new information entirely.

The first option is a little more productive in that we utilise the separate pieces of information to come up with a beneficial or balanced solution. Knowing that smoking is bad whilst wanting to smoke may result in someone deciding to quit or distract themselves. Justification can take us along a different journey, however, where counter-arguments are provided and negotiations are made in order to circumvent the opposing viewpoint. Ignoring the new information altogether is another more pernicious response to dissonance. Refusing to believe the new perspective, thus maintaining the current premise, is a rather dangerous mindset to maintain. This may be the most ignorant of responses and is responsible for many a narrow-minded perspective that damages our progress as a species. Even worse is that the more important, emotive, or potentially embarrassing the situation may be, the greater the level of dissonance and the stronger our response is likely to be. Interestingly, the same is found in the Dunning-Kruger effect in terms of estimated ability.

"Cognitive dissonance is a deeply ingrained human trait. The more we have riding on our judgments, the more we are likely to manipulate any new evidence that calls them into question."

Matthew Syed[17]

Matthew Syed's *Black Box Thinking* again discusses cognitive dissonance at length. He shows how the issues surrounding its effect have had major impacts on particular disciplines and industries. As previously discussed, the aviation industry has 'taken on board' (pun entirely intended) its major failings and reacted accordingly. Instead of ignoring or blaming something else for the mistakes that narrow focus incurred, they have embraced more beneficial solutions to resolving their own cognitive dissonance. Unfortunately, Syed also discusses the less than optimal approaches found in medicine and law, where the culture appears less conducive to behaviour change as a result of dissonance. In fact, Syed finds that in the face of new and contrasting information, it actually makes people more convinced that their initial assumptions were right. He cites examples of DNA evidence that exonerated previously convicted killers, only to find the prosecutors and detectives are now even more sure that they were the guilty party.

"So, here's the second option: denial. We reframe the evidence. We filter it, we spin it, or ignore it altogether. That way, we can carry on under the comforting assumption that we were right all along."

Matthew Syed[17]

"Facts are meaningless. You could use facts to prove anything that's even remotely true!"

Homer Simpson[18]

The certainty that surrounds some people's beliefs is such that no other information is permitted to enter their minds. We become instinctively stubborn in order to protect our sense of self and avoid blame. This is one of the catalysts behind 'blame cultures' that develop within organisations. Without a culture that embraces more constructive ways of resolving the relatively inevitable dissonance that will occur, we are destined to fall into a world of sheer force of will or blind ignorance. This reluctance to weigh up the balance of information and take the appropriate course is a reluctance to initiate transition into conscious incompetence. By maintaining our viewpoints, we are belligerently anchoring ourselves within the known or the Yin. We are making a metaphorical statement regarding the chaos of new information and our refusal to let in the light of further wisdom. We are in a sense not really living and not really growing.

"We can easily forgive a child who is afraid of the dark; the real tragedy of life is when men are afraid of the light."
Plato[19]

"False and doubtful positions, relied upon as unquestionable maxims, keep those who build on them in the dark from truth. Such are usually the prejudices imbibed from education, party, reverence, fashion, interest, et cetera."
John Locke[20]

This stubbornness can often manifest itself outwardly, not just in refusal and denial, but in assertion of opinion. Much like the Dunning-Kruger effect, it is often the less informed who fall into this trap of trying to convince others of their ill-founded truths. The idea that the less informed are a little more 'enthusiastic' about their knowledge is thousands of years old. From Western to Eastern philosophy and throughout the ages, we see examples of the arrogance associated with poor knowledge.

"One who knows does not speak
One who speaks does not know."
***Lao Tzu*[21]**

"Wise men speak when they have something to say, fools speak because they have to say something."
***Aristotle*[22]**

It appears that those truly in possession of more knowledge actually speak of it less than those without. Perhaps this is a lack of confidence in the knowledgeable ones, as previously discussed. Or perhaps the wiser among us also realise that they have less to prove. After all, the truly wise realise that they don't know that much after all. The motivation to demonstrate their knowledge seems likely caught up in a poor attachment to ego and self-worth. Making sure that people 'see how intelligent you are' by showing off whenever you can is a damaging compulsion that we will discuss shortly. With regard to our state of opinion though, it is why the loud among us are not just misinformed, but are misaligned internally. What's more is that the less able have also been shown to react poorly to feedback provided, meaning that they fail to learn of their shortcomings and therefore address them.[23] Unfortunately, the task of setting someone on the right course is rather difficult, meaning that the perpetual cycle continues to turn until the wheel is broken by greater wisdom and forethought.

"It is with narrow-souled people as with narrow necked bottles: the less they have in them, the more noise they make in pouring out."
***Alexander Pope*[24]**

"It is one thing to show a man that he is in error, and another to put him in possession of the truth."
John Locke[25]

FINAL THOUGHTS

Our cognitive biases come in many different formats. Some we are more prone to than others, but needless to say we are all at the mercy of cognitive biases at some point. Awareness, though, is key to escaping them. The more we are aware that we may naturally seek evidence that supports our current view, the more we can begin to search for ideas that contradict our beliefs. The more aware we are as to why we are subject to cognitive dissonance, the more we can strive to alleviate it.

Appreciating how much our understanding and opinions can be skewed by our biases should surely tell us that not only resolute belief in our own points of view may be misguided, but that espousing those to everyone else in the world may also not be advisable. Instead, taking the time to further investigate and seek clarification can help remove us from being at the mercy of biased thinking. You may be forgiven for thinking 'how then are we to act if everything we think may be wrong?' We will answer this in the next part.

PART C – AN ANSWER TO IGNORANCE

Considering our predetermined or socially influenced perspectives, inflated estimations of knowledge, and the biases that plague our interpretations, it seems that ignorance may be more expected than not. Given how knowledge is acquired and worldviews are formed, ignorance is more like a default setting than anything else. We all start from a place of little or no knowledge and awareness. The question is not therefore 'are we ignorant?', but rather 'how ignorant are we?' Nudging ourselves along the continuum of ignorance towards a more enlightened position (whatever the topic) forms the basis of our 'answer to ignorance'. Much like the content of chapter 2, achieving this means staring into the darkness. It means a readiness to assess our position of knowledge that dictates our responses, no matter what we find. It means embarking on a journey, voluntarily, where greater knowledge or *truth* is found. Or at least that should be the objective, even if it is somewhat unattainable.

THE SEARCH FOR TRUTH

To overcome the trap of ignorance and the prison of poor assumption, we must make a fundamental change in mindset toward opinions and knowledge. Defeating our own ignorance requires the initiation of a new relationship with knowledge, one where we engage with the unknown. It is more than simply learning something new, for that new information could feed an existing cognitive bias. Instead, we must actively seek to prove ourselves wrong and test our opinions as objectively as possible. This is a very different narrative and one that may be hard to hear. The ancient philosophers believed that the only way to defeat our ignorance was with knowledge itself.

Again, not just that which fits your existing confirmation bias, but a knowledge that challenges it. This was known to be the search for 'truth', in the strictest of senses.

Truth itself is a difficult philosophical position. Without wanting to labour on the debate of whether it is possible to ever really obtain the 'truth' or absolute reality of something, we can take the position of truth meaning 'the most accurate assessment, information, or perspective we can attain'. Perhaps this is indeed definitively unattainable, yet the pursuit and yearning for truth is what becomes the prevailing theme. A desire to explore and to grow our knowledge of what is going on is the metaphorical aim. Much like the relationship between chaos and order, it is the 'conversion', the search, and the struggle that is the most important aspect, not the possession of order. It is a mindset, not a tangible possession. Once we settle for order, we are no longer searching, no longer finding, no longer growing.

"Knowledge is true opinion."
Plato[26]

"There are very few lovers of truth, for truth's sake, even amongst those who persuade themselves that they are so."
John Locke[27]

With a love of truth, we are taking responsibility for our own thinking. We are saying to the world that I intend to further my knowledge and challenge that which I believe to be so. The statement invigorates the mind with activity and a reluctance to just accept what is given. What if the source of information is poor? What is the impact of my assumption on both myself and others? What if I am wrong? Thinking in this way creates a thirst for knowledge that Pope would argue requires a very large glass indeed. It is thinking on the new information gained that leads to greater wisdom and a quieter disposition. It's what separates those who jump to a conclusion from those who are happy to not know; for they may not have all the pieces of the puzzle. Not yet.

"He who learns but does not think is lost! He who thinks but does not learn is in great danger."
Confucius[28]

"For it is the mark of an educated person to search for the same kind of clarity in each topic to the extent that the nature of the matter accepts it."
Aristotle[29]

PROVE YOURSELF WRONG

In the search for ways to prove ourselves wrong, we have a few hurdles to overcome. Initially, we must set our minds to more objective sight, rather than the subjectivity that is all too common. We have to take ourselves down from our self-made pedestal and allow those around us a turn. We have to accept that our intellectual downfall can come from anyone at any time and that no one is above reproach. You may believe someone else's knowledge to be 'beneath' yours and yet, as per the science experiment analogy, it only takes one occasion to disprove even the most expert of theories. Divergent thinking 'geniuses' (children) are those who would automatically be seen by society as 'less knowledgeable' by nature, due to their age and lack of experience. But consider this once again and you may find a new perspective when talking to a 'less experienced' individual. Subsequently, they may find a less arrogant or sanctimonious individual in you.

"Accustom yourself not to be disregarding of what someone else has to say: as far as possible enter into the mind of the speaker."
Marcus Aurelius[30]

Another issue in front of us is that of openly acknowledging the limits of our knowledge. This is a combination of both conscious incompetence and awareness of our capacity to understand that which evades us. I make this distinction not to urge people back into a fixed mindset of 'not being intelligent enough' to understand or learn something, but rather to reinforce the idea that you may not be there *yet*. Take a 'children's movie' like *Toy Story*, for example. There are many references, jokes, and pieces of dialogue that will be understood to varying degrees by the majority of viewers. The younger audience will likely not understand the subtle humour in relation to adult experience and why should they? Of course, they do have the capacity to learn and appreciate this in the future, but their current state is oblivious to this content or concept.

At this point, they are generally unaware of their naivety either, thus reinforcing the notion they we 'don't know what we don't know'. Consider, then, what concepts and information are potentially outside of your limitations? What do you already know, or have experienced, that you may not truly understand until you are wiser or more experienced? What might this mean for your opinions today?

"In all affairs it's a healthy thing now and then to hang a question mark on the things you have long taken for granted."
Bertrand Russell[31]

"But you who seek to give and merit fame,
And justly bear a critic's noble name,

Be sure yourself and your own reach to know,
How far your genius, taste, and learning go;
Launch not beyond your depth, but be discreet,
And mark that point where sense and dullness meet."
Alexander Pope[32]

Pope once again illustrates our need to rein in our self-belief in light of our potential limitations. Whilst he is referring to the role of a critic, the idea of understanding the extent of your reach is a valuable one. Genuinely acknowledging the extent of our 'genius, taste, and learning' is still, however, subject to our cognitive bias. It is therefore no easy task, but one that must be embarked upon nonetheless. Perhaps Shunryu Suzuki had it right when he suggested that we all need 'a beginner's mind', where we are not constrained by what we know, but rather freed to absorb whatever new stimulus comes our way. By doing so, we are not just acknowledging our limitations, but removing our presuppositions altogether. We are emptying our proverbial cup of assumed knowledge, readying us to receive more and more.

*"**Moat**: It is hard to fill a cup that is already full.*
***Jake Sully**: My cup is empty. Trust me. Just ask Dr Augustine. I'm no scientist."*
From the movie 'Avatar'[33]

Emptying your cup is about removing the rigidity that comes with assumed knowledge. If you think you know a lot about something, you are saying that your cup is pretty much full. If it is full, then you can't put any more in it. Thus blocking yourself off from allowing new knowledge in. This is metaphorical, of course, for I am not suggesting that we actively forget information in order to 'make room' for new knowledge. What I am suggesting is adopting a mindset that is open. Consider it like opening the gates of your mind, rather than closing them.

Lastly, from my perspective at least, is the necessity for courage. The courage to be prepared to be proven wrong and to not appear knowledgeable, skilful, or wise. This may sound confusing given that you are reading this book and, in doing so, are hoping to learn something from someone 'more knowledgeable'. However, what I am again referring to is a state of mind. Of course we can still share our thoughts and opinions, and also look to 'more knowledgeable' people for wisdom and guidance. What I am suggesting is twofold. One is that with a more open-minded approach to knowledge development and truth, the thoughts and opinions are more balanced and thorough in the first place. The more we can bring to the table, the more informed and cultured that conversation becomes. Second, being prepared to be wrong helps negate the competition that arises between people that restricts the search for truth in favour of 'winning the argument' or appearing to be more knowledgeable.

There is an interesting book entitled *The Courage to be Disliked*, by Fumitake Koga and Ichiro Kishimi, that discusses courage as a form of disengagement with the ego.[34] The book is based on the premise of Alfred Adler psychology mixed with Western philosophy, where one must summon the courage to separate the tasks of our lives. Tasks that are for us and tasks that are for other people. In the book, this is focused upon the idea of being 'liked', but can equally be applied to that of being seen to 'be right'. It is our task to look after the development of our own knowledge and it is the task of others (if they see fit) to judge our competence. If we involve ourselves with the issue of how other people see us, we become less concerned with our own task, distracted by our neighbour's viewpoint. Instead, if we focus our attention purely on the acquisition of knowledge and not on how we appear to others, we can more easily maintain perspective.

"Do not live to satisfy the expectations of others."
Ichiro Kishimi[34]

The courage to be wrong is a bold statement of intent. It says that I do not hold myself in such regard that I can neither be proven wrong, nor am I actually prepared to be wrong. In that sense, being 'wrong' is the issue. What actually is the danger in being wrong, or in others seeing you being 'wrong'? Yes, there are of course real-world implications for things like professional reputations. Being seen to be wrong may make you question someone's authority to guide you. But I would ask you this—would you rather listen to someone who can acknowledge their wrongs, making every effort to put them right, or someone who makes mistakes and allows you to believe them as correct forever more? Not even Einstein was right about everything he said and thought.[35]

As mentioned in the chapter on learning and needing to fail, we see that being wrong is exactly what is required for us to develop. If we are not brave enough to be wrong, we are once again lowering our ceiling. Not to mention we are probably frustrating those around us. If we can bring ourselves to detach from right and wrong as representative of good and bad, we can begin to see new information as opportunities for progressing our knowledge and state of mind. Opportunities for growth; opportunities and desire to find out that we were wrong.

"If I am walking with two other men, each of them will serve as my teacher. I will pick out the good points of the one and imitate them, and the bad points of the other and correct them in myself."
Lao Tzu[36]

"A man should never be ashamed to own he has been wrong, which is but saying in other words, that he is wiser today than he was yesterday."
Alexander Pope[37]

The love of truth is reliant upon our willingness to chase after being wrong, with as much gusto as we can muster. It is an acceptance of our fallibility, not as weakness, but of strength or necessity. In turn, using those instances to create behaviour change is what helps move from conscious incompetence onward, from pre-contemplation to action and more.

"If someone can prove me wrong and show me my mistake in any thought or action, I shall gladly change. I seek the truth, which never harmed anyone: The harm is to persist in one's own self-deception and ignorance."
Marcus Aurelius[38]

A CALL TO ACTION

It is easy to feel that constantly searching for the limits of our knowledge might leave us paralysed and fearful to act. The necessity for openness, both to new information and to potentially being wrong, might stifle our progression through life. However, this could not be further from the point. On the one hand, we do need to know where to draw the line. From the perspective of accumulating knowledge in different areas and on different topics, focusing on the ones most pertinent to you and your situation is clearly a good starting point. If you do not really need to learn about shoe manufacturing and design, as that knowledge can relatively safely be awarded to Nike, then do not concern yourself with becoming an expert. However, if you have just taken up jogging, a little more knowledge of design and mechanics may be the difference between a repetitive strain injury that directly impacts your future health and enjoyment. Likewise, if your political knowledge is somewhat lacking, you may want to invest time in learning more, given the fact that we can vote (those old enough, of course).

The other perspective might be on how far you need to go before you're ready to act. In some aspects of life, we will have a greater amount of opportunity for cultivating a strong level of knowledge before needing to apply it (or ever applying it). Though in many cases, action is a prerequisite for existence and we can ill afford to be wasting time or potentially never even starting. But as we will see, we can have the best of both worlds in a healthy and positive way.

"Activity and reflection should ideally compliment and support each other. Action by itself is blind, reflection impotent."
Mihalyi Csikszentmihalyi[39]

Acting is how living is done. Like the balance of Yin and Yang, to act is in harmony with the act of contemplation. If we do not act, we cannot enjoy what life has to offer. We would never achieve flow or live out both the pursuit and acquisition of our goals. Then how are we to marry these two ideas appropriately? This conundrum is discussed really well in the book *Superforecasting: The Art and Science of Prediction* by Tetlock and Gardner. They give the example of the Prussian Military General Helmuth von Moltke, who developed a system of war based on the uncertainty of existence.[40] Moltke stated that everything in life is uncertain and that we should never completely trust our plans. Yet, whatever you choose to do, do so with commitment. He also stressed that you have to be open to changing your course of action when superior knowledge comes your way. Not to change in the face of improved understanding is to encourage defeat. Or like the famous saying goes:

"When my information changes, I change my mind. What do you do?"
Paul Samuelson[41]

We can't spend every moment investigating the world or we would never get anything done. However, remembering that we are subject to the quality of information and the level of investigation should help us remain open-minded and flexible. Marrying the 'nothing is certain' idea with strong commitment might seem counterintuitive. However, it is not. It is saying 'make the best decision you can through your open-minded journey towards truth and commit to it fully'. Yet, allow yourself to be open to new possibilities and that you may need to disregard your plan when better information is found. The problem only arises when we believe that we can't change. Or worse, that when in the face of greater awareness and understanding, we shouldn't have to change.

FINAL THOUGHTS

Our minds are extremely complex entities with a degree of ignorance built in to boot. Whilst they have the capacity to make our lives easier through certain heuristics, our minds are not always so helpful. Our assumptions, convictions, and opinions can be influenced by our biases. Sometimes we focus on information that supports our current views, so that change is unnecessary. Sometimes, we will seek not just an easy answer, but even an easy question, that helps us avoid mental distress or dissonance.

Fortunately for us, there is light at the end of the tunnel. That light is knowledge itself and a genuine search for truth. The truth will indeed 'set you free'; free from a life of mental stubbornness and naivety. The price we pay, however, is an exchange of courage and humility for a more open mind. A mind that is willing to do battle with the forces of chaos, the strength of the ego, and the belief in everything we believe and rely upon to be true. But if we can balance this with the willingness to act and commit, without closing off our minds to new information, we can successfully navigate this otherwise paralysing reality.

"In the highest level a man has the look of knowing nothing. These are the levels in general. But there is one transcending level, and this is the most excellent of all. This person is aware of the endlessness of entering deeply into a certain Way and never thinks of himself as having finished. He truly knows his own insufficiencies and never in his whole life thinks that he has succeeded."

Yamemoto Tsunetomo[42]

"I would never die for my beliefs because I might be wrong."

Bertrand Russell[43]

"'I am not the Messiah!'
'I say you are, and I should know. I've followed a few.'"

Monty Python[44]

PART 3: THE JOURNEY

CHAPTER 8

OVERCOMING ADVERSITY AND RELISHING CHALLENGE

"Life is so hard, Tommy. Sometimes I think it's the hardest thing there is."
***Chucky, from 'Rugrats'*[1]**

"Just remember what ol' Jack Burton does when the earth quakes, and the poison arrows fall from the sky, and the pillars of Heaven shake. Yeah, Jack Burton just looks that big ol' storm right square in the eye and he says, 'Give me your best shot, pal. I can take it.'"
***Kurt Russell, from the movie 'Big Trouble in Little China'*[2]**

Adversity; something that we all face and if brave enough, dare to overcome. But of all the adversity tackled in our lives, why do we seem to forget the steps taken, the lessons learned, and the robustness gained whilst doing so? Why are the feelings of anxiety and frustration that were so easily replaced once the impending crisis was averted, so readily accepted again in the coming storm? Are our trials and tribulations the problem, or is it the perception of those issues that really makes the difference? As with everything, it seems, the problem lies with us and not with life. If only we could appreciate how fleeting is the difficulty and how lasting is the gain, then we would all find solace. So why not take comfort in the knowledge that if anything, we are the ones who hold the advantage, for we can already see the impending entropy and the chaos that quickly follows, carried on the wheels of the Tao. All that remains is for us to arm our minds accordingly and overcome once more.

PERCEPTION OF ADVERSITY

Before we talk about overcoming of adversity, it is first important to address the precursor for adversity in the first place, or rather our perception of events. Philosophically at least, there is no problem and no hill to climb if we do not perceive there to be so. You may think at this point I am suggesting we just ignore the obvious issues of life and be on our merry, if not naïve, way. Far from it, though. What I am suggesting is that our perception of what is and isn't adversity plays a major role in determining our common responses and psychological reactions. The more we perceive an issue to be large in nature, the larger that issue becomes. The smaller we perceive it, well, you get the idea. The idea of this perception-based viewpoint has its roots in ancient Greek philosophy, through to modern psychology, with much in between. The Stoics pioneered the concept of acceptance of reality rather than objection to difficulty, offering a change of narrative for the otherwise perturbed individual.

"Do not seek to have events happen to you as you want them to, but instead want them to happen as they do happen, and your life will go well."
***Epictetus*[3]**

Epictetus is suggesting that regardless of what comes your way, accept it as being appropriate nonetheless. This is not about playing the role of the positive thinker or kidding yourself that 'you wanted *that* to happen anyway'. Rather, what you want is for things to just happen as they do and that you will accept whatever outcome transpires. We will discuss the concept of passivity later, but essentially what I am suggesting presently is not a state of 'not caring', nor is it a state of blind ignorance. What Epictetus is asking for is a mental shift of perspective, so as not to evoke an emotional response. We can look to Shakespeare for further clarification:

"There is nothing either good or bad, but thinking makes it so."
From 'Hamlet' by Shakespeare[4]

Shakespeare is showing that our reality is shaped by our perception of it and nothing else. Whether we deem a situation favourable or not is purely down to that; how we deem it. The last chapter showed us how important perspective is. Here, we explore how it pertains to our mood, our resilience, and our vigour.

"I have come to the frightening conclusion that I am the decisive element in the classroom. It is my personal approach that creates the climate. It is my daily mood that makes the weather..."
Haim G. Ginott[5]

Ginott's quote captures the essence of the power we wield over our minds. Whatever the events that come our way, they are exactly that; events. How we choose to perceive those events is what causes our subsequent reactions. Instead of our usual understanding, imagine the events of your life, past, present, and future, to be a movie on a screen. Now, consider your consciousness as being you, but sat in the audience. Rather than 'feeling' every event, you are 'viewing' every event. Now when something good happens, you too can share in the delight. When something bad happens, you can say "that is not happening to me", for you are your consciousness, not your physical self on the screen. Our perceptions, our thoughts, can be separated from our experience. Just like Shakespeare was saying, we can decide what is either good or bad. The movie of life will continue to play, but we can choose how we react to the good bits and to the bad bits.

"Change: nothing inherently bad in the process, nothing inherently good in the result."
Marcus Aurelius[6]

The choice of mentality allows for the acquisition of rationality and a tranquillity that allows for simplicity. Removing the emotion associated with directly 'feeling' the event provides a state of mind that is in a better place to tackle difficulty. Given that problems often require a significant cognitive response, removing the additional thoughts that clutter the mind allows for a more streamlined thought process. Much as in chapter 3, this de-cluttered result gives the individual more freedom to be creative in the problem-solving itself. Or indeed, provides the clarity from which to arrive at the intended destination in as direct a fashion as possible, without the unintended detours that irrational thoughts incur.

"In a contemplative fashion,
And a tranquil state of mind,
Free from every kind of passion,
Some solution let us find. Let us grasp the situation,
Solve the complicated plot –
Quiet, calm deliberation
Disentangles every knot."
W. S. Gilbert[7]

"The fastest route between two points, will always be a straight line."
Chinese proverb[8]

This rather simplified viewpoint, taken at face value, does not allow for the overcoming of obstacles. However, the saying goes much deeper than that. The straight line also refers to arriving at the answer, as much as anything else. It is the removal of unwanted destinations or the unhelpful considerations that often cloud the mind and therefore the journey between the two points. As the Gilbert quote illustrates, the quiet calm enables the 'disentanglement of any knot' by helping you get to the answer in an unfettered way. The removal of undue stress associated with considering the problem at hand also allows for a rational appreciation of how patient you must be, what you must do, and how you must do it. Therefore, the individual can be both more open to new strategies and enthusiastic about the effort required to execute them. If we can see a problem as merely a puzzle that needs solving, we can be better placed to take the steps needed. Thus, overcoming is less about dealing with emotional pain, exhilaration, and anxiety and more about solving a proverbial sudoku, if you will.

"Do you have the patience to wait till your mud settles and the water is clear? Can you remain unmoving till the right action arises by itself?"
Lao Tzu[9]

"When it is obvious that the goals cannot be reached, don't adjust the goals; adjust the action steps."
Confucius[10]

"Obstacles don't have to stop you. If you run into a wall, don't turn around and give up. Figure out how to climb it, go through it, or work around it."
Michael Jordan[11]

Lao Tzu's view poses somewhat of a challenge to all and a call to arms. Resisting the temptation to overreact or become too embroiled in the melee that is the difficult situation requires an effort to remove oneself. Perhaps effort is not the right word, but either way it is a conscious decision and action, something that Zen practitioners would call 'non-action'. Mud in the water illustrates the disturbance caused by problems that distort your view of otherwise clear waters, or a rational mind with clarity of thought. You may even find that the stepping back from problems in order to wait for the emotion and mud to dissipate is actually a therapeutic experience. Being able to do so is to acquire a new skill that leads towards self-improvement and higher cognitive ability. We may even begin to enjoy the challenge of a problem for what it brings us in return.

"Enjoy your problems."
Shunryu Suzuki[12]

"I smile at obstacles."
Tiger Woods[13]

CHALLENGE VERSUS THREAT

The concept of how we perceive events has also been explored in modern psychology. In particular, the theory of 'Challenge and Threat States' covered briefly in chapter 1 is very similar to the ideas mentioned by Suzuki and Woods. The theory is predicated on an individual's perception of the impending task as either a challenge (thus motivating and invigorating), or as a threat (thus inhibitory and overwhelming).[14] Again, the key here is 'perception' of the impending task or issue. The result is a very different physiological and psychological response to what is otherwise the same problem. If viewed as a challenge, the increase in psychological arousal, adrenaline, and other neurotransmitters in the brain are helpful. However, a threat triggers similar activity of the sympathetic nervous system, but with a different combination of neurotransmitters that add to stress levels, like cortisol.

The idea that we are not equipped to meet the demands of the task is based on our perception of our ability versus the perceived level of complexity, pain, or difficulty of whatever is in front of us. Given that human beings are notoriously bad at accurately estimating this sort of thing, the psychological repercussions are rather important. As the eminent professor Daniel Kahneman states:

> *"Claims for correct intuitions in an unpredictable situation are self-delusional at best, sometimes worse."*
>
> ***Daniel Kahneman***[15]

This misguided belief in our ability in unpredictable situations is mirrored by another phenomenon of note: 'Illusory Superiority'. Related to the Dunning-Kruger effect from chapter 7, this is where the large majority of people surprisingly self-assess their ability to be above average (an obvious statistical impossibility) in comparison to the ability of others. It is a form of cognitive bias that humans are very susceptible to, increasing the lack of reliability for human perception. Interestingly, when we assess our ability in relation to others, we overestimate, but when we perceive potential threats, we tend to do the opposite. Jonathan Haidt discusses this in his book *The Happiness Hypothesis* where he discusses that human beings react to negative and threatening stimuli more than they do positive stimuli, producing a bias towards assessing difficult situations as threats. The brain is pre-wired to see a threat before it can rationally assess the potential good.

"Most people's minds have a bias toward seeing threats and engaging in useless worry..."
Jonathan Haidt[16]

"Bad is stronger and faster than good..."
Roy Baumeister[17]

In the face of actual danger, the bias towards seeing threats is obviously a beneficial and evolutionarily valuable tendency. One could argue that this habit may be a fundamental reason behind the success of the human race in lasting as long as it has. However, when that same mindset is taken towards the assessment of problems and challenges, the associated lack of confidence can be rather stifling. Again, this is not to say that the fear of bad repercussions is not a powerful motivator, but keeping them all in perspective may be the answer. Psychologists have actually extolled the benefits of using a major threat as a motivator for action, with positive results in certain instances.[18] Generalising this as a good and all-encompassing strategy for life, however, is another thing entirely. I picture it like choosing to be chased by a shark in order to make you swim faster; it'll definitely work for a while, but it'll probably end up biting you in the butt eventually.

It would appear that we have a tendency toward seeing threats and thus evaluate our ability to meet external demands as sub-standard, but generally speaking, overestimate our ability in relation to other people. Or in other words, we are anxious and scared by default, but don't let it stop our ego claiming superiority. Clearly, we are a very complex animal. Would it therefore not just be better to overestimate our ability as a default setting, to reduce the associated stress that comes from threat assessment? You could argue that this would be rather delusional at best, potentially subjecting an individual to a crushing realisation when their shortcomings become evident.

We are not necessarily talking about life and death situations. For the most part, our everyday, personal, and professional lives provide more than enough challenges for us to exercise a little assuredness in our ability to meet external demands. Especially given that the sense of calm provided to disentangle every knot reduces stress levels so that we feel better about the task of solving every problem. Again, this is not a case of 'ignorance is bliss'. Either way, you still have to face the problem in front of you, right? A change in perception of your ability does not change the problem at hand, but may alter the probability of your triumph and the health of your state of mind.

Our ability to lean towards challenge assessment rather than threat assessment is wrapped up in our sense of self and the consequences involved thereafter. What are the consequences of your actions? As we discussed in chapter 5, the perception of what it means to fail is of major importance to our success. The evidence provided may have already convinced you that failure is necessary or even sought after. For many, though, evidence is one thing, but to change how we really 'feel' in relation to failure is another. It may be very difficult to escape the 'failure equals bad' feeling. But why is that the case? And why should that affect your approach and subsequent stress levels towards tackling the problem?

Well, all roads lead back to emotion. Emotion attached to your sense of ego (again, see chapter 2). Emotion attached to associating success or failure as a definition of who you are. If we are attached to the result and allow it to define us, we are clearly going to be more emotionally caught up in the process. Whilst the desire to overcome can be an extremely powerful motivator, it is something that also needs to be kept in tow. If you can view the challenge as simply that, a challenge, whilst maintaining a sense of reality that is not caught up in the outcome, you will be more equipped to engage rationally with the problem.

So rather than seeing this as 'not caring' about the outcome, see it as caring deeply about the task at hand, but not letting the outcome define you either way. That way, the drive to succeed can be as strong as ever, without some of the associated worry that can cripple the creativity and effort required to achieve the desired result. This is especially important when we imagine the concept of being the 'underdog'. The underdog is not expected to win and may not do for a long time. They may battle against the odds for years until they eventually triumph. If they were attached to every outcome, the recurring feelings of failure would no doubt destroy any remaining enthusiasm. But we find that the perception of challenge, along with the idea of growth and mastery, produces an enduring and burning desire that is not easily extinguished.

"Winning is not always the barometer of getting better."
Tiger Woods[19]

BECOMING ENDURING

Much like most things to do with our personal psychology, our approaches are partly predetermined genetically and are part actionable and changeable characteristics. Indeed, our predisposition toward a particular bias of positivity or negativity is now quantifiable. Some people have higher anxiety levels genetically than others, as Jonathan Haidt describes in *The Happiness Hypothesis*.[16] Losing the 'cortical lottery', as he puts it, means that some of us are born with more of an anxious, negative, and threat-sensitive disposition. However, we do have the power to action change for the better. The idea that we can become more enduring in the face of adversity has a great deal of potential to benefit a great deal of people. But what does it mean to be more enduring and how do we go about doing so? Well, concepts such as robust positive thinking, acceptance of the nature of life, lack of attachment to outcomes, and a more balanced view as to fighting versus perseverance are the common themes.

From a positive thinking perspective come the more meme-based, assertive mantras that we see on social media. Forgive any hint of cynicism there, as repetitions of strong assertions have a great deal of value. One only need see the success of Tony Robbins and the like to see how powerful these mindsets and practices can be.

"Whatever you hold in your mind on a consistent basis is exactly what you will experience in your life."
Tony Robbins[20]

"Mind precedes all mental states. Mind is their chief; they are all mind-wrought."
Buddha Guatama[21]

If your thoughts are of metaphorical defeat, being beaten down by life and adversity, then that is likely how you'll feel. The prevailing thoughts and perceptions become the dominant discourse in what is a fairly fluid concept of mental state. As a result, choosing the affirmative option of bravery, achievement, and robustness will likely generate similar internal feelings.

"But man is not made for defeat. A man can be destroyed but not defeated."
Ernest Hemingway[22]

Hemingway speaks of not letting a loss, a failure, or some form of hardship defeat you. It means to rise once again in the face of the oncoming onslaught. It is the faint smile that appears when you look upon a significant challenge or threat, knowing that you may be beaten up in the process, but you'll give it all that you have to offer regardless. Feel free to use your own inspiring quote here in order to arouse the right sentiment itself. The mere use of one is what matters at this point.

ANTICIPATION AND ACCEPTANCE

Anticipation and acceptance of entropy is again either your friend or foe, depending on how you deal with the idea. With emphasis placed upon anticipation, we can obtain either anxiety and pain, or preparedness and flexibility. Aristotle once said that "Fear is pain arising from the anticipation of evil".[23] Anticipation essentially means 'to change your course of action in relation to a future event', often to avoid something ill-natured. In that regard, anticipation can be seen as something beneficial and frankly necessary for prosperity. However, it does take a degree of acceptance in order to avoid the mind dwelling on the hardship, or fearing the impact of its manifestation. Likewise, acceptance when a bad thing actually does occur bolsters our ability to be able to both deal with it and remain undeterred.

"'It is my bad luck that this has happened to me'. No, you should rather say: 'it is my good luck that, although this has happened to me, I can bear it without pain, neither crushed by the present nor fearful of the future'."
Marcus Aurelius[24]

"Enjoy when you can, endure when you must."
Goethe[25]

Aurelius puts another emphatic spin on the acceptance of hardship, combining it with the mantra-based techniques of Tony Robbins and the like. Turning 'negatives into positives' comes to mind. However, with Stoics like Aurelius, the emphasis is again on acceptance of the event, rather than viewing it as being inherently good or bad, desirable or un-desirable. That way, if ten potentially negative events come your way, the overwhelming deluge is less detrimental than if we attributed them with value.

REMOVAL OF ATTACHMENT

The removal of attachment has already been discussed as beneficial to our ability to overcome adversity. Conceptually, the removal of attachment is a removal of ego and expectation. Ego, in the sense that we often allow what happens to us to define our sense of self. That means that when we engage with a problem, we are often not just considering the issue, but also the question of what it means for me if this goes wrong, especially in other people's opinions. Allowing the results to define you provides an additional context that exists outside of the situation. We are essentially inserting a problem into a problem. This may seem completely logical. How else am I supposed to think and behave, right? Especially if this adversity is painful, or even completely destructive. Once again, the philosophical answer is to remove the emotional bonds that treat our physical self as 'us' and that treat outcomes as indicative of our self-worth.

"Heaven is long-enduring and earth continues long. The reason why heaven and earth are able to endure and continue thus long is because they do not live of, or for, themselves. This is how they are able to continue and endure."

Lao Tzu[26]

Lao Tzu is highlighting the link between 'things that endure' and things that do not get wrapped up in their ego. These entities that do not live for their ego are therefore separate from it. If something were to be broken, that entity would still exist in its current form. It would not capitulate under the weight of its own expectation, its grief of opportunities missed, or scars worn. It would just be. Consider that for a moment. Whatever befalls you does not become you. If you wear the scars of proverbial life battles, you are still you. Much as the Earth continues to spin, your life continues to play out. But how do we marry this with the ideas of desire for improvement, success, and achievement? Lao Tzu again suggests an appropriate strategy of emotional removal:

"He who perseveres is a man of purpose,
He who does not lose his station will endure."
Lao Tzu[27]

To lose your station; having expectations that are perhaps beyond your capability, beyond what are realistic, or even having expectations at all? The idea that you might 'deserve' a particular outcome brings with it a fragility that threatens your ability to carry on in the face of adversity. If what you deserve does not manifest, how will you likely feel? I'd imagine you'll feel disheartened, embarrassed, and angry. None of which are likely to help you endure life's struggles. To endure is to continue in the face of whatever comes, so perhaps the removal of all expectation is what is required.

The psychologist and author of *The Chimp Paradox*, Steve Peters, discusses this aspect and the alteration to your personal vocabulary.[28] Instead of 'this should happen', change it to 'this could happen'. The removal of expectation creates a shift in reaction. 'Could' allows for multiple possibilities. 'Should' suggests a likely or even inevitable outcome and thus an associated weight of expectation. If we expect and do not receive, we are surprised, disappointed, and hurt. But what of our dreams and aspirations? Does the removal of expectation therefore remove desire for a better life? Would the removal of emotional investment reduce the motivation to overcome and achieve? Jim Carrey explains this well (on getting what you want):

"As far as I can tell, it's just about letting the universe know what you want and then working toward it while letting go of how it comes to pass."

Jim Carrey[29]

The emphasis here is 'letting go' of what happens. There is no less effort expended. In fact, the very nature of 'letting the universe know what you want' suggests incredible effort need be invested to increase the chances of success. Make a metaphorical noise so loud that the heavens cannot help but hear, but let go of your attachment to the outcome. That way, you are both driven and free all at the same time. Freedom that invigorates the individual, probably allowing for greater effort in the first place and a greater sound to be made.

"Those who seek knowledge, collect something every day. Those who seek the Way, let go of something every day."

Lao Tzu[30]

"Trade your expectations for appreciation and the world changes for you."

Tony Robbins[31]

A MORE BALANCED PERSPECTIVE?

The philosophical approach being discussed is one of perseverance, not a battle of force. To overcome with force suggests a gut-wrenching journey that may strip you of everything before you triumph. To persevere conjures images of contemplated and calculated effort.

There is an old golf saying coined by Greg Norman: 'in the breeze, swing with ease'.[32] Much like Lao Tzu, the focus is not on trying too hard to overcome what troubles you, but rather keeping your wits about you and remaining calm. Lao Tzu also extols the idea of passivity at length in the Tao Te Ching, but again this is more to do with the removal of emotional struggling and less to do with just 'letting things happen to you'.

However, remaining calm enough to persevere and 'stay the course' in the face of countless setbacks is a very difficult thing. Yet, doing just that is apparently what wins out in the long run. If we begin this journey under the assumption that all things worth attaining are hard to achieve, then the need for staying the course is as paramount as anything else in this book. Some even refer to this ideal as true bravery, displaying the fortitude revered by anyone and everyone.

"All good things are difficult to achieve, and bad things are very easy to get."
Confucius[33]

"The bravest sight in the world is to see a great man struggling against adversity."
Seneca[34]

INNER BELIEF

But much like the earlier references to Tony Robbins, inner belief appears to be a strong factor in building a resilient and stoic mindset. Yes, each problem should be viewed rationally, unemotionally, and as a separate event that needs solving. But the idea of not being dismayed by the repeated bullying that life can bring is still a big feat for many. The solution appears to be taking small step after small step, in something you know you can do. As Seneca once said "sometimes even to live is an act of courage". So, let those acts of courage begin with what may seem to be rather benign at the time. Much like the notion of making your bed in the first chapter, the idea of 'getting back on the horse' in order to right the wrongs of chaos may start with something as simple as putting one foot in front of the other.

"I know what I have to do now, I've got to keep breathing because tomorrow the sun will rise. Who knows what the tide could bring?"
Tom Hanks, from the movie 'Cast Away'[35]

"Just keep swimming. Just keep swimming. Just keep swimming, swimming, swimming. What do we do? We swim, swim."
Dory, from the movie 'Finding Nemo'[36]

Keep breathing, keep swimming, and keep moving forward. And if you can't move forward? Well, move left, move right, up or down, around or over. But keep breathing and you'll generate the courage required to shake the heavens. Add this unwavering commitment to movement with constructive intentions and we may have a recipe that is hard to match. If your intentions are genuine and well advised, the setbacks become momentary blips in what is otherwise a grand and beneficial plan. When those minor details cease to be an issue, what remains is the journey, or your personal story of success.

"If you pursue evil with pleasure, the pleasure passes away and the evil remains; If you pursue good with labour, the labour passes away but the good remains."
Cicero[37]

With each successful step comes more confidence in your ability to endure. Ultimately, what is manufactured is not a sense of infallibility, but one of resilience. You 'know' that whatever comes your way may have you down, but not defeated. It may cause the slightest detour, or it may shock you to your core. But you will know as sure as anything else in life, that whatever is left within you will be enough to pick you up once again and move forward. The Japanese have the word *nintai*, which means 'with perseverance we can endure the unbearable'. This belief in enduring spirit is a sentiment that was never so well expressed as in the poem *Invictus* by William Henley.

"Out of the night that covers me,
Black as the pit from pole to pole,
I thank whatever gods may be
For my unconquerable soul.

In the fell clutch of circumstance
I have not winced nor cried aloud
Under the bludgeonings of chance
My head is bloody, but unbowed.

Beyond this place of wrath and tears
Looms but the Horror of the shade,
And yet the menace of the years
Finds and shall find me unafraid.

It matters not how strait the gate,
How charged with punishments the scroll
I am the master of my fate,
I am the captain of my soul."

***William Henley*[38]**

He speaks of the pain and bludgeonings of life causing hurt, but never tempting resignation. The 'horror of the shade' and the impending 'menace of the years' encapsulates the chaos and entropy already well documented. Yet come what may, if you make it so, it will find you ready and willing to tackle. It matters not how difficult or narrow the path and how many bludgeonings arise, you still and will always have control of your destiny. For in as much as you can choose how to react to the strife, you can forever remain the captain of your soul.

We are all the same when it comes to our juxtaposition with life. Inevitably, life will batter us all to within an inch of our patience, strength, and courage, so it is important to acknowledge this fact. If we acknowledge, we prepare. Telling a child that everything will be sunshine and roses hardly prepares them for the struggle that lies ahead. There is a reason that the most enduring stories in human history are those of triumph over evil, making order out of chaos, and overcoming adversity in order to secure victory when the day is done.

From the *Enuma Elish*, otherwise known as the Mesopotamian creation myth, the rise of Zeus over the Titans, the trials of Thor and Hercules, to virtually every fairy tale or movie of the last few centuries, overcoming adversity is not just a powerful message, but is probably the greatest good we can achieve. What we must therefore do is acknowledge the struggle. Without which our story would have no plot, no adversary or demon in the darkness. Once acknowledged, we can focus on the realisation that we have the power to overcome it. We can smile in the face of the impending danger, safe in the knowledge that any loss is both temporary and not a measure of our self-worth.

"If you can laugh if the face of adversity, you're bullet proof."

Ricky Gervais[39]

"The world breaks everyone, and afterward, many are strong at the broken places."
Hemingway[40]

The opposite approach can be temporarily seductive. To ignore the pain or cover it up somehow can temporarily alleviate our mind. However, the crashing of reality appears more debilitating than beneficial. The cocktail created when combined with a measure of fear only heightens the damage. Better to face our hardship with eyes wide open, rather than the alternative. Convincing yourself that 'well, I didn't really care about that relationship anyway' is not as beneficial as dealing with the loss itself. Ignorance, once again, seems far from bliss.

"Numbing the pain for a while will make it worse when you finally feel it."
Harry Potter and the Goblet of Fire[41]

Our strife can, however, become our sense of power. Our losses educate our wins to come, our pain elevates our celebration yet to be realised. If we choose to take our knocks and press forward, our movements are on top of our past, like a house on top of foundations.

"Oh yes, the past can hurt. But you can either run from it, or learn from it."
Rafiki, from the Lion King[42]

"For he lives twice who can at once employ
The present well, and e'en the past enjoy."
Alexander Pope[43]

This 'education' from life helps us clarify who we are, what we are made of, and what to do or not do. If taken on board, our troubles can be used like the knife that cuts away the clay of a sculpture, revealing that which we desire, or can become enmeshed in the clay itself, distorting and perverting its intended design.

"Some bodily pains are worth enduring to ward off others like them."
Epicurus[44]

"A gem cannot be polished without friction, nor a man perfected without trials."
Seneca[45]

FINAL THOUGHTS

What appears clear is that the ability to overcome is wrapped up in our perception of the adversity in the first place. Both the Stoics and Taoists would suggest a balanced and rational outlook is the key to keeping things in perspective. Personally, I like to think of a balanced mind very much like a spirit level, where the bubble is our mental state. Using our objectivity, we can maintain balance, resisting the temptation to overreact to external stimuli, forcing our bubble outside of the lines. When it does fall outside of those borders, the hormones start to flow and our mind is overtaken. Now, this is not to say that I wish for positivity and joy to be limited, but rather kept in perspective. For just as with the balance of Yin and Yang, or Newton's Law of Motion, every action has an opposite and equal reaction. The sugar rush that creates the high is inevitably followed by the crash. To try to maintain the high will ultimately cause an unhappy mind and an unhappy pancreas. But if we can remove our ego, our expectations, and our fear, we can tackle the onslaught of life and maintain our balance. We can build the confidence that reinforces our ability to cope. A mindset that facilitates our ability to breathe, to swim, and to persevere when all could seem lost. Only then can we learn the lessons from our losses and stay the course of our journey. Sure, bad stuff will inevitably happen, but you know that, don't you?

"Pain is neither unenduring nor unending,
as long as you remember its limits and do not
exaggerate it in your imagination."
Marcus Aurelius quoting Epicurus in 'Meditations'[46]

"Take courage, my heart: you have been through
worse than this."
Homer, 'The Odyssey'[47]

"The flower that blooms in adversity is the most
rare and beautiful of all."
The Emperor, from the movie 'Mulan'[48]

CHAPTER 9

RISKING IT ALL

"And the day came when the risk to remain tight in a bud was more painful than the risk it took to blossom."
Elizabeth Appell (misattributed to Anais Nin)[1]

"Stupid risks are what make life worth living."
Homer Simpson[2]

They can be paralysing or inspiring, stifling or liberating. They can open up the unimaginable or forever stay in the imagination. They are everything we can be, every possibility and every opportunity, or they are the forgotten dream and the mundane made reality. Risks are the key to change and the initiation, cessation or maintenance of existence. Yet, for every one risk taker there are likely nine safety dwellers, for in the uncertainty lies fear, in the initiation lies a debt of effort, and in the new lies the habits of old. The risk, it seems, is laden with reasons not to pursue and to stay safe inside the bud. But why do these reasons overcome that of the alternative? Why is the allure of what may come any worse than the expectancy of what currently is? When all life is change, why do we not take a chance on a desired change; one that brings us closer to our dreams? We are in fact a product of our risks, both taken and not. We are exactly what we should be, because of what we risk we could be.

WHAT IS RISK?

The mere definition of risk has inbuilt suggestions and inferences. Generally speaking, it is the potential for loss or harm. When we discuss taking 'risks' we are in fact discussing only the likelihood of something negative coming our way. Consider the one-sided mindset that is surely to follow a notion like that. We are not discussing a term of equivocal nature. Instead, we find ourselves firmly in one camp, already placed in negativity or expectance of some degree of hardship. No wonder, then, that the relationship between human endeavour and risk is so skewed.

From an evolutionary perspective, risks were a case of life and death. Sleeping in this cave rather than that cave might have been the difference between a good night's sleep and a rather less-than-comfortable altercation with something furry, hostile, and full of teeth. When our decisions have such devastating consequences, it only makes sense that caution be more dominant than our sense of adventure. As discussed earlier, there is a reason that 'bad' is faster and stronger than 'good', neurologically speaking. That is why our limbic system that hosts the amygdala (what people often refer to as our 'lizard brain') developed first and remains the dominant entity in our reactions to stimuli. The lizard brain was initially thought to just respond to fear, however, better interpretations see it as an organ for classifying stimuli and deciding on what to do about it. People with a damaged amygdala are thought to lack fear, due to its inability to accurately classify situations and stimuli (see Klüver-Bucy syndrome).[3] Well, in monkeys at least, but we can infer a similar response in humans.

For much of society, the days of life-threatening decisions are relatively few and far between. Instead, our 'risks' are more generally caught up in financial, physical, or emotional loss. Yet with the decrease in severity of the potential loss, there is not necessarily a decrease in sensitivity to loss. This may sound silly at first. Just to get into your car is a risky undertaking with potentially disastrous consequences. Statistics suggest that UK motorists have a 1 in 20,000 chance of dying whilst driving, in any given year.[4] That figure rises to 1 in 240 across a lifetime. But for want of a better phrase, these 'risks' are rather expected and thus less stimulating to the brain. Driving is seen as such a common activity that is not only done by most people, but is also seen as somewhat of a prerequisite for 'normal life'. Oddly, the fact that 'this could end in death' hardly seems to be on the mind of each motorist.

However, the average human being still appears reluctant to take on 'risks' that are by nature much safer than the risks associated with our primordial ancestors. Take the common deathbed revelations expressed in Bronnie Ware's *Top Five Regrets of the Dying*. The most common theme was that of dreams unfulfilled, chances and risks not taken.[5] Many of our ideas and plans remain just that; ideas and plans. We far too easily let our enthusiasm for execution be suppressed by our fears, becoming a more sensible and cautious version of ourselves. It may appear that the amygdala is still the dominant entity in our reactions to events of the world, regardless of their severity.

"Nowadays people die of a sort of a creeping common sense, and discover when it is too late that the only things one never regrets are one's mistakes."

Oscar Wilde[6]

"Everything you've ever wanted is on the other side of fear."

George Addair[7]

The idea of fear as the dominant discourse in our mind may be accurate for many, but not for all. If it is for all, then there are people among us who are able to bypass this emotion in order to more rationally appraise a situation. Think of the great entrepreneurs of the world who took a risk and defied the odds to become the successful individuals we know today. Of course, statistically for every one success story there are likely many disasters. But even so, those that experienced 'disaster' were brave enough to take on the risk in the first place. Given that the most common deathbed confessions are to do with regretting opportunities missed and dreams not fought for, Oscar Wilde seems to have hit the nail on the head. Even a loss in today's world is not that bad. It appears that those who interpret risks from an emotional perspective may indeed activate their primordial response, convincing them once again to remain in the bud or their existing cave. Whereas those that can think more rationally about the risks, charge their growth mindset and back themselves to 'give it a go', are the ones who explore the chaos and the unknown.

"The trouble with most people is that they think with their hopes or fears or wishes rather than with their minds."
Will Durant[8]

"All men dream: but not equally. Those who dream by night in the dusty recesses of their minds wake in the day to find that it was vanity: but the dreamers of the day are dangerous men, for they may act their dreams with open eyes, to make it possible."
T. E. Lawrence[9]

THE BIOLOGY AND PERSONALITY OF RISKS

The concept of risk is not exactly straightforward. The psychologist, Elke Weber, has studied risk at length and has divided it into five specific domains: recreational, financial, social, health and safety, and ethical risk.[10] In each category, human beings undergo a complex weighing of perceived risk (chances of something bad happening/happening to me) versus the perceived benefit. A key element here is that of subjective perceptions. Gender and personality impact this perception and seem to create the differences we can so easily observe between people in everyday life.

Generally speaking, women are more risk-averse than men.[11] The gender differences seem to be as a result of intra-sex competitiveness between males for female attention. This has led to an evolutionary difference whereby males have a naturally greater predisposition for risk-taking. Women still take risks of course, but just less on average. That being said, women have been shown to take more risks in a certain domain, that of 'recreational risk' and are more likely to make significant career changes later in life.[10] The 'big five' personality traits of extraversion, neuroticism, openness, agreeableness, and conscientiousness also have an effect on someone's approach to risk.[12] An example might be that those who 'lost the cortical lottery' (measure higher in trait neuroticism) are also more inclined to view the potential drawbacks of a particular risk as much greater than the potential gain. Age also appears to be a compounding factor in that the average individual takes less risks as they get older.[11]

Despite the variations highlighted, an individual's attitude to risk within each domain is relatively stable. But much like their personality traits, which are also relatively constant, they can indeed change if addressed.[10] Given that each decision regarding risk is a subjective analysis of the repercussions of that risk, it can be altered with changes in perspective. Just as the untimely wisdom of deathbed revelations would suggest, opportunities lost were based on "the choices they had made, or not made".[5] A dying woman's personality has not changed that drastically that this now appears obvious, but rather her perception of the potential repercussions has. Now that she 'knows' what was to become of her based on the choices she did in fact make, she now realises how negative her perception of the risks truly were. Coincidently, the third most common regret among the dying was of not having the courage to express their feelings fully. Again, the 'risk' associated with being honest was seen to outweigh the benefit. That these confessions appear to be somewhat ubiquitous among the dying suggests that whilst we humans do in fact take risks, we might not be taking the ones we should be.

BEING COMFORTABLE WITH RISK

The inherent emotion associated with risk appears to centre around loss or harm. If we consider the material of previous chapters, the ego plays a large part in that perception of loss. If you were to 'lose' in this proverbial game of risk, what difference would it really make? For some, the level of risk associated may be greater than others. Financial commitments with severe consequences could just be seen as bad risks, or unmitigated ones at least. Losing your house as a result of bad investment would definitely fall into that bracket. However, for the purposes of this chapter, let's consider the more realistic alternative that can still lead to dizzying heights of success.

The majority of risks will likely see significant loss if we fail, but not loss of our safety; rather simple, tangible objects like money, or emotional perceptions like our sense of self. Objects can be rebought, money can be made once again, and our ego can be rebuilt (or let go of completely). So what then of the 'loss' incurred? What are we really risking? Are we thinking like empowered drivers of our lives, or are we thinking like victims in the passenger seat? Again, our 'perception' of what it means to be taking a risk becomes intrinsically linked with how prepared we are to do so.

Let's consider for a moment the plus side of taking calculated risks. In doing so, we increase our autonomy, change our mindset, self-determine our action, increase our relatedness, and action steps towards self-actualisation and our realisation of potential. Does this not outweigh the former? Perhaps it is not as simple as a mere balancing act of 'pros vs cons', but worth breaking down a little more.

DEALING WITH CHANGE

With risk comes uncertainty. Some even define risk this way, as an 'active engagement with uncertainty'. This uncertainty reflects the unknown, the less dependable or familiar possibility. The patterns of our life that bring us comfort also bring stagnation. If we are too heavily entrenched in order, we are nowhere near the 'divide' that helps us grow and develop. For many, this safety is perceived as therapeutic, allowing tranquillity and peace. Yes, the world is at the mercy of entropy, yet that entropy is more predictable and stable. I can recognise and relax into the patterns of my life. If I stay in the bud, I build the illusion of being able to mitigate or limit the risks. For any change in my circumstances brings with it a wealth of uncertainty that floods in from the chaotic world around me. As a result, change in itself becomes an object of fear.

Change is a strange concept. We now know that the universe is pre-set towards constant change, yet our ability to accept it is often poor. The famous book *Who Moved My Cheese?*[13] is a fantastic analogy of the all-too-common human response to change. In short, the book describes two little humans and two mice inside a maze controlled by 'regular humans'. Each day cheese is deposited in the same place and each day both the mice and humans travel to this destination to dine. Then one day the cheese is not there. The mice respond accordingly, looking elsewhere for their meal. The humans decide to wait, for this must be some sort of mistake, and expect the cheese to be there once again if they are patient.

What then ensues is a cascade of human emotion in relation to dealing with change. Patience turns to disbelief, disbelief to despair, and despair to self-pity. The little humans spend a huge amount of time debating the risk of leaving this location, just in case the cheese gets put back there. All the while, the mice have been enjoying their newly found cheese ever since the change in location, all due to responding accordingly to what is unfamiliar territory, or just a simple change.

Change is often feared and dwelled upon rather than embraced and dealt with. No wonder, then, that taking risks is often avoided as we are in effect placing ourselves at the mercy of uncertainty and becoming victims of change. An alternative mindset sees change as opportunity. A chance to better a situation and find more cheese, so to speak. Instead of being 'let down' by chance, we are provided with a new possibility.

"Is someone afraid of change? Well, what can ever come to be without change? Or what is dearer or closer to the nature of the whole than change? Can you yourself take your bath, if the wood that heats it is not changed?"
Marcus Aurelius[14]

The new possibility is unfortunately located in the unknown. Opportunity is therefore not dependable. It requires active engagement forming a battle with chaos, where winning or losing is what is at stake. However, many people would rather just watch from the audience, afraid to get punched in the face, or indeed to do the punching.

"Life opens up opportunities to you, and you either take them or you stay afraid of taking them."
Jim Carrey[15]

"Our lives are defined by opportunities, even the ones we miss."
From the movie 'The Curious Case of Benjamin Button'[16]

Our perception of opportunity versus negative change is inherently linked with our mindset. The challenge and threat states discussed earlier and the growth mindset offer a context within which to observe this conundrum. Gravitating towards one rather than the other reflects your approach towards challenge and therefore the unknown. Believing that you have, or will subsequently acquire, the skill set to deal with the change in circumstance solidifies opportunity within the idea of risk. The original definition of risk is therefore redefined, so as to incorporate uncertainty with improved possibility, rather than impending doom. Again, this change in perception, to include that of challenge, also increases the utility of loss or failure. If I lose or fail, that is okay. Failure provides vital information that helps with the next challenge. Therefore, the risk is mitigated by virtue of the reduction in severity of consequence.

"When you take risks you learn that there will be times when you succeed and there will be times when you fail, and both are equally important."
Ellen DeGeneres[17]

In addition to the above, we need remind ourselves that we are not defined by outcomes. This idea of separating ourselves from the outcomes that befall us will be explored later on. Presently, the notion that we are not the outcomes of our life is often hard for people to swallow. If not the outcomes of our life, then what? Outcomes are the product of the processes that have come before, combined with the circumstances placed upon us. Processes are things we can change and modify. Poor outcomes or 'failures' are then just momentary situations or eventualities. They do not encapsulate everything we are as a human being. Just as boiling some water does not mean that it will forever stay hot, a momentary outcome does not have to stay that way, or indeed be indicative of its true nature. The condition of water can change, so too can circumstances, outcomes, and most importantly, so can you.

"You can't keep blaming yourself. Just blame yourself once, and move on."
Homer Simpson[18]

NOT 'KNOWING YOUR POSITION'

For many, the uncertainty of risk and the adventure of the unknown is like sailing into the abyss. Not 'knowing where you are' becomes as important as being able to accept the nature of change. If we consider this along with the notion of being the driver, steering into the unknown may seem a little strange. 'What if I don't know where I am going?' The uncertainty can make you feel stranded or marooned. But there is an alternative view.

"All that is gold does not glitter. Not all those who wander are lost."
J.R.R. Tolkien (from the movie 'The Lord of the Rings')[19]

Instead of seeing wandering as aimlessly milling around, see it as actively exploring. When we explore, we are actually trying to uncover new ground and expand the reaches of our awareness. The very idea of unknown territory is that it is uncharted. So moving in the direction of that which you have not experienced is not to be lost, but to be invigorated by the opportunity to explore in the first place.

When we consider our destination, however, things can get a little tricky. The idea of working towards a goal is of course important, however the definition of that goal may be even more so. Being specific about your goals and ambitions is seen as a good thing (SMART goals for example), but in uncharted waters the goal might just be to find land, regardless of what that land might look like. We may have a vision of how we want this new world to look, but that does not mean that the eventual reality will fit the description, or that it is inherently bad if it does not.

Thus, the idea of a general goal that becomes clearer the more we explore may be just as important and liberating as having a very specific goal to which you can hold yourself accountable. In the former situation, it is the act of venturing forth that has ultimate value. It is the spark that ignites the fire within you and determines that there will indeed even be a potential destination.

Consider a frustrated employee, beaten down by the incessant bureaucracy and uninspiring work, who longs for a job with some 'meaning'. For this person, the sheer desire to become self-employed is actually a goal or destination that helps to alleviate the occupational crisis they are currently experiencing. At this point, they may not know what their future business will be, look like, or specialise in. Yet, the goal of working for themselves is enough to create movement and begin the voyage. As the journey begins, the vision may become clearer, or perhaps even change completely. The point, though, is that whilst destinations are of value, we do not need to get married to one specific kind of destination or goal. Whether you are journeying towards a very clear objective or setting off in a general direction and building a clearer objective as you go, you have to at least set sail.

"A ship in harbour is safe, but that is not what ships are built for."
John A. Shedd[20]

When we reconsider the idea of the journey and the uncertainty, we change the narrative of existence. To journey toward uncertainty is to engage with the universe. Not knowing where you are is therefore evidence of the liberation from the known. In the known, you knew exactly where you were. But maybe knowing exactly where you are means actually being lost. Lost in a sense that you have no direction, no inspiration, and no wind in your sails.

"I'm not lost for I know where I am. But however, where I am may be lost."
Winnie the Pooh[21]

Taking risks could therefore be a prerequisite for progression and true experience. If we take on no risk and therefore no adventure, we risk never breaking free from the known. Understanding that this is where our growth and fulfilment takes place, a lack of adventure would surely lead to a less-than-glorious existence. Your development (and thus potential) is rooted in the adventure. By definition, failure to engage with uncertainty is to guarantee certainty. Certainty that you will not change, grow, or move forward progressively. As in a previous chapter, you may be moving through life, but should not confuse this movement with action.

"The biggest risk is not taking any risk. In a world that's changing really quickly, the only strategy that is guaranteed to fail is not taking risks."
Mark Zuckerberg[22]

SELF-BELIEF

Philosophically at least, the idea that engagement with the unknown leads to prosperity is relatively well described. We have already discussed the premise a little in the first chapter, however the conviction to carry through with your journey or even your proposed journey is another matter. The initiation of process seems to take a degree of self-confidence that some may find out of reach. However, self-confidence, like many aspects of psychological perception, can be a learned capacity or even a mere choice. Granted, choosing to be confident in a given situation is no simple thing. But given the relationship between perceived competence (which may not even be accurate—see chapter 7) and self-confidence, we can see that the choice to be confident is not based primarily on fact or a consistent ideal.

Consider someone's confidence levels in a hard maths exam versus the confidence they may feel teaching maths to their five-year-old daughter. With a different context comes a different level of perceived confidence. Our perception of our competence in relation to the situation impacts on our confidence, but can be adjusted. If we relate that to embarking on a potentially risky journey, our confidence to take the first step is again something malleable in nature.

"Magic is believing in yourself, if you can do that, you can make anything happen."
Von Goethe[23]

With the initiation of movement comes a substantial benefit. You have actively engaged with uncertainty and chaos. You have stared into the void, deciding to move forward nonetheless. You have proven to yourself that you are prepared to overcome the proverbial darkness and shine your light. Consider what that means for you psychologically, regardless of the outcome. Farrah Shorr wrote in her book *The Discomfort Zone* that clinical psychology shows us how exposing yourself to that which you are afraid of doesn't make you less afraid, it actually makes you braver.[24] In the same way, if you have overcome your fear of a potential risk once, you are more likely to be able to do it again. In doing so, you are more likely to be successful, for you can't win if you don't play the game, after all.

"The only way to pass any test is to take the test. It is inevitable."
Marlo Morgan[25]

"Ask, and it shall be given you; seek, and ye shall find; knock, and it shall be opened unto you."
***Matthew** 7:7*[26]

The quote from the book of Matthew speaks metaphorically about obtaining that which you seek, merely by seeking it. This is a powerful message. By engaging with a topic, you are indeed finding that which you seek. A door will likely not open if not knocked upon. You have to take the first step if you want to experience the ones thereafter. In that regard, risk is but a chance for possession. To 'ask' is to put yourself in a position to receive, rather than just having something done for you or merely holding out your hand expecting a gift. This is what Jim Carey discussed in the last chapter when he mentioned 'letting the universe know what you want'. He goes on to say:

"So many of us choose our path out of fear disguised as practicality. What we really want seems impossibly out of reach so we never dare to ask the universe for it. I'm the proof that you can ask the universe for it."
Jim Carrey[27]

You may have read *The Secret* or know someone that has. For reference, the book discusses the relationship and 'laws of attraction' of the universe.[28] Now, I am not putting this down at all, but want to make a distinction between 'asking' in order to receive and a law of attraction with the universe. In the previous paragraph I am highlighting the metaphorical need to initiate, engage, and move forward. I am not suggesting that this is a mystical process, but rather a very logical one. If we work toward something, we are far more likely to achieve it than if we did not. Many find comfort in *The Secret*, however that is possibly a conversation for another day. For the purposes of this book, the choice of behaviour based upon increased knowledge is the fuel provided to start your journey.

"Some people want it to happen, some wish it would happen, others make it happen."
***Michael Jordan*[29]**

PERSEVERANCE

To minimise risk, the conviction to begin must be met with a commitment to continue and persevere. We have already discussed the importance of this from the perspective of learning, but in this context, it is in reference to living out our dreams. We mentioned previously that nothing good is ever easy to come by. If we are prepared to negotiate risk, we must be doing this for a valid reason. We have chosen, rightly or wrongly, to delve into a new venture. Yet for many, cessation of this activity is far too common. How many of us know of someone who has embarked upon a dream, only to give it up for some reason or another? Perhaps this is you? I would propose that if we cannot muster enough motivation to follow through on our intent with consistent effort and determination, then there was never any risk at all. Instead, it was an absolute certainty that you would fail.

Seeking in order to find is not transactional in nature. It is not a one-time effort that finds immediate reward. To 'seek' is to actively and consistently engage with the task at hand (much like deliberate practice). By doing so, we reduce the inherent risk with every ounce of sweat expended. This is not to say that all our quests are worth seeing to the end. Having the foresight to let go of a less than beneficial journey is a mark of wisdom. There is an old poker saying about 'getting married to your hand', or in other words, not knowing when to fold because you feel too invested in the hand.

The ability to let go of a bad idea is a big part of the process of learning and growing. It is part of the experience that informs our future endeavours. Consider the alternative. If one idea turns out to be not as great as we thought, do we give up on the concept of ideas forever? If we are truly committed, we will use this information to change course for a new port and intensify our efforts.

"Go all the way with it. Do not back off. For once, go all the goddamn way with what matters."
Ernest Hemingway[30]

EFFORT AND COMMITMENT

The commitment and effort required therefore alters the semantics around risk and 'trying' to make something succeed. If we again assume that a lack of commitment results in an associated increase in risk, then even the purpose of 'trying' seems flimsy at best. To try would suggest a less committed and almost optional behaviour. It is the metaphorical 'dipping of the toe' into the waters of whatever risk you are currently flirting with. Dipping the toe however, is not commitment. Much like Hemingway says, 'going all the way' shows that the thing you pursue really matters. If you continue with this approach, your effort is not optional but rather more definitive.

This may sound slightly contradictory with regard to the aforementioned conscious incompetence, in that we should not believe we 'know' and therefore move forward in a gung-ho fashion. However, the point here is not that we should refrain from acting and committing to action, but rather that we should commit fully whilst remaining open to new information and direction as they present themselves.

You are either in the game or you are not. As a result, the word 'try' not only becomes irrelevant, but can be viewed as a halfway house of effort; like a light switch in perpetual limbo between 'on' and 'off'. If this is the case for most people, there is no wonder why many a risk or hardship endured subsequently upsets the delicate balance and all too easily nudges us to the 'off' position. Even though that is sure to leave us in the dark and take the end goal out of sight.

"Do, or do not. There is no try."
Yoda, from 'Star Wars Episode V'[31]

"The beginning is the most important part of the work."
Plato[32]

"In the realm of ideas everything depends on enthusiasm... in the real world all rests on perseverance."
Goethe[33]

RISK AND REWARD

The balance of risk and reward is a tempestuous one. The common mindset is that the greater the risk, the greater the reward. Personally, I do not believe things to be that simple. Take a lottery ticket, for example, where one risks a very small sum for the chance to acquire a very large sum. Or indeed the tendency for someone to risk a lot in order to gain very little. Keep in mind that since 2011, 259 people have died whilst taking selfies in dangerous situations and you'll have some idea as to what I mean.[34] With these examples, the former premise does not hold up at all. To think that there is a direct and positive relationship between them is misleading and potentially foolish. It is the sort of thing that may encourage the 'stupid risks' that Homer Simpson offered us at the start of the chapter. Especially when some may try to portray themselves as, or even believe themselves to be, big 'risk takers'.

Like a practical-joke battle that quickly escalates out of hand, the big risk taker can easily fall into the trap of taking larger risks in order to maintain the high or even prove others wrong. In that regard, risk-taking becomes a drug, with the allure of greater gains through greater potential sacrifice. However, I would argue that the term 'sacrifice' should be revised and realigned. Rather than sacrifice our livelihood and the livelihood of those around us on a whim, we should see it more as sacrificing a part of ourselves on the chance of greater good. Whether that be our time, effort, or ego, our sacrifice is something we can give in the knowledge that we can apply more if required. Of course, money and the like are probably going to be associated, but perhaps not as irresponsibly as the reckless might have it. What we cannot escape from, though, is that with any reward, large or small, there is an inbuilt risk or toll that we must pay.

"No sacrifice, no victory."
From the movie 'Transformers'[35]

"It seems to be a law of nature, inflexible and inexorable, that those who will not risk cannot win."
John Paul Jones[36]

"He who is not courageous enough to take risks will accomplish nothing in life."
Muhammed Ali[37]

COURAGE VERSUS FOOLISHNESS

Muhammed Ali speaks of the courage required in order to take risks that lead to achievement. Whilst that may be the case, at what point does courage to take on the risk become foolishness? The more romantic view of this chapter is that of the aspiring individual battling against the odds to realise their potential and succeed in the end. As we have discussed, to some degree this is inevitably true. The prerequisite of risk for reward, the drive and commitment to minimise the chance of losing the dream, and the courage to both embark on the journey and feel at ease whilst possibly being lost, are all tied up in the balance. However, the idea of courage suggests that not to take risks is cowardly. For the most part, it would seem that this is true. What generally holds us back from taking the chance we've always dreamt of may indeed be fear and therefore an element of cowardice. Taking a chance on the uncertain means paying in to something that may never pay you back. Bravery, then, may still be the ego talking. The delusions of grandeur that have seen the demise of many may only be a circumstance or two away from sheer brilliance.

"Courage is the commitment to begin without any guarantee of success."
Goethe[38]

"For fools rush in where angels fear to tread."
Alexander Pope[39]

How then does one navigate this treacherous path? Perhaps there is no easy answer. Maybe only the outcome decides. Or maybe the answer lies in the act of courage over fear and what seems the best way of living. At the extremes of the continuum, is it better to be a brave fool or a perceptive coward? The clinical literature cited earlier from Shorr would favour the brave (much like fortune). In the inspiring mind, the brave commit themselves to their goals and their desired fate. The cowards, who miss their chance to live time and time again, kill their dreams and thus their possibility of life with every risk avoided. Hence the following quote:

"Cowards die many times before their deaths; the valiant never taste of death but once."
***William Shakespeare*[40]**

Caution, then, can either sharpen the nose of the individual or paralyse them altogether. How we choose to use it is up to us. Being aware of the downfalls, managing them accordingly before then taking the risks, may be the virtue of the brave rather than the vice of the scared. Being careful can therefore be complimentary to our sense of risk, rather than inhibitory where our sense of adventure erodes. Hemingway also once wrote:

"No, that is the great fallacy: the wisdom of old men. They do not grow wise. They grow careful."
***Hemingway*[41]**

"Take risks: if you win, you will be happy; if you lose, you will be wise."
***Swami Vivekananda*[42]**

The second quote highlights the connection with risks and fulfilment. The happiness that comes with having taken a shot at what you desire to be brings only benefit. For even in the loss you are still to gain. The suggestion of risks, plural, indicates a way of living where risk-taking is the norm. Again, the converse would be the paralysis of caution and therefore a lack of fulfilment. You may suggest that such a lifestyle would be unimaginable or even unmanageable. How often would the circumstances work out in your favour? How often would you be in a position to make it work in the first place? Unfortunately for us, it would seem that life rarely provides a completely safe or sound footing from which to climb.

If we wait for one, we will likely miss our opportunities and credit caution for our 'wisdom'.

"Fate rarely calls upon us at a moment of our choosing."
Optimus Prime, from 'Transformers'[35]

Missing the opportunity is thus the price we pay for an over-cautious nature. Much like chapter 3 and the stress placed upon living for today, waiting for tomorrow is adversely related to our fulfilment. Tomorrow may hold an abundance of opportunity, but it cannot escape the questions of your life. The dreams you hold now will likely be forgotten, or sold back to your mind as too risky in the first place and that you were therefore 'right to avoid the risk'. However, the element of finality that life presents could possibly shed light on those risks.

Steve Jobs was famed for his views on taking risks, using the premise of impending death as a way of clearing the mind of the clutter that comes with apathy, fear, and caution. Given both his success and his unfortunate end, perhaps he has a good point. Though it is also worth noting that his attitude did lead to him refusing modern medical treatment in search of alternative and less 'proven' cancer remedies, possibly shortening his life. This only further stresses the need for the appropriate weighing of options, benefits, and consequences when taking a potential risk.

"Remembering that I'll be dead soon is the most important tool I've ever encountered to help me make the big choices in life."
Steve Jobs[43]

FINAL THOUGHTS

Whatever your views on risks, they are and forever will be present in life. What we choose to do with them, however, can make the difference in what impact we have on both our own lives and those of others. Of course, some things are not worth the risk. But that judgement should probably come from a place of rationality and prudence, rather than fear or apathy. If we let the idea of uncertainty or imminent loss dominate our minds, then the smallest and largest opportunities for self-actualisation and achievement will likely pass us by. Given that life itself is at a constant risk of being extinguished, is it not better to play a game you choose to play, rather than one that you are forced to play? If my mind is open to failure, my will focused to persevere, and my ego freed from the outcome, am I really risking anything at all? Ships are made to sail, after all. As, indeed, we were made to live.

"Don't worry about failures, worry about the chances you miss when you don't even try."

Jack Canfield[44]

"If you risk nothing, then you risk everything."

Geena Davis[45]

CHAPTER 10

CREATIVITY AND PASSION

PART A: THE HUMAN NEED FOR CREATIVITY

"Whatever you can do, or dream you can, begin it.
Boldness has genius, power and magic in it."
***Von Goethe*[1]**

It not only distinguishes us from our ancestors and competitors, but provides a window to our soul. It not only calms our minds, but invigorates our spirit. It is the expression of curiosity that inspires and the transcendence of ourselves in material form. From the simple to the sublime, creativity is an exercise in human functioning and one that brings significant benefit to both creator and beholder. Yet, does everyone have it in them to be creative? Or is the ability confined to but a few 'talented' ones? Is creativity limited to the painting of pictures, or is it simply the creation of something that did not exist at all before? There are many questions that we can ask of ourselves in relation to being creative. Most of which will likely centre around whether we are 'good enough' to even try. But like most things in this book, it is the act of engagement that is the most important thing, not the end product.

"We are born only once and cannot be born twice, and must forever live no more. You don't control tomorrow, yet you postpone joy. Life is ruined by putting things off, and each of us dies without truly living."

***Epicurus*[2]**

CREATIVE HOMO SAPIENS

Creativity is often the vehicle that people use in order to explore their passions and in turn create their joys. Creativity is largely born of passion, curiosity, and enjoyment. This mirrors that of our pleasurable pursuits, providing a strong premise for their connection. Creativity is therefore a core tenet of doing what you love. Producing art, music, or the opportunity to do these things for a living, is creativity at its maximum. Even a professional athlete is considered an artist of their trade, once again channelling their efforts to stand out above the crowd. Creativity, though, is more than just a potential opportunity for expressing oneself. Many now believe that creativity is at the heart of Homo sapiens' success over other species, an innate drive that we must satisfy and the key to true experience and living.[6]

"Let your light so shine before men, that they may see your good works, and glorify your Father which is in heaven."

***Matthew 5:16*[3]**

You may have read books such as *Sapiens* by Yuval Noah Harari, in which he depicts the development of the human race as we know it.[4] His work has postulated that creativity and cooperation are the biggest factors in our success over the likes of Neanderthals. Our ability to orchestrate ourselves in large numbers is likely what made us dominant over our bigger, stronger, and even larger-brained counterparts. That orchestration comes from our creativity, in terms of our ability to create stories that guide our collaborative efforts. Harari discusses the idea that physically and genetically we are still very similar to chimpanzees and socially we are still very similar to many other species. What sets us apart is our ability to create stories and our language skills with which to convey these stories. As a result, the human race creates a world of inspiring tales to help us collaborate in very large groups. This ability is unique to human beings and is key to our success.

"You could never convince a monkey to give you a banana by promising him limitless bananas after death, in monkey heaven."

***Yuval Noah Harari*[4]**

Harari argues that very few of the things that we humans have created in order to foster collaboration actually exist outside of our minds. For example, believing in a religion that therefore creates a code of existence that nurtures mutually beneficial collaboration is unique to humans. At times this belief is contradictory, causing catastrophic outcomes or war and conflict, but for the most part our stories work to create collaboration. The modern 'western world', which is largely predicated on Judaeo-Christian beliefs, is a great example. The general code of ethics promoted under these faiths leads to a society that is happy to co-exist and work together. Harari also describes even the use of money and the creation of companies to be excellent evidence of how humans are willing to believe in stories and therefore substantiate non-existent entities in their minds. Money is nothing more than an 'I owe you' and Google is not actually a thing like maybe 'wood' is considered a thing. It is a belief in an entity made up of contracts, logos, and buildings. None of which are actually 'Google'. It is a social contract and one that wields significant power. Harari's sentiments are also shared by Augustin Fuentes, who has discussed the creative spark and imagination as being the biggest factors in our success and subsequent global domination.

IN THE INDIVIDUAL

Creativity, it seems, is a precursor for human innovation and development. If it separates us from the rest of creation, then it is at the heart of who we are as a species. This large-scale creative collaboration articulates the progression and evolution of humans, but again on a grand scale. What of the importance to the individual? Does each of us have the potential for creativity and do we need to exercise that potential? In a word, yes.

Remember the work of Ken Robinson where he highlighted the findings of divergent thinking in 5-year-olds, showing that a startling 98% were divergent-thinking geniuses. Consider then the evidence that supports divergent thinking as the most accurate predictor of creative achievement and we can easily extrapolate that everyone has creative potential.[5] Much as Einstein implied in the last chapter, education often impedes this creative spark by telling students that there is already an answer for each question, so you need not do any original thinking of your own. Hence the progressive reduction in divergent thinking as we grow older. The challenge then is maintaining your divergent and creative mind in the face of education, naïve opinion, and the passing of time. Strangely enough, this sentiment has been recognised by many forward-thinking individuals.

"Every child is an artist, the problem is staying an artist when you grow up."

Attributed to Pablo Picasso[6]

"The creative adult is the child who survived."
Ursula Le Guin[7]

Intelligence is another factor that people would often regard as a key element of creativity. Fear of not being intelligent enough could easily form a psychological barrier, preventing people from exploring their potential. Fortunately, whilst evidence suggests a link between creative potential and intelligence, it is a small one.[8] Further research has gone on to suggest that intelligence is related to creativity, but only in as much as a certain level is required for creativity; above that it does little to increase creativity (at least until the extremes of intelligence).[9] Indeed, the creation of something completely novel and 'outside of the box' has been shown to be linked with intelligence, however we are currently discussing the innate creative capacity that resides in humans. In that case, much like Malcolm Gladwell's findings in *Outliers*, one only need be 'intelligent enough' to be creative. Divergent thinking, therefore, is still the dominant force and one that we all possess.

EXERCISING OUR CREATIVITY

Given that it is both in our evolutionary nature and that we all have the capacity, one could argue that exercising our creative ability is a determining factor in why some people are happier and more fulfilled than others. If only some of us have the inclination to utilise the creative spark, or are in a position to do so, clearly observable differences would arise between a population that essentially starts off on the same foot. What then, is the resultant effect of being creative? What is the impact of using or not using this natural drive for producing something original and new?

Research has shown that creativity is strongly associated with self-actualisation and therefore reaching one's full potential and fulfilment.[9,10] Reaching the peak of Abraham Maslow's famous 'psychological needs' hierarchy is therefore dependent on creativity, among other things. If we do not exercise that ability, it would seem, we do not become our true and optimal self. Maslow believed that self-actualisation created a being who was more at one with themselves and everything around them. They are more confident and independent, curious, courageous, self-confident, and more autonomous.[11] They are more willing to embrace chaos rather than seek the sanctity of order. Again, the connection between creativity and self-actualisation seems to rest at the feet of autonomy, much like in previous chapters on self-determining one's actions and embracing challenge. It would appear, then, that creativity is a psychological need that can either inhibit or facilitate our movement towards a truer experience and realisation of potential.

"Our healthy subjects (more self-actualised) are generally unthreatened and unfrightened by the unknown... They accept it, are comfortable with it, and, often are even more attracted by it than the known...
They do not cling to the familiar, nor is their quest for the truth a catastrophic need for certainty, safety definiteness and order..."

Abraham Maslow[12]

"Curiosity about life in all of its aspects, I think, is still the secret of great creative people."

Leo Burnett[13]

Being creative is also 'right brain soothing'. In other words, it calms the mind, reducing cortisol levels associated with stress and anxiety. Daily creativity has been shown to help regulate our emotional and psychological well-being, releasing neurotransmitters and endorphins that make us feel better.[14] It is also a common precursor to 'mindfulness' that we discussed in chapter 3. When we engage with something creative, we are 'present in the moment' and not thinking about anything else.

The need for creativity is also closely associated with excellence and competence. As discussed earlier, competence (or the need to demonstrate competence/excellence) was initially seen as an innate drive and latterly as a core part of self-determination theory and the building of esteem. We might then consider that creativity, excellence, and overall competence are enmeshed with one another and the quest for self-actualisation.

"The secret of joy in work is contained in one word – excellence. To know how to do something well is to enjoy it."
Pearl S. Buck[15]

SOMETHING NOVEL

Exercising creativity helps people to pursue what they love. They can be creative in their spare time, engaging in pursuits that really speak to them, providing an outlet for their creative spark. People can also find opportunities for and ways to exploit their creativity in their daily work. Others go as far as to make their living from their creativity, developing their own path. This does not necessarily have to be an artistic form of creation. Starting your own accountancy, plumbing, or computer business would also be the creation of a new entity. In the latter sense, developing a project yourself or in collaboration with others is as strongly associated with creativity as writing a song or painting a picture. The advantage here is that we can engage with our creative self and our business enthusiasm simultaneously, enjoying the best of both worlds. What is important is that you are building something that does not already exist or providing unique solutions for problems because you have a desire or passion to do so. You are not passively waiting, but rather actively chasing your goals. Whichever option you choose, securing a creative outlet is what is important.

"Creativity is a natural extension of our enthusiasm."
Earl Nightingale[16]

"Think left and think right and think and think high. Oh, the thinks you can think up if only you try!"
Dr. Seuss[17]

"Imagination is the beginning of creation. You imagine what you desire, you will want what you imagine, and at last, you create what you will."
George Bernard Shaw[18]

Finding your outlet is to identify a path towards self-actualisation and intellectual freedom. You afford yourself the opportunity to invest yourself in something that connects with you internally. This is an important sentiment. There needs to be a real connection with what you are doing in order for it to be fulfilling. As a result, your ability to regularly interact with this opportunity needs to be protected, or in the event of something preventing this, alternatives must be found. Too often people lose their creative outlet and don't replace it with a new one. Needless to say, the psychological repercussions may be significant and troublesome for the individual as their road to self-actualisation is blocked.

"If you've got a talent, protect it."
Jim Carrey[19]

"The aim of art is to represent not the outward appearance of things, but their inward significance."
Aristotle[20]

Aristotle mentions the inward significance of things as the aim of art or creativity in this sense. It is worth noting that the ancient Greek philosophers considered 'creativity' as more of an act of 'discovery', rather than producing something new. That being said, the sentiment here is about its importance to the creator or explorer. The inward significance is what is felt by the individual during the process and the meaning behind the exploration in the first place. The creator is therefore invested in their creation, as it not only contains within it the effort expended, but it also represents a piece of themselves. We humans can therefore not resist but be emotionally attached to that which we create, whether that be a sculpture or a business.

Think about the pride you once had in school project creations. That terrible plaster of Paris sculpture, that poorly crafted spice rack or whatever 'object' you produced in class was of huge importance to you and your family. Why? Because you are the one who made it. The rather obscure item was a manifestation of your imagination and effort into something tangible and real. The feeling of associated pride is all too regularly forgotten as we grow older. We become institutionalised in our 'real' work, too embroiled in TV or the internet (someone else's creative endeavours), or too busy with unimportant pursuits. The very idea that we can express ourselves in some creative way becomes an afterthought. Much like Picasso said, we need to retain our artistic spirit in whatever guise that may be if we are ever to feel that sense of pride once again.

The expression, pride, and enjoyment is what puts the love in 'doing what you love'. As previously stated, whether this is professionally or recreationally, doing what you love is something that we all need. Producing opportunities for us to live out our creative spirit day to day may possibly be the pinnacle of this thought. Yet regardless of whether you can make a living doing what you love or you just regularly engage in that pursuit, its beginning need come from you in the first place. Remember, autonomy is as important for self-actualisation as anything else. For the purposes of the remaining content, we will continue under the idea of 'doing what you love' as doing that for a living, but it is equally applicable to following your passions in any form.

Creating your own opportunities in life will simultaneously incur an increased emotional investment. As a result, you will likely be more engaged with the pursuit than if it were an opportunity afforded you by someone else. This is the reason that so many of us are able to move from one job to another with relative ease. However, the more of yourself you put into that job, the more the emotional investment will shackle you to the walls. Hence the difficulty that some people have in leaving their job, even though they have grown to dislike it greatly.

Much like the poker reference previously mentioned, we can all become 'married to our hand'. But for the self-created opportunist, the shackles are not chains; rather more like the ties that bind parent and child. Your creation is your proverbial baby and one that needs nurturing and love. That is a very different relationship to what is felt in a normal employment situation and is what feeds the burning desire to see it become successful or thrive.

Think Bill Gates and Microsoft; a manifestation of a love for code writing and a sharp business acumen. Whilst employees can be motivated to help improve the future of a company, its father will likely care that little bit more. Much like any good parent, the motivation to work all hours, think carefully about progress, and stop at nothing to keep safe become natural instincts for the creator. Not only that, but they have not waited for things to happen. They have developed their own school project equivalent for which they can be passionate and proud. Thus, they have paved the way for their own future. What could be more autonomous than that?

"The future cannot be predicted, but futures can be invented."
Dennis Gabor (often attributed to Abraham Lincoln)[21]

"I learned many great lessons from my father, not the least of which, was that you can fail at what you don't want so you might as well take a chance on doing what you love."
Jim Carrey[22]

Importantly, many a 'successful' person will speak of passion and enjoyment as being the key ingredients. For them, 'doing what you love' supersedes success in that domain. Success is nothing more than a potential outcome of doing what you love. For Bill Gates it was the love of writing code, for Michael Jordan it was playing basketball. Their love of the task is what drove their effort, resilience, and creativity. They explored the realms of their craft because they wanted to, not because they were asked to. The fame and fortune was the result of that love, not what produced it.

"Paul and I, we never thought that we would make much money out of the thing. We just loved writing software."
Bill Gates[23]

"The law of work seems unfair, but nothing can change it; the more enjoyment you get out of your work, the more money you will make."
Mark Twain[24]

FINAL THOUGHTS

Human creativity is a wonder to behold. It is the inspiration behind da Vinci's *Mona Lisa* and Michelangelo's *David*, the vision behind the Great Wall of China, and the joy behind the finger painting of a 3-year-old. We are as it seems—creative animals. Whilst we have felt the sheer pride that comes from creating something, many of us rarely exercise that inbuilt desire anymore. However, doing so brings with it an array of benefits that help keep our minds and bodies both happy and aligned. Our greatest challenge, it seems, is fighting back the demons of doubt and the perceived opinions of society. You do not need to be a genius, a prodigy, or an expert. You just need you and a willingness to start expressing what it is that is inside of you.

PART B: FINDING YOUR CALLING

"Where a man feels at home, outside of where he's born, is where he's meant to go."
***Hemingway*[25]**

Finding your 'purpose' or 'calling' in life is more than just participating in something you enjoy. We cannot just sit on a beach in a tropical climate, sipping cocktails out of a coconut. That would never truly satisfy us. We human beings need to engage with something that excites and stimulates us. Some people make their living in a way that incorporates their passions, providing daily fulfilment at a level beyond that of just 'enjoying your job'. The old phrase of 'do what you love and you'll never work a day in your life' is something we have all heard, but rarely bring to fruition in our own lives. Regardless of whether your passions are realised in your work or personal life, one thing seems to be for sure; humans require fulfilment from engaging with things that truly speak to them. We need to involve ourselves with something that lights the proverbial fire in our belly, the thing that we desire to pursue when we wake up in the morning, the thing that never feels like a chore, and the thing we would still do even if we never made a dime from our efforts. They are the things we must do because we would not be 'us' if we did not.

"Choose a job you love, and you will never have to work a day in your life."
***Attributed to Confucius*[26]**

A SEARCH FOR PURPOSE

Finding your calling is perhaps the trickiest of puzzles. If we could only find that thing that excites and invigorates us, we could either obtain a job where we do it, or create a job in order to do it. Unfortunately, that may not be as easy as it sounds. Finding or manufacturing our calling requires some form of foresight, imagination, or experience. However, no one is to say that we don't all have this capacity, or that we have to figure it out right away.

We have discussed at length the creative spark that rests in all of us. Couple that with the experiences obtained by an inquisitive and curious mind and we have a recipe for exploration. Your calling can therefore be found at any time, for which no arrival is too late. Perhaps all we need do is listen to our childish artist and our imagination, then let it run wild with possibilities. This is not a one-stop shop, however. We can have many callings, big and small, paid or unpaid. What is important is not settling for an uninspiring existence where you watch your dreams, motivations, and potential float by.

"The imagination is always restless and suggests a variety of thoughts, and the will, reason being laid aside, is ready for every extravagant project."
John Locke[27]

"The only way to do great work is to love what you do. If you haven't found it yet, keep looking. Don't settle."
Steve Jobs[28]

"There comes a time when you ought to start doing what you want. Take a job that you love. You will jump out of bed in the morning. I think you are out of your mind if you keep taking jobs that you don't like because you think it will look good on your resume. Isn't that a little like saving up sex for your old age?"

Warren Buffet[29]

Perhaps the answer to the challenge of finding our calling can be found in what the Japanese call 'ikigai'.[29] Ikigai is essentially our 'reason for being'. The Japanese characters that combine to make this word are ones for 'life' and 'to be worthwhile'. Figure 7 shows the graphical representation of how (from a professional perspective at least) your ikigai is found and nurtured. Combining 'what you love', 'what you are good at', 'what the world needs', and 'what you can be paid for' creates an intersecting area that forms your ikigai. Now, this is not to say that it is easy to find. On the contrary, many will go a lifetime searching for this golden occupation or reason for being. The intersection of each pair does provide some hope, however, with interesting ideas around what makes your mission, passion, profession, and vocation. Perhaps focusing on these areas first may provide some insight into what truly speaks to you and whether or not you can turn this into something more than just a pastime or ambition.

As usual, the Western philosophers of old have also remarked on this before. Aristotle once remarked that "Where your talents and the needs of the world cross, there lies your vocation". Not exactly the same as the ikigai description, but only as far as the missing distinction between profession and vocation. Aristotle's thoughts seem clear, though, that focusing on matching your talents with what the world could use more of seems a pretty good way to go.

Figure 7. Adapted from *Ikigai: The Japanese Secret to a Long and Happy Life*[30]

"Find what you like doing best and get someone to pay you for doing it."
Katherine Whitehorn[31]

"You can be creative in anything – in math, science, engineering, philosophy – as much as you can in music or in painting or in dance."
Sir Ken Robinson[32]

Consider for a moment how long we all spend in employment or work. Depending on the average life expectancy of your country and your academic history, you are likely to be 'in work' for upwards of 40 years. This is a huge amount of time. On the one hand, you could argue that length of time is far too long to waste doing something you hate. On the other, it may not be long enough if you do something you love. Either way, a 40-year professional career does afford plenty of time for figuring out what it is that you want to do. Unfortunately, many of us feel stuck in our misinformed career choices, especially after taking on the responsibility of such things as mortgages, partners, and children. During even this challenging time, do we not have the opportunity to work towards our ikigai, even if this is on a small scale? It would certainly make us more fulfilled to engage in that which we love. We would also be a more self-actualised person and therefore a better employee, partner, mother, or father. So again, even if this search takes all of the 40+ years or more, it would still be worthwhile. Especially when we consider the alternative.

"Your work is going to fill a large part of your life, and the only way to be truly satisfied is to do what you believe is great work. And the only way to do great work is to love what you do."

Steve Jobs[28]

An important thing to realise here is that there is an ikigai (at least to some extent) for everyone. This is not a quality exclusive to one section of society in particular. We all have something we enjoy and something we do better than we do something else. When we factor in the content of the chapter on learning, we have also found that we can get better at anything, meaning that the seemingly difficult part of the diagram (what you are good at) can be covered with mere application and determination. What remains is identifying what the world needs and then getting someone to pay you for the pleasure. Regardless of your success in the latter, we all have the opportunity for seeking and exploring something more meaningful to us. What's more is that this thing needs to be genuinely important to us and not just something we believe we should probably do.

Your ikigai will never be found by following trends in society or attempting to live up to parental and societal expectations. Even the proposed future of playing video games in your bedroom whilst still in your underwear has some modern-day potential for making you a living. Of course, some choices may be more likely than others, but they are our choices nonetheless. More important though, is the idea that we can find our ikigai if we are so inclined. However, this may take a great amount of persistence, resilience, and drive in order for it to become reality.

"Just don't give up trying to do what you really want to do. Where there is love and inspiration, I don't think you can go wrong."

Ella Fitzgerald[33]

"Everyone has been made for some particular work, and the desire for that work has been put in every heart."

Rumi[34]

Our ikigai does not need to be something grand and awe-inspiring. Whilst the romantic view of hugely illustrious work is something we would all ideally aspire to, the worldly heights of Steve Jobs and co. are not for everyone. However, everyone has their thing. Comparing yourself to the rest of the world (and therefore being ego-driven) is probably the last thing one needs to do when searching for greater purpose. As is often the case, purpose can be found in the simple or rather uneventful. People enjoy all manner of things that to us would seem strange, and our professions and passions are no different. Regardless of the activity, passion is the foremost driver.

"If it falls your lot to be a street sweeper, go out and sweep streets like Michelangelo painted pictures. Sweep streets like Handel and Beethoven composed music. Sweep streets like Shakespeare wrote poetry. Sweep streets so well that all the hosts of heaven and earth will have to pause and say, here lived a great street sweeper who swept his job well."

Martin Luther King, Jr.[35]

For many, nagging self-doubt or the opinions of inexperienced others can be hugely detrimental to our ability to follow our passions. Unfortunately, the dreams of one person may seem ludicrous to another and hence receive criticism. Some people are even so beset by the enthusiasm of others that instead of embracing the creative spark that they see in their neighbour, they choose to tear them down, ignoring their inner demons. Shortly, we will expand upon the idea of separating from the ego, but here we can see perfect examples. The more we are concerned with other people's opinions, the more we will second-guess our efforts. The disbelief of others is more likely to be a reflection of their own fears and jealousy than it is an objective view of your endeavours. This is not to say that everything you do or choose to pursue is a good idea, however, consulting experienced professionals and researching your ideas thoroughly is the way forward.

"The future belongs to those who believe in the beauty of their dreams."

Anonymous[36]

"New opinions are always suspected, and usually opposed, without any other reason but because they are not already common."
***John Locke*[37]**

The historical view of creativity was one of pragmatic exploration. However, if we take the more modern or post-enlightenment era viewpoint, creativity is by definition producing something new and unique. With regard to our choice of pursuits, business ideas, and artistic efforts, we are likely doing just that. We are creating something that does not already exist. As a result, it will likely be met with scepticism, as humans often fear that which they do not know. These ideas are the 'unknown' or 'chaos' for everyone else and are thus considered dangerous and unpredictable. Perhaps it is easier for us creators if we observe the negativity of others in that way.

As John Locke says, the natural instinct for many is one of suspicion, but that is all it is. Opposition is just an obligatory reaction to an automatic response and, as such, should not be taken personally. Taking on that negativity and convincing ourselves that this is being 'rational' is to let the emotive knee-jerk reaction of others become a controlling influence. Far too many of us become surrounded by this natural aversion that it becomes so easy for us to confuse suitable caution with 'sensible' negativity. Much like a previous quote from Oscar Wilde, our creativity can die from this 'creeping common sense' that is acquired from caring a little too much about the world's responses and how eager it seems to be to share them.

"The chief enemy of creativity is 'good' sense."
***Pablo Picasso*[38]**

"Living creatively is really important to maintain throughout your life. And living creatively doesn't mean only artistic creativity, although that's part of it. It means being yourself, not just complying with the wishes of other people."
***Matt Groening*[39]**

If anything, the negative opinions of others can or maybe should be seen as a good sign. As discussed, if your creations are truly unique, then by nature they are the unknown. An individual who makes their metaphorical home in this land might be considered somewhat strange for doing so. This may be the root of why the creative and exceptional are often seen as that much more eccentric. Those that embody a sense of chaos are hardly going to be viewed as representative of the rest of the population. Creative people almost represent the wild animal, whose unpredictable actions induce fear. They are the ones who see a different world to others, who see possibility where some see limitation, and hear music where some hear noise. So do not be afraid if people shun your work as nothing more than delusion. Maybe we should be more worried if they do not?

"No great mind has ever existed without a touch of madness."
***Seneca*[40]**

"Creativity is seeing what everyone else has seen, and thinking what no one else has thought."
***A paraphrase of Artur Schopenhauer*[41]**

LET GO OF THE OUTCOME AND JUST BEGIN

The outcome of your labour is not as important as the labour itself. Much like the principles around learning, it is the struggle that is most valuable. The act of doing is the act of exercising the creativity that resides deep inside you. In that regard, the outcome almost seems irrelevant, if it were not for the need to sell your wares for the purposes of business etc. There is a reason that many see the benefit in removing the importance of the outcome and just allowing people to play at being creative. When we remove the outcome, we can more easily enjoy the process. The self-consciousness that is wrapped up in your potential creation dissipates, leaving you with a more mindful headspace for revelling in the act itself. Out of this play comes the more natural and unadulterated expression of what lay inside you.

When we consider what others might think, we let that become the dominant discourse in our minds. As a result, our creativity is perverted by external influence. Our creations are ours. Sure, we may intend sharing it with the world, but at that first stage it is nothing more than our expression for the sake of simply expressing. Consider this for a moment. How often is what you do affected by your projections of other people's comments or opinions? Why do you let one of your most natural drivers required for a fulfilling existence immediately be polluted with the imagined thoughts of others? This is not a simple case of ignoring the inevitable. Of course, the opinions of the world will likely follow any creation made public. However, that is at the back end of the process. The challenge therefore is not to let the inevitable ruin the fun. We must simply allow ourselves to create whatever it is that is inside us, regardless of what may come our way afterwards.

"If you want creative workers, give them enough time to play."

John Cleese[42]

"Don't think. Thinking is the enemy of creativity. It's self-conscious, and anything self-conscious is lousy. You can't try to do things. You simply must do things."
Ray Bradbury[43]

FINAL THOUGHTS

Our true calling, our ikigai, is to be found in what we love doing, for that passion is what drives creativity in the first place. But this does not mean that everyone need be the next Pablo Picasso or a future Bill Gates. We do not need to create our own business empires or artistic legacy in order to be exercising creativity. Our calling, our outlet for passion and excellence can be found in anything. It is unique to us and not restricted by public opinion. It is whatever we need to do in order to have even the smallest outlet for our creative drive. But make no mistake, engaging with it is a must. If we do not, we will never truly be us, we will never truly make our mark or contribute our verse. We will fall into the grips of sensible rationality and convince ourselves that we cannot do it or, even worse, that we don't need to.

"Perhaps imagination is only intelligence having fun."
George Scialabban (often attributed to Einstein)[44]

"You can only become truly accomplished at something you love. Don't make money your goal. Instead pursue the things you love doing and then do them so well that people can't take their eyes off of you."
Maya Angelou[45]

"A thing of beauty is a joy for ever:
Its loveliness increases; it will never
Pass into nothingness."

John Keats[46]

PART 4: CULTIVATING VIRTUE

CHAPTER 11

LIMITING DESIRES AND BEING CONTENT

PART A: NEEDS VERSUS WANTS

"Bart! With $10,000, we'd be millionaires! We could buy all kinds of useful things like...love!"
***Homer Simpson*[1]**

What do we desire and why? What will eventually satisfy us? Is it enough to possess, or do we want to possess in excess? What does it mean to be rich and how do we qualify being rich in the first place? Is the contented individual 'wealthier' than the discontented, regardless of their many belongings or monetary value? Many philosophers and psychologists have extolled the importance of limiting our desires for material things and appreciating what we already have. But in a world where marketing, social media, and status play such a large role in society, how difficult is it to remain balanced and content? Doing so means addressing the balance of our wants and needs. It means the removal of attachment to 'things' that do not necessarily make our lives better. It means not inserting your sense of self-worth into them, for they do not encapsulate you as a human being.

DESIRE—WANTS VERSUS NEEDS

Desire is essentially to long or hope for something. We may all possess many desires, not necessarily detrimental in nature. A desire to alleviate our physical suffering from illness is a great example of a desire that will bring greater happiness. Commonly, desire relates to our needs and wants where the distinction between the two may prove to be most vital. Much like everything within our mental scope, 'needs' are subjective.

What one person feels they need may be very different to what someone else views as such. A 'want' may be limited to things or situations that are less necessary. A nicer car than the one you have is probably just a 'want', whereas actually owning a working vehicle may be a 'need' as it pertains to you getting to work on time. Your own personal definition of what it means to 'need' something is then of paramount importance. The story you tell yourself in order to justify your needs is perhaps the thing that requires attention. Blurring the lines between the two, or increasing our attachment to our wants, is something that philosophers of old have often discussed.

From a historical point of view, 'desire' is often written about as a 'want'. Perhaps more specifically it is 'wanting to excess' or rather being dependent on the acquisition of our wants for happiness. Granted, there is evidence that suggests wealth can indeed make us happier to a certain extent (explored later in the chapter), but the reliance on such is what the Stoics, Buddhists, and Daoists would all advocate against. One could even argue that it is our individual approach to assigning value to material things that actually makes the attainment of those things pleasurable in the first place. In a society where money is not required, having more of it would not bring you greater happiness. I know how silly that may sound, given that money is virtually a universal constant in our world, but you see my point. If we ascribe value to something, the attainment of it will make us happier. Coincidently, if we ascribe value to something and then lose it, the opposite will occur.

What the aforementioned philosophers tried to do was encourage the limitation of our 'desires' (our wants rather than needs) so that we were not dependent on them or even a slave to them. Again, I am not suggesting here that we cannot desire something or work towards the attainment or acquisition of something, material or otherwise. If that were the case, we would never get anything done, nor achieve anything of worth to us or the rest of humanity. What I am suggesting is that we take a leaf out of the philosophical book and readdress our wants both in terms of our classification of them and our attachment to them.

"Know contentment and you will suffer no disgrace.
Know when to stop and you will meet with no
danger. You can then endure."
Lao Tzu[2]

The Stoics had a particularly strong outlook on desire (referred to as 'wants' for the remainder of the chapter). They believed it to be one of the four passions that misguide us towards unhappiness, with the other three being fear, pleasure, and distress. Desire was seen to be attending to something outside of our control. If we long for something, or a certain circumstance, we are choosing to place the locus of control outside of ourselves. Instead, the Stoics taught self-reliance and as such moved away from concerning themselves with things not in their control. In that regard, it meant that once you had done all you could in order to achieve a goal or obtain and item, you did not concern yourself with its acquisition thereafter. Nor did you attach your sense of self-worth to obtaining it either. Epictetus, a major exponent of stoicism, believed that the removal of desire in totality was a key to happiness. Exercising restraint from falling into the trap of desire was a skill to be credited and respected. Aristotle also shared the sentiment to some degree, treating desire as somewhat akin to that of animal drives in that it was not born of rational choice or cognitive processes.

"Freedom isn't secured by filling up on your heart's desire but by removing your desire."
Epictetus[3]

"Restrict yourself to choice and refusal; and exercise them carefully, within discipline and detachment."
Epictetus[3]

Epictetus describes succumbing to desire as bowing to the inferior. Allowing ourselves not to exercise restraint and therefore being taken in by the allure of the inferior was seen as a poor way to live. He suggested that mistaking the inferior for something good (focusing on material wealth as a source of happiness at the expense of one's personal health) would put someone at odds with the world and themselves, incurring anxiety, stress, and disappointment. In other words, desire causes us to concern ourselves with the superficial that will never bring us true happiness or fulfilment.

"We are responsible for some things, while there are others for which we cannot be held responsible. The former include our judgement, our impulse, our desire, aversion and our mental faculties in general; the latter include the body, material possessions, our reputation, status –in a word, anything not in our power to control.
The former are naturally free, unconstrained and unimpeded, while the latter are frail, inferior, subject to restraint –and none of our affair."
Epictetus[3]

The same thoughts were shared by Marcus Aurelius—"very little is needed for a happy life". Epicurus echoes this sentiment with the notion that those taken by desire for more will never truly feel content. The restraint suggested by the Stoics as being a key virtue is also seen as a perspective change for many. Altering the narrative of what it means to enrich our lives is something that adds a new worldview for those that need realignment.

"Nothing is enough to one for whom enough is very little."
Epicurus[4]

"We are enriched not by what we possess, but
by what we can do without."
Immanuel Kant[5]

Here, Immanuel Kant is doing just that. 'What we can do without' is showing the need for removal of desire and detachment from possessions in order to be truly fulfilled. Interestingly, the major poets of history have also come to similar conclusions about desire and its connection with unhappiness.

"Blessed is the man who expects nothing, for he shall
never be disappointed."
Alexander Pope[6]

"Some say the world will end in fire,
Some say in ice.
From what I've tasted of desire,
I hold with those who favour fire."
Robert Frost[7]

Here, Frost is comparing fire with desire, suggesting that it is desire that will be the end of all things. He portrays desire as being a more destructive force than even hate, bringing about greater calamity and despair. The pairing of these carnal passions are also the focus of Dante's *Inferno*, where he also suggests a descent "Into the eternal darkness, into fire and into ice" as a journey into purgatory and perpetual hell.

WHEN SATISFYING OUR DESIRES (WANTS) ACTUALLY MAKES US HAPPY

Before we go any further, it is worth discussing how the acquisition of things can actually make us happier and more fulfilled. This may sound rather contradictory, but just humour me for a while.

Initially, psychologists Van Boven and Gilovich found that generally speaking, if we are to spend money on something in order to make us happier, then 'experiences' do a better job than material possessions.[8] The reason being that the happiness benefit brought about from material gain reduces over time, or even causes a degree of 'buyer's remorse'.[9] People often end up comparing their belongings to those of other people, again causing a drop-off in the happiness associated with acquiring 'things'.[9] With 'experiences', that comparison is much harder to make.

Things are rarely that simple, though. Purchasing things can indeed bring us happiness when they are linked to our personality[10] and when they are 'things' that create experiences.[11] The former occurs when what we purchase is deemed as reflective of who we are. Things that help to portray our genuine personality (clothing related to our identity, for example) or even the settings in which they were purchased (drinks in a bar for an extrovert) help to create a sense of happiness in those purchases.[9] The latter relates to purchases we make that lead to good experiences. Purchasing a canoe for the family that brings with it years of enjoyment is a great example.

To complicate matters even more, research has also found that buying things can make us happier than purchasing experiences, depending on what we buy.[12] This research found that the highs of experiences were more intense, however the happiness from certain things was more frequent (things with greater utility over a period of time). So what does this mean for us all? Well, it seems as if there is no one-size-fits-all formula for 'buying happiness'. People will respond differently to different types of purchases. However, the evidence suggests that if you are to buy things, then buy things that are indicative of who you are and that are likely to give you repetitive bouts of joy over long periods of time.[9] In other words, avoid material purchases that are likely to make you compare them to other people's, or that are purchased on a whim, through vanity or through unnecessary collection.

You may be forgiven for thinking then that 'I can buy my way to happiness'. Whilst we have shown an element of truth in that, the real question lies in the motivation behind the purchases and how 'required' they are for the flourishing of your existence. What we need to do is balance the philosophical views around our desires with the psychological literature.

For many of us, the allure of collecting belongings is all too strong. If we were to really dissect the purchases we have made over the years, we may indeed find that many of these have fallen into the 'unnecessary' category. This is partly due to the temporary fix that we feel when purchasing something, which is somewhat similar to that of the dopamine release obtained through 'likes' on social media.[10] We covet something and then acquire it.

In some regard, this closing of the loop may explain the psychological benefit we feel at the time. One could even argue that it helps you convert some chaos (not owning that object) into order (now owning it). As discussed earlier, though, this is not necessarily the same as the process of conversion. Merely purchasing something like that is not making a valuable contribution to your state of mind or sense of accomplishment. Instead, it is a superficial prize and one not often earned in a metaphorical sense. It may have been purchased through money earned, or on a credit card, but is not necessarily a healthy result of the lessons learned or sacrifices made.

> *"**Marge**: This chair is $2 000! We could buy a whole living room set for that.*
> ***Homer**: Marge, there's an empty spot I've always had inside me. I tried to fill it with family, religion, community service, but those were dead ends! I think this chair is the answer."*
> ***The Simpsons**[13]*

BUYING HAPPINESS—MONEY

Across the world, research appears to support the idea that money correlates to happiness and well-being.[14] The rather huge 'Our World Data' study, showed that richer countries were on average happier than less affluent ones (with some exceptions that we will discuss shortly).[14] Data within countries also showed that wealthier people are on average happier than less wealthy individuals. This might suggest then that money does indeed buy happiness. Yet, there is a little more to the story.

A recent research paper claimed to have found the figures at which happiness and well-being peak in terms of annual individual income.[15] The study found that $95,000 (approximately £68, 840) annual income was required for peak 'life satisfaction' and that approximately $60,000–75,000 (£43,478–54,347) was required for peak 'emotional well-being'.[16] This study by Jebb and colleagues in 2018 built on previous work where figures of $75,000 were found.[17] Both studies found a fairly linear relationship in that the closer someone got to those figures, the more their well-being and happiness increased.

Now, this might sound like very compelling evidence. However, there are some significant caveats. Increases above those figures actually saw a decrease in happiness. In other words, more money does not equal more happiness above these levels. This is thought to be due to an increase in comparison with other people and therefore ego involvement, the obsessive need to earn more or buy more, and the restrictions on time and freedom that come with doing the jobs that are likely to earn those sorts of incomes.[15,16,17] What's more is that the international data shows how areas like Latin America are actually happier than their income figures would suggest, showing that even aspects of culture can contribute to the perception of wealth and happiness.[14]

"I think everybody should get rich and famous and do everything they ever dreamed of so they can see that it's not the answer."

Jim Carrey[18]

Remembering that these figures are based on average levels is very important. Yes, it does appear that for most people earning more money (up to the figures given) does make us happier. But this is across large populations and does not take into account specific individual differences. Our perception of the situation and what we choose to do with our money and time can make a big difference. As Rachel Sherman (a sociology professor) stated, "people can have exactly the same amount of money and feel totally different about whether it's enough for what they want to buy and enough to feel secure".[17]

This brings us back to what the philosophers of old were suggesting before and the apparent contradiction. If we change our perspective on what it means to want something and what it means to be content with what we have, we can be happier with less (or indeed even happier with more). Bear in mind that the average

UK pre-tax income is £22,400 (as per 11/2019) and that the peak life satisfaction figure of £68,840 would place someone in the top 5% of UK earners and we have a potential need for addressing our monetary perceptions.[19] With the right mindset, we can indeed bring our perception towards our current income and perceptions, rather than having to rely on bringing our income to our perceived level required for happiness.

FINAL THOUGHTS

The dynamic interplay between needs and wants provides a landscape upon which to build. Re-evaluating our perceptions of what will make us happy can help to shed new light on our motivations for purchases and for earning more money. Granted, certain purchases and experiences may only be possible through the acquisition of money, but what we choose to spend that money on is more important. When our purchases reflect who we are, are necessary, or provide long-term enjoyment, they are more beneficial to our overall happiness. But more and more of the 'wants' does not translate into more and more happiness. Instead, our interpretation of what it means to want and what it means to have are what require framing accordingly. What we really seek is contentment, not abundance.

"I cannot tell if what the world considers 'happiness' is happiness or not. All I know is that when I consider the way they go about attaining it, I see them carried away headlong, grim and obsessed, in the general onrush of the human herd, unable to stop themselves or to change their direction. All the while they claim to be just on the point of attaining happiness."

Chuang-Tzu[20]

"And you may know how little God thinks of money, by observing on what bad and contemptible characters he often bestows it."

Thomas Guthrie[21]

PART B: LETTING GO OF ATTACHMENT

"There is no crime greater than having too many desires;
There is no disaster greater than not being content;
There is no misfortune greater than being covetous.
Hence in being content, one will always have enough."
Lao Tzu[22]

If the acquisition of things can make us happy, then why can buying anything you want not bring you more happiness? If money brings life satisfaction, why do vast sums of it not bring elation? The relationship between the acquisition of things and happiness is not that simple. There are inherent components in the equation that cause the waters to muddy. The components are *you* and the role of existence and human flourishing itself. Our attachment to things and our perspective of them becomes the differentiating factor in being content with what we have and striving for more. If we can adjust our relationship with what we have and don't have, we can free ourselves from the prison that is mass consumerism, the desire for status, and keeping up with the Joneses. We can of course still work hard towards our goals, including that of possessing material objects. A bigger house may indeed be more comfortable for the family and thus make everyone happier. But when material belongings are not the marker of success, or a prerequisite for happiness, we enjoy life for how it *is* rather than how it *would be* 'if only I had that'.

CONTENTMENT

Being content with what we have may be somewhat of a cliché. But again, something being a cliché does not diminish the value of the statement in itself. Actually, the fact that such a poignant sentiment is considered a cliché is what is most concerning. It is as if people are prepared to say "yeah, everyone says/knows that", yet proceed to practise the opposite in their daily lives. Much like the earlier chapter on perspective and revelations, there is a difference between hearing wisdom and exploring or feeling it. Just because something is common does not mean it is fully grasped or understood. Contentment is one of these things.

Being content is about removing our attachment to things and what it means to possess/acquire them. Earlier we discussed the idea that ascribing value to something is what gives it value. In this sense, attachment to belongings is due to a value we 'give' to things and what they will therefore do for us physically and psychologically. We are allocating value outside of ourselves. But as we have seen, this 'value' is not constant (in that it does not continue to bring us more and more happiness) and as such is a poor strategy for long-term happiness. In fact, chasing greater and greater highs eventually makes us less happy.

OTHER PEOPLE'S PERCEPTION

> *"How do you let go of attachment to things? Don't even try. It's impossible. Attachment to things drops away by itself when you no longer seek to find yourself in them."*
>
> ***Eckhart Tolle***[23]

Tolle is talking about the insertion of our egos into the things we own or are yet to own. It is the idea that people are looking at you and judging you that compels the need to portray a particular image. How you want to be perceived is therefore more important than how you perceive yourself. Think of the majority of Instagram accounts and consider whether what you see is how things really are, or how they want you to see them. The incredibly straightened and aligned desks that show how organised and tidy we are, the selfie taken at optimum angles to portray how slim or muscular we are, and the meal picture that shows how great our diet is. How much of this is for your benefit and how much is for everyone else's?

Of course, it is easy to fall into this sort of trap, given how the dopamine release in the brain upon receiving 'likes' and 'views' is the same as that from certain drugs, sugar, and so on.[24] Yet these are all a temporary fix and not a true panacea. We cannot fill the gaps inside us with 'likes'. If we try to do so, we spend our lives in search of the next like, the next pat on the back, or the next display of admiration from the crowd. The ego is therefore the thing holding us back from true fulfilment. Instead of finding fulfilment within, we look to find it outside of ourselves. As a result, our material and external environment becomes more important than our internal one and the accumulation of belongings and status begins.

"To what base ends, and by what abject ways,
Are mortals urged through sacred lust of praise!"
Alexander Pope[25]

SEEKING VALIDATION

The work of people like Eckhart Tolle highlights the playing of 'roles' as the manifestation of the self or ego, again reinforcing the notion that valuing outward appearance is to make our ego the driving force of our lives. Seeking validation of our self-worth from others is to place the permission of happiness in the hands of everyone else, rather than in our own. We create and maintain a façade in order to meet the supposed needs of the world, rather than our own needs (creating more and more 'wants'). When we stop trying so hard to impress people, we can begin to really see what we *need.*

"I don't know how to put this but I'm kind of a big deal. People know me. I'm very important. I have many leather-bound books and my apartment smells of rich mahogany."

Ron Burgandy, from the movie 'Anchorman'[26]

In Tolle's work, he describes the ego-driven mind as "a dysfunctional relationship with the present moment". Going back to chapter 3, we can see that living in the present is to live in our true nature. This nature is to be 'us' in the 'now' and not a projection of ourselves for the future. Our true nature is therefore the truth of us and not a concocted fiction, or an effort to attain favour from the crowd. Removal of ego and living presently puts us back in the driver's seat, where recognition is but a small bump in the road.

"The esteem of others is outside our control; we must attend instead to healing ourselves."

Epicurus[27]

"The high-minded man must care more for the truth than for what people think."

Aristotle[28]

This sentiment may seem healthy and internally progressive. However, I am sure that some will point out the potential existential issues surrounding what may appear to be living inwardly focused lives and not concerning ourselves with others. Some may even perceive these approaches as selfish or harbouring the development of some sort of alternate egoism. To not seek the opinions or admiration of others is to value your own views, happiness, or behaviours over all else? But that is not the impact that these philosophers are trying to have. Nothing is stopping you from consulting others in order to help guide your actions or choices. The emphasis is instead on being open to opinion, knowledge, and recognition from others, but not being attached to whether that is positive or negative in nature. To do so is to be seeing this feedback as relating to your sense of self and reacting with your ego. Perhaps a better way to view a more functional reality in terms of our relationship with the world is found in the words of Immanuel Kant:

> *"Seek not the favour of the multitude; it is seldom got by honest and lawful means. But seek the testimony of few; and number not voices, but weigh them."*
> ***Immanuel Kant***[29]

Kant is focusing on the quality of feedback from the world that adds value to your life, rather than just praise, favour, and recognition. The valuable and meaningful contributions (the weight of them) therefore help guide you to the 'truth' mentioned by Aristotle earlier. If your ego is held in check, you will seek feedback in whatever guise it comes, either negative or positive, because it will help you live more effectively, rather than just momentarily boosting serotonin levels.

FILLING A VOID

The acquisition of unnecessary objects or our more trivial wants for the sake of acquiring them, again has a lot to do with our lack of fulfilment and happiness in the rest of our lives. For some, the lack of control that people feel in the large motivates them to purchase things and thereby exercise control or autonomy. This is a hollow sense of autonomy, nonetheless. For others, the acquisition provides more opportunities for social media posts, likes, and simultaneous serotonin boosts. Some people also seek a shiny new object in order to fill the hole inside of them that should probably be filled by self-love, acceptance, or social connections.[30,31] What we end up with is more and more self-justification for why we should acquire something, thus alleviating cognitive dissonance and burying our worldview out of sight.

"It is the preoccupation with possessions, more than anything else, that prevents us from living freely and nobly."
Bertrand Russel[32]

"Well, we're living in a material world and I am a material girl... Or boy."
Adam Sandler, from the movie 'The Wedding Singer'[33]

The different philosophical views discussed previously all have their own way of describing the metaphysics of existence. By virtue, they would then provide explanation as to our relationship with the physical world. Interestingly, none of them seem to provide much in the way of justification for acquiring physical objects for the sake of the development of happiness. Instead, all appear to maintain that our attachments to the physical world only hinder our spiritual, internal, or existential journeys.

Our preoccupation with possessions becomes somewhat of an obsession in the belief that 'the next item I covet will really make me happy'. In doing so, we fail to see the triviality of the possessive cycle. We are replacing our existing items with new, shinier, more glamourous or fashionable ones. But under that philosophy, those items that we are replacing were the ones that gave us our initial 'sense of completion or happiness' in the first place. So, our need for possessions is therefore less about the item itself and more about the idea of acquiring something we want, something we can show off about, and something that brings us momentary relief from our real existence.

"There's no money, there's no possession
*Only obsession. I don't need that s**t."*
Papa Roach[34]

"Don't ruin the things you have by wanting what you don't have,
but realise that they too are things you once did wish for."
Epicurus[35]

REMOVING EXCESS DESIRE

So how then are we to free ourselves from the shackles of desire and the slavery of want? Well, first of all we may try to once again change our perspective on what it means to desire something and what it means to acquire it or not. We have already discussed the ideas that desire is largely born of the egocentric mind, concerned with appearance, incorrect assumptions of self-worth, or shallow fulfilment. Let us consider the alternative. What if you did not attain all these worldly possessions, wealth, and status? What would this say about you?

"Ask this question of every desire: what will happen to
me if the object of desire is achieved, and what if not?"
Epicurus[35]

What are the repercussions of not obtaining that new (more extravagant) car? This may take some deliberation. The philosophers and poets would say that with true introspection, you will find that nothing would change. Your world is not made immeasurably better through somewhat petty acquisitions. To attach ourselves to this outcome would have only enslaved you further, after all. By assessing the alternative to attaining something, we can realign our perspective and get to grips with the core value of that supposed acquisition. What would this do for my life, really? What would happen if I didn't acquire it? It can also help realign our attachment to things already in our possession. What would happen if this became faulty or if it were stolen? Again, what would this mean to me? What would it say about me? When we debate these questions internally, we begin to assess what it means to acquire and what it means to be content. The latter is the goal of the Stoics, Buddhists, and Daoists. With contentment we are rich and not in what we have, but in that we do not desire more.

"Not to be attached to something is to be aware of its absolute value. Everything you do should be based on such an awareness, and not on material or self-centred ideas of value."

Shunryu Suzuki[36]

"The greatest wealth is to live content with little."

Plato[37]

Contentment is the management of expectations toward what is in your control and what is not. It is an understanding of the superficial nature of belongings and recognition, or the inferior, as Epictetus would say. It is a self-awareness of what you are doing and what that means, along with an appreciation for what you currently have. Contentment is thus a powerful idea and one that we can utilise more often. In the world of online shopping and ever-more-rapid delivery systems, the opportunity to 'purchase happiness' has never been closer. Yet to know contentment is to know that these belongings do not always add value to our lives in the strictest sense of accumulation.

One of the prevailing ideas from philosophy is that of lower expectations from things and thus higher satisfaction. Another is the idea of diminishing returns, where with greater wealth or material possession, the impact of any new possession acquired is reduced.

"It is not the man who has too little, but the man who craves more, that is poor."
Seneca[38]

Further research into happiness has also highlighted the depth of human connections and relationships as a significant factor. The longest happiness study in existence, conducted by Harvard University and run by Robert Waldinger, has repeatedly shown that these are the 'possessions' most strongly correlated with a long and happy life.[39]

So it would appear that happiness (using whatever definition or measurement tool conceivable) is far from an easy thing to assess. What the research does show though, is that happiness and fulfilment are complex entities and go far beyond that of simple wealth and material gain. What appears clear is that a possible answer to the quest for happiness lies in our belief of what actually brings happiness and fulfilment. Our internal appreciation is what makes the difference in our perception of a situation. Contentment and happiness is nothing more than a state of mind and one that can be attained in virtually any environment. Of course, I am not suggesting that we abandon all possessions, or indeed the drive towards acquiring certain things. Rather, I am suggesting that we maintain a healthier appreciation for what our belongings actually bring us and what it would mean if they were no longer there. It may be nice to have something new, but that does not mean that we are more complete as a result. If we are to be truly happy, we must first learn to be okay with not having the material things we want in life. Focusing our efforts on that which brings real value (of the superior kind) is therefore the way forward.

"He who knows contentment is rich."
***Lao Tzu*[40]**

It would appear, then, that the wisest among us are those who can properly align their expectations and their mindsets towards a healthy appreciation of material things. Those who can, enjoy a freedom from attachment, a freedom from desire. Much like the earlier comments, the esteem of others is also nothing more than a trivial possession; we just can't necessarily hang it on our wall. So consider your actions and desires at the next available opportunity. What is my motivation for having this? What would happen if I did not?

"The greatest blessings of mankind are within us and within our reach. A wise man is content with his lot, whatever it may be, without wishing for what he has not."
***Seneca*[38]**

FINAL THOUGHTS

If we are not careful, our desires can consume us. Convincing us that in some way, they will actually improve our lives at a deeper level. In today's world it is all too easy to judge yourself or your neighbour by what they have, rather than who they are. We are also far too preoccupied with 'what people may think of me' or 'how many likes this may get on social media' than we are with our true motives. The philosophers of old believed this to be a root cause of unhappiness and rather unanimously recommended re-evaluation. For them, limiting desire is to make rational decisions, assessing the true value of something. It is also a case of focusing our efforts on what we can control, rather than what we cannot (like the opinions of others). When we remove the ego from the equation, we can better see the inferiority of our desires and the superficial nature of our actions. With our eyes opened, we can learn to appreciate what we currently have and who we are, becoming more content in the process.

Contentment brings with it a wealth of the immaterial and one that cannot be stolen away by any other. In that sense, the only person in charge of your wealth is you. You are the one that decides whether you are poor or rich. You may indeed still aim for greater achievement and work hard to better your situation. However, your sense of self-worth will not be combined with the belongings that may come along with them. Instead, you will be both richer and wiser; for you will know that no possession can define you.

"Care about people's approval and you will be their prisoner."
Lao Tzu[41]

"In the end, only three things matter: how much you loved, how gently you lived, and how gracefully you let go of things not meant for you."
Buddhist saying[42]

"All in exact proportion to the state:
Nothing to add, and nothing to abate.
Each beast, each insect, happy in its own,
Is Heav'n unkind to Man, and Man alone?
Shall he alone, whom rational we call,
Be pleased with nothing if not blessed with all."
Alexander Pope[43]

CHAPTER 12

A PATH TOWARD VIRTUE

PART A: THE ORIGIN OF VIRTUE

"But where's the man, who counsel can bestow,
Still pleas'd to teach, and yet not proud to know?
Unbias'd, or by favour or by spite;
Not dully prepossess'd, nor blindly right;
Though learn'd, well-bred; and though well-bred, sincere;
Modestly bold, and humanly severe?
Who to a friend his faults can freely show,
And gladly praise the merit of a foe?"

***Alexander Pope*[1]**

"It is our choices, Harry, that show what we truly are, far more than our abilities."

***Dumbledore, from the movie 'Harry Potter and the Chamber of Secrets'*[2]**

What is it to be virtuous? Is virtue itself a forgotten… virtue? In a modern-day world of individual wants and desires being so easily prioritised and satisfied, is the idea of virtue a dying one? The ancient philosophers prioritised virtuousness as above pretty much all else, and for good reason. Our possessions, our status, or anything else of 'inferior' note is nothing compared to who we are as individuals and how we conduct ourselves. Compound that with the cumulative effects of society and we have a recipe for a better world. But rather than focus on the masses, let's just focus on ourselves for now. We cannot control the actions of others, but we can control our own. Therein lies great power, for we can choose to be what we want to be. The emphasis here is on choice. Even if we do not consider our virtues consciously, we nonetheless have them.

Whether we wish to acknowledge it or not, we are choosing to act a certain way, even if that choice is made through ignorance alone. Perhaps then, we would all benefit from gaining a greater understanding of virtue and how it can help our lives. From ancient times to the present, many have expressed the need to live a better quality of life by assessing our own actions. Whilst we can't be perfect, that does not provide justification for remaining as we are. We have the opportunity to be better people. What's more is that when we are better people, we arguably reach an existence of a higher plane and a higher quality; a place where our actions can create a catalyst for others to follow suit. The Jordan Peterson quote from earlier resonates once again, "What better do you have to do with your time?" Personally, I struggle to think of a valid answer.

WHAT IS VIRTUE?

Virtue is a tough concept to consider. Whilst we may all have a generally implicit understanding, we may find it hard to explain. We may also all understand the need for it, but not necessarily the reasons why. This is a difficult thing to get our heads around. Why do I believe I need something, or that it is important, when I don't exactly know what it is? Questions like this have sparked many a philosophical debate and a multitude of moral philosophy writings.

Virtue can often be considered as desirable qualities that are also seen to be morally sound or good in nature. This is a little ambiguous, but maybe treat this as an overarching statement that encapsulates what it means to be a moral, just, and good person. Virtues then, are any qualities that bring that person closer to the realisation of 'good' (in a sense of admirable moral quality). Of course, there are many examples of virtues that achieve this in some small measure: being kind, genuine, charitable, honest etc. Virtues define us as individuals through our choices and behaviours, rather than our physical self. One might argue that our virtues are a more accurate reflection of who we are, given that they are a manifestation of what we hold inside and can influence, rather than just the image everyone sees the rest of the time.

"I have always thought the actions of men the best interpreters of their thoughts."

John Locke[3]

"By their fruits ye shall know them."

Matthew 7:20[4]

What then of virtue in a modern world? I think we would all agree that fostering qualities that make us inherently good or moral is just as important as ever. If our virtues are seen in our actions, then our actions become most important. How we interact with our neighbours and society in general becomes a window into our soul. We may say we are a certain type of person, however if our actions betray this image, no one will ever believe us. How we manage ourselves in an array of situations will likely tell a greater story of 'us' than we could ever knowingly articulate.

"If you would read a man's disposition see him game, you will then learn more of him in one hour than seven years of conversation."
Richard Lingard (often attributed to Plato)[5]

"Behaviour is the mirror in which everyone shows their image."
Goethe[6]

Many philosophers and religions espouse the idea that our behaviours demonstrate who we are inside. In reality, many things can end up affecting our behaviours, to the detriment of our true nature. 'Mob mentality' comes to mind as an example of how outside conditions can make us significantly betray our moral compass. Yet, awareness of our virtues and fostering better ones where required is something we can all do to shift our behaviours more toward the good side of the moral continuum. As per other chapters, addressing the core beliefs that we hold to be true can impact our worldview and thus affect our interaction with the world. The same can be said for our moral qualities. If we put more focus on them, cultivate and develop them, it will manifest itself outwardly for all to see. If we do not, then the opposite will be true. Your poor qualities will rise to the forefront of your behavioural norms and impact upon your neighbour accordingly. Adjusting our core self in light of this is mythically the premise of redemption and reconciliation. We must first identify and then battle with our basic, underlying self in order to see our actions change for the better. There is a great passage in the bible to illustrate this:

"Even so every good tree bringeth forth good fruit; but a corrupt tree bringeth forth evil fruit. A good tree cannot bring forth evil fruit, neither can a corrupt tree bring forth good fruit."

Matthew 7:17–18 (King James version)[7]

If our tree is not good, then nor will be our fruit. Try as we may, our actions will betray us and reveal who we are. It is impossible for us to hold something in our hearts and act as if it is not there. Eventually, we will either cave in or be 'seen through' regardless.

"It is impossible for bad men not to act in character."

Marcus Aurelius[8]

Our intentions, then, must be to improve ourselves and grow a tree that bears more beneficial fruit. This does not mean we do so at the expense of both living in the now or being content with our lot (in a material sense). Instead, see it as still living in the moment, but making better choices in those moments. Choosing to adopt a 'better' behaviour upon reflection of previous situations still provides the opportunity to be fully immersed in what we are doing. You would still be doing something, after all.

What we have discussed thus far may also have provided the necessary fuel for those who wish to maintain that 'we cannot change who we are'. At this point, I would like to make it clear I am not talking about our ability to change a pathological disorder. Frontal lobe damage or abnormal development believed to be the precursor for psychopathy, for example, is not about to be 'cured' through careful consideration of our virtues, behaviours, and choices. Instead, I am suggesting that the majority of us have the ability to address the less primordial and pathological; the more commonplace and malleable tendencies that impact our everyday lives. As Carol Dweck would recommend, a growth mindset is all we need in order to help us foster a more caring, open-minded, and generous disposition, rather than remain in our current and possibly fixed virtuous mindset.

"Out of the crooked timber of humanity, no straight thing was ever made."
***Immanuel Kant*[9]**

A BACKGROUND FOR VIRTUOUSNESS

Virtuousness is steeped in literary history. From the oldest myths of ancient heroes, to the new genre of comic-book saviours, desirable human virtues have been displayed, discussed, and replicated for many centuries. The Mesopotamian creation myth of the *Enuma Elish*, where Marduk overcomes the tyrant and gives metaphorical birth to civilisation, is the first known example of its kind. The same types of myths have been ubiquitous ever since. You may be more familiar with the Egyptian battles of Set and Osiris, where Set is representative of every undesirable quality. Set is eventually defeated by Horus, who not only rids the world of Set's tyranny, but shows even greater bravery and generosity by venturing into the underworld, donating his recently reassembled and recovered eye to Osiris, thus bringing his father back to life.

Historical myths like this often centre around virtues of bravery, wisdom, and sacrifice. These ideals have then become synonymous with any tale of heroism and form the basis of any triumph over chaos, establishing and returning things to order. Likewise, the Greek term *arete* that generally means 'excellence' was often used to describe the heroic exploits of Homer's famous characters. *Arete* was therefore synonymous with moral virtue and being an effective human individual, and was revered as the ultimate quality to possess.

The majority of Ancient Greek myths also seek to critique the vice and virtue of Man, in an attempt to reinforce that which is desirable and good. The *arete* of humans is therefore the qualities that make them excellent and able to live excellent lives. Or in other words, the qualities that 'bringeth forth good fruit'.

"It takes a great deal of bravery to stand up to our enemies, but just as much to stand up to our friends."
Dumbledore, from 'Harry Potter and the Philosopher's Stone'[10]

In the East, a similar development of the human ideal can be found. Anyone who has read Confucius will have seen the repetition of the term benevolence, later translated as *ren*. *Ren* is a fundamental premise of Confucianism and represented the shining example of what it meant to behave like a great human being. At its heart are qualities such as respect, humility, courage, kindness, and righteousness. Possessing and displaying these qualities are what made the difference in the functioning of society and what separated the 'gentlemen' from the 'small men', metaphorically speaking. The benevolent gentlemen were praised as being more morally just and ethically sound, whereas the small men were seen as contemptuous and somewhat petty. Having *ren* was no easy thing, either. In fact, cultivating this type of quality was what Confucianism and Daoism saw as a major focus of human activity and purpose. We had to work at being better people, regardless of our belief as to exactly what that looked like.

Similarly, if we fast-forward to more modern approaches, the moral philosophy of Immanuel Kant contained elements of these moral virtues. His idea was one of moral duty above all. This was identified through what he called *The Categorical Imperative*, which helped clarify if our actions were in support of our duty. The premise was based on two questions: "Can I rationally will that everyone act as I propose to act?" "Does my action respect the goals of human beings rather than merely using them for my own purposes?"[11] If we were to answer "no" to either of these, then we should not do whatever was in question.

All of these philosophies support somewhat of an idealism-oriented worldview, and the list of potential frameworks is by no means exhaustive. However, the ideals of human history are there for a reason and should not be sniffed at. Cultivating greater virtue than possessed previously is hardly a bad thing. Yes, true *ren* may be almost impossible to attain, yet what better thing to aim towards. As long as we keep our efforts and goals in healthy perspective (not dwelling on them or over-interrogating ourselves), we can maintain a movement towards a greater level of being and a greater version of ourselves, without driving ourselves to distraction in the meantime. Aiming higher after all, is well, higher.

"If I should bow my head, let it be to a high mountain."
Maori Proverb[12]

You may be forgiven for having such thoughts as 'I am a moral person, so why does this apply to me?' and in some respects, I agree. If your moral compass is accurate and you are a generally respectful and courteous person, then perhaps you have ticked a sufficient number of boxes. However, the degree to which we are those things can always be questioned. Not only that, but there are a whole host of other virtues that we may cultivate in order to become better versions of ourselves. For example, you may be kind, but how generous are you? You may be generous, but how brave are you? By actively cultivating these aspects, we attempt to conduct ourselves in ways of which we can be proud, ways that maintain a more honourable self and a better quality of life for everyone.

"Life is never incomplete if it is an honourable one. At whatever point you leave life, if you leave it in the right way, it is whole."
***Seneca*[13]**

"To be able under all circumstances to practice five things constitutes perfect virtue; these five things are gravity, generosity of soul, sincerity, earnestness, and kindness."
***Confucius*[14]**

Our pursuit of virtue, benevolence or *ren*, is neither easy nor short. With so many possible qualities that are beneficial to our existence, it can be a bit of a minefield to navigate. Perhaps then, we should begin with those that pertain to us first and others second.

CONSISTENCY AND DILIGENCE

One aspect of virtuousness to consider is that of consistency. If we are to be a more virtuous individual, do we need be so more often than we aren't? If not, we possess nothing more than temporary glimpses or hollow promises of a better self. The mere display of a good-quality pales in comparison to consistent reproduction. We may all be able to be gracious in defeat once. However, to be a gracious competitor is another thing entirely.

"One swallow does not make a summer, neither does one fine day."
***Greek proverb*[15]**

"It's not what we do once in a while that shapes our lives. It's what we do consistently."
Anthony Robbins[16]

In this vein, the ability or rather the motivation to uphold our virtues is of great importance. Making these desirable behaviours commonplace or habitual should therefore be something we work upon. Old habits die hard, they say; so we should probably make them good ones. Adopting habits of good intent, even in some small measure, can help to lay the foundation for our long-term behaviour changes. Repeating intentional actions has been shown to develop lasting changes in human behaviour. Unfortunately, the science on this is not exact, as there are far too many variables at play. The previously reported 'minimum of 21 days' of Maxwell Maltz before a behaviour is assimilated into automatic action is a little misleading. Recent research has shown that on average 66 days of repeated action is required in order to change behaviour, however with a great degree of variation from the mean (ranges from 18–254 days for people to change behaviour).[17] Whilst these examples are generally limited to minor habits and daily actions, the same can be said of our deeper and more meaningful behaviours. Whatever the length of time, our actions and behaviours can be practised and absorbed into our lives.

"We are what we repeatedly do. Excellence, then, is not an act but a habit."
Will Durant[18]

"If you quit once it becomes a habit. Never quit."
Michael Jordan[19]

The quotes above both express the need for consistency of action, but inadvertently reveal an inherent difficulty in doing so. The temptation to take easier roads than land us squarely back in a world of order is often too great for anyone to withstand. So how then are we supposed to maintain our virtues when all those around us are losing theirs? In the face of emotion, stupidity, anger, and incompetent bosses, our struggles become all the more real and all the more difficult. Perhaps then, the answer lies in two key points: expectation management and diligence.

Managing our expectations as to the extent of change, the length of time required, and the impact of making mistakes appears key to behavioural change. Much like the chapter on failing, we need to appreciate that: one, we cannot maintain perfection (virtue is a matter of degree); and two, that it is okay (no, actually required) that we make mistakes. If our intentions are good, little slip-ups are absolutely fine. They will be beneficial if viewed in the right way (like in the chapter on learning). Diligence then, is our ability to maintain effort and focus towards our goal. It also stands for more than just persistence, as it has the undertone of valuing work over laziness; duty and responsibility over avoidance.

"Weaselling out of things is important to learn; it's what separates us from the animals... except the weasel."
***Homer Simpson*[20]**

"I never could have done what I have done without the habits of punctuality, order, and diligence, without the determination to concentrate myself on one subject at a time."
***Charles Dickens*[21]**

Once again, Mr Simpson provides a shining example of what not to do in life. Being the individual that sticks to their commitments with conscientious effort will always see greater results and greater trust from others. As Dickens goes on to say, it is diligence that separates us from what we often are and what we desire to be. Diligence is perhaps the key that unlocks all virtues, or keeps them hidden forever.

> *"Running taught me valuable lessons. In cross-country competition, training counted more than intrinsic ability, and I could compensate for a lack of natural aptitude with diligence and discipline. I applied this in everything I did."*
>
> **Nelson Mandela**[22]

"What is firmly rooted cannot be pulled out;
What is tightly held in the arms will not slip loose;
Cultivate it in your person
And its virtue will be genuine."

Lao Tzu[23]

FINAL THOUGHTS

We cannot be perfect. Virtues are by their nature a matter of degree. Yet we can still aim for them. The admirable qualities proclaimed by the philosophers of old have just as much power now as they did then. So we can still value them. But it takes more than just valuing virtues for them to really have an effect. We need to embody them and display them through our actions. Our actions demonstrate who we really are, where who we really are is a dynamic entity. We can change and develop ourselves. We can make 'good' behaviours and qualities more of a part of our lives than they were before. With consistency and diligence, we bring about lasting change that not only benefits us, but also everyone else.

PART B: INWARD VIRTUES

"Preference of vice to virtue, a manifest wrong judgment."
John Locke[24]

"Lisa, if you don't like your job you don't strike. You just go in every day and do it really half-assed."
Homer Simpson[25]

If I am to be more virtuous, which ones should I focus my attention upon? Are some better than others? Do I concentrate on those that pertain to me, or to others? In many respects, there is no right or wrong answer to any of these questions. The study of virtue-based philosophy is a huge topic in itself and one that struggles to provide concrete answers. Answers, it seems, are what we seem to gravitate towards. Yet, if we are to embrace the philosophies of the East, we realise that sometimes definitive answers are not just unattainable, but unrequired. Often, arguing over semantics and debating the finest of details stops us from actually engaging in the thing we originally sought after. Instead, if we embark on an exploration of virtues, we can begin to take on ideas that benefit our lives and the lives of those around us. There really isn't an exhaustive list of virtues, but as with the rest of this book, perhaps beginning with *us* is the way to go.

HONEST AND GENUINE

Many things in this chapter, or even this book, will seem completely obvious almost to the point of unnecessary inclusion. However, just because something appears obvious, does not mean it is realised, practised, and promoted. It is obvious that calorific intake exceeding that of expenditure will make us put on weight. Everyone 'knows' this and yet many of us are overweight. Knowledge does not automatically elicit action. In the same way, many of the things in this book are included in order to make us look beyond what we know and question our actions, thought processes, and beliefs regarding this knowledge. With regard to honesty and genuineness, we may all assume their obvious requirement for life and qualification of virtue. Yet how often do we practise it and bring it into reality? How often does the metaphorical cessation of dietary discipline responsible for our weight gain impact upon how genuine or honest we are?

"Fine words and an insinuating appearance are seldom associated with true virtue."
Confucius[26]

In the same way that our knowledge of calorific balance does not instantly translate to a diet of calorific balance, speaking words of honesty does not make us honest people. Much like Mr Robbins said earlier, the consistency of action is what really matters. We have to go beyond that of just what we say if we are really to be an honest individual. Especially given that dishonesty has a rather compounding effect, where one lie requires many more in order to keep the story afloat. It is all too easy for any one of us to fall into a world of 'selective' truths. Philosophically, even the smallest of lies is still a lie nonetheless. Honesty could be seen as an absolute term and as Sheldon Cooper from *The Big Bang Theory* mentioned earlier, 'it is not subject to gradation'. We are either honest, or we are not. However, given that virtues are a matter of degree, being 'more honest' is perhaps the way forward.

"Oh, what a tangled web we weave, when first we practice to deceive!"
Sir Walter Scott[27]

"He who tells a lie, is not sensible how great a task he undertakes; for he must be forced to invent twenty more to maintain that one."
Alexander Pope[28]

Being 'economical with the truth' is another perspective around honesty. Neglecting to tell the truth or act in an honest manner is arguably as dangerous for our sense of virtue as being dishonest itself. Again, it is easy for this type of mindset to creep into our everyday existence. Often in life, we are happy to stand by and allow something to happen, for lies to be retold, or for information to be left out. For the most part, we may not consider these things to directly reflect our own behaviour. But is being honest and genuine as simple as just what pertains directly to ourselves, or do half-truths, witnessed wrongs, and white lies tell us more about just how virtuous we really are?

"There can often be wrongs of omission as well as commission."
Marcus Aurelius[29]

One of the issues we can have with honesty is the difficulty it can often place us in. Some of the aspects already discussed can often place us in difficult positions, where knowledge of less scrupulous behaviour and actions places us at odds with our desire to be an honest individual. Take, for example, the knowledge of a friend's infidelity and the desire to not get involved in other people's business.

In those situations, how do we balance the ideas of personal honesty versus that of another moral or attribute? In addition, honesty is not always welcomed and not always advantageous in life. 'Going along to get along' is another type of behaviour that can again put someone at odds with their desire to be genuine. In those situations, we are inclined to supress our honesty in favour of not 'rocking the boat', so to speak.

The repercussions of our honesty can often spell the ruination of the delicate office environments we call home, and the forever awkward political dances in which we may unwillingly participate. But what does this mean for us? What impact does this have on our ability to call ourselves honest and genuine (if that is what we desire, of course)? There is no easy answer to this dilemma. However, I am inclined to say that our choice of action is ours to make and ours alone. For those of us more highly principled, transparency will always win out. For those of us who are possibly subjected to more political issues, perhaps a balancing act is required. Weighing up the pros and cons, so to speak, may be all we can do to answer the difficult question of "should I, or shouldn't I?" As far as our conscience is concerned, we will always be better off maintaining our virtue. But we may need to keep in mind that this may not always be welcomed in the dishonest environments we sometimes inhabit.

"Honesty is for the most part less profitable than dishonesty."

Plato[30]

"Dignity does not consist in possessing honours, but in the consciousness that we deserve them."

Aristotle[31]

Let's take this idea with a pinch of salt, though. Whilst honesty should generally prevail, little white lies that protect people's feelings and don't compromise your moral virtue are perfectly acceptable. "Do you like my painting, father?" may not need to be met with a particularly harsh (yet completely honest) critique. In some respects, there is an element of common sense required in relation to the application of honesty from a moral perspective.

When it comes to our own actions, acting in accordance with our nature (as Aurelius might say) is the most important thing. This provides the basis for a genuine self and one not subject to pretence or deception. If you disagree with something or are witnessing something you do not condone, then making yourself heard may be the appropriate thing to do. The difficulty there is assessing whether your view on that particular issue is actually right or wrong in the first place, but we will leave that to your self-reflective processes. This does not mean excusing all behaviour as 'that's just who I am', but rather a rationale for trying to act consistently in a manner becoming of your ideal self and of the virtues you wish to embody. To be genuine is to practise what you preach, show yourself for who you really are, and play no metaphorical game of illusion.

"Do not pretend to love and practice wisdom, but love and practice wisdom in reality; for we need not the appearance of health but true health."

Epicurus[32]

"Always do sober what you said you'd do drunk. That will teach you to keep your mouth shut."

Hemingway[33]

One way of ensuring that we are genuine is not to give us things to be ashamed of in the first place. Acting in accordance with your virtues whilst visible is nothing in comparison to acting that way in private. Are you the individual to pick up that piece of litter when people see you doing it, but walk by the same piece when no one is around? One potentially good action should not be mediated by a simple change of circumstance. What is right to do, is right to do. If we can be who we should be regardless of the circumstance, then we are all that bit closer to being genuine. Couple that with the removal of intention to portray a favourable image for the sake of looking a certain way and we have a recipe for virtue.

"Do nothing in your life which would cause you fear if discovered by your neighbour."
Epicurus[32]

MODESTY AND CONFIDENCE

Modesty, or rather 'being unassuming in the estimation of one's abilities and behaving in a way intended to avoid impropriety or indecency',[34] is somewhat complex. In today's world, confidence is an admirable and attractive quality that often places people in positions above their level of competence.[35,36] 'Confidence' can often seem to be attributed to anything from being self-assured to efforts in celebrating your individuality. As a result, confidence (as it is sometimes practised) does not always satisfy the idea of a healthy virtue and can sit in opposition to modesty. However, confidence and modesty can be held together as long as confidence does not become arrogance or narcissism.

"He who speaks without modesty will find it difficult to make his words good."
Confucius[37]

If we do indeed want to embody honesty and humility, we need to question the motives behind our actions and words. What is your main driver for behaving this way? Are you as competent as you think you are? Are you verging on narcissism? By doing this, we can begin to unpick our thought processes. Think about something like social media. What are your motives for making that post? Do you seek recognition and status or are you just sharing what is going on in your life? The fact that you have 'followers' suggests that the latter is entirely possible. Much like the chapter on creativity, large-scale communication and sharing is a part of what makes us a successful species. On an individual level, though, is that really what you are doing?

I am not suggesting that social media posting is evil and should be banned, but I am suggesting that it is worth questioning our motives behind what we post and how frequently we do so. What are you trying to prove, and to whom? Are you being genuine, or are you creating an impression of what you want people to perceive? Moving away from social media, our actions in life can be put under the same scrutiny. Why are we doing them, saying that, or reacting this way? When I am being modest, am I truly being honest, or am I just laying a proverbial modesty trap for people to walk into? How often do we strategically respond in a way that feigns modesty, only to secretly wait for the gratification and recognition that is surely to follow? As long as I appear modest initially, my hunger for recognition will be more covert and less arrogant in nature?

"Modesty is only arrogance by stealth."
Terry Pratchett, 'The Long Earth'[38]

"For, as blushing will sometimes make a whore pass for a virtuous woman, so modesty may make a fool seem a man of sense."
Alexander Pope[28]

"It's not much of a tail, but I'm sort of attached to it."
***A.A. Milne, 'Winnie-the-Pooh'*[39]**

To be truly modest, we have to have less care for credit and less need for self-indulgence. This is difficult to do, but again goes back to ideas like intrinsic development rather than extrinsic reward. In doing so, we remove the shackles of public acknowledgement, freeing us to get on with the achievement of the thing that would truly make an impact on our lives. Rather than striving to receive compliments about how we look in the mirror, try doing more of the thing that will improve our physical appearance. The desire to feel more attractive is not an inherently bad thing. What I am suggesting is that internalising your development is more important than whether or not you get credit for it. In a grander sense, how much of our lives is spent desiring recognition for something we have done, rather than doing the thing we want or need to do? Instead, if our actions exceed our desire for recognition of those actions, we are by nature more modest.

"A superior man is modest in his speech but exceeds in his actions."
***Confucius*[37]**

"A great man is always willing to be little."
***Ralph Waldo Emerson*[40]**

The removal of desire for applause also provides more opportunity for sharing the spotlight. Helping those around us provides even greater intrinsic value and aids in the development of society. When we become less preoccupied with the pat on the back, we become more concerned with doing something worthy of the praise, regardless of whether we will ever see it. It is this that feeds our modesty, rather than feeding our selfishness and ego.

"It is amazing what you can accomplish if you do not care who gets the credit."
Charles E. Montague[41]

"That will do extremely well, child. You have delighted us long enough. Let the other young ladies have time to exhibit."
Jane Austen[42]

HUMILITY

To be humble is another quality of great virtue. Believing ourselves not beyond reproach is a healthy way of maintaining modesty and humility. It prevents us from falling into the trap of believing ourselves superior, or believing ourselves devoid of the need to follow rules. Being humble means not to regard ourselves above our own station and not to judge others as such. It is maintaining perspective of what it means to exist in society and what it means to appreciate our efforts and those of others.

Humility provides a foundation for accepting criticism. The humble person does not see this is a critique of what makes them who they are, but of their actions or efforts. As such, the humble person can take on the criticism and move forward, regardless of whomever gave the criticism. For many of us, this is a difficult concept. What if the person in question is not as 'knowledgeable' as I am? Should I give merit to their opinion? The humble individual would be able to take on board and weigh a suggestion regardless of the purveyor's status, rank, or position.

Ask yourself, how much do I qualify someone's right to bestow their opinion upon me? How much does it matter to you who they are, rather than what they are saying? Even our worst enemy could make a correct analysis of a situation. From whom the information comes should be of no importance. Good critique is good critique, after all. Or are we too grand an individual to see this? Just as the quote from Aurelius earlier in the book stated, 'If someone can prove me wrong and show me my mistake in any thought or action, I shall gladly change. I seek the truth, which never harmed anyone'. If the leader of the Roman Empire can achieve this level of humility, I might suggest we all can.

"He who is not a good servant will not be a good master."
Plato[43]

You may then think, 'What about someone's misguided opinion? Should I treat that the same as a more informed one?' However, this is missing the point a little. Someone trying to tear you down on social media, for example, may not be worth dwelling on. But that does not instantly mean that what they had to say was not true. A broken watch is right twice a day, as the old saying goes.

Importantly, the idea is about never finding yourself above reproach and not taking criticism personally as some form of attack on your self-worth. If you can do that, you can separate yourself from the comments as just potential information to be taken in and weighed accordingly. Nothing more. When we attach our ego to the comments, this unwanted 'noise' can be very distracting and depressing. The difference is your perception of what it means to have someone 'criticise' you. They are just words and ones that may be true and may also be false. If you then introspect genuinely and effectively, you'll find out which one it is.

Another aspect of humility is that of hubris, or overconfidence, and severe pride. How often have our mouths got us into trouble by biting off more than we could chew? Hubris was the failing of many a Greek subject. The inability to let go of pride, assess our true ability, or brag uncontrollably can cause a multitude of negative situations in our lives. But even with all the mythological examples and real-life experiences, we somehow find the ability as a species to sometimes write cheques that we cannot cash, so to speak. The promise of something to come that is never fulfilled.

The same can also be said for misrepresenting ourselves or even taking credit for the actions of another. The combination of pride and greed does wonders for our ability to associate ourselves with achievements unearned. The more humble and less pride-stricken among us are able to maintain their dignity and the dignity of others, and give credit where it is due. As Pope states at the start of this chapter, gladly praising the merit of a foe is a mark of a humble and grounded human being. Acknowledging the contributions of our peers is something that many a business leader could do with recognising. We might all feel a little more appreciated if that were the case. Isaac Newton once captured this perfectly:

"If I have seen further it is by standing on the shoulders of Giants."
Isaac Newton[44]

The motivation behind many of the aforementioned frailties is the desire not to be found inferior, or rather to show our strength and dominance. Our own insecurities give way to the social pressures of status and the temptation to seek position, by any means; for the opposite is scary as we are vulnerable and potentially weakened. Yet showing and acknowledging our vulnerability is a mark of strength and arguably a necessity in the quest to overcome adversity and chaos. We must know how we are to be harmed before we can protect ourselves. If we can reframe our 'displays of weakness' as something more akin to acknowledgments of opportunity, we may have a healthier route to our goals. Hiding our vulnerability only masks our frailty, leaving us susceptible to far greater ruin if ignored. Better to be prepared for what is to come, rather than exist in ignorant or naïve disbelief.

"We need never be ashamed of our tears."
***Charles Dickens*[45]**

"The best people possess a feeling for beauty, the courage to take risks, the discipline to tell the truth, the capacity for sacrifice. Ironically, their virtues make them vulnerable; they are often wounded, sometimes destroyed."
***Hemingway*[46]**

"In a scholarly dispute, he who loses gains more because he has learned something."
***Epicurus*[32]**

Unfortunately, the need to protect our sense of self (as we believe is perceived by others) can lead to many an error in judgement and action. The inability to admit we are wrong, for example, is the hallmark of the insecure. Those who wish to hide their vulnerability and portray a vision of what is real, rather than what actually is real, are victims of their own crimes. The defensive among us are such people that perceive their vulnerability to be avoided at all costs. Cognitive dissonance is rectified in all too common a way and never in the admittance of fault. To them, fault equals bad and bad equals 'terrible for me'. As such, their actions are dictated by the avoidance of the terrible, rather than the embrace of virtue.

"The vulgar thus through imitation err,
as oft the learn'd by being singular;
So much they scorn the crowd, that if the throng
By chance go right, they purposely go wrong."
Alexander Pope[28]

COURAGE

Courage has always been a prized virtue. The aforementioned myths and stories that have been passed down through generations for longer than the written word has existed have always contained overarching themes of courage, sacrifice, and perseverance. Courage is thus a core element of righteousness, benevolence, and virtuousness. Our ability to actually practise the virtues discussed relies heavily on our ability to maintain our actions in the face of potential adverse repercussions, ridicule, and torment.

"Courage is the most important of all the virtues because without courage, you can't practice any other virtue consistently."
Maya Angelou[47]

Courage often has a more grandiose impression. It is often synonymous with great physical strength and bravery to tackle situations that may cause bodily harm. Yet, virtually all of the virtues discussed so far have required courage in order to stand by principles, show our vulnerability, and maintain our genuine and heartfelt intentions. Courage has more to do with moral fortitude than physical strength, with solidarity rather than aggression. In this way, the virtue of courage is more about facing our mental chaos, which underlies all physical chaos.

Even in the case of an imminent physical altercation, is it the thought of the injury that scares us, or what that might mean to our appearance, reputation, and status? Our internal chaos is a metaphorical land of chaos and the battlefield for our victories or losses. Courage, then, is our proclivity or willingness for tackling said chaos in spite of what struggle, effort, or embarrassment may arise. It is the belief in taking on the challenge, regardless of the expected outcome, merely because it is a challenge that needs facing.

"God grant me the serenity
to accept the things I cannot change;
courage to change the things I can;
and wisdom to know the difference."
Serenity Prayer—Reinhold Niebuhr[48]

"To teach how to live without certainty, and yet without being paralyzed by hesitation, is perhaps the chief thing that philosophy, in our age, can still do for those who study it."
Bertrand Russell[49]

Our greater achievements and our greatest self lay just beyond our greatest fears. Courage is our key to unlocking them and our key to proving that the dragon can be tamed, that the prince can free the princess, and that civilisation can be saved. Courage grants our self the opportunity to proceed on the right path, even if it is not the popular one.

"Courage is grace under pressure."
Hemingway[50]

"To lead an orchestra, you must turn your back on the crowd."
Max Lucado[51]

Even in the most dire of conditions, the human spirit has the ability to remain steadfast and unwavering. There are many reports of the atrocities of Man, including imprisonment, torture, and slaughter, wherein individuals maintained their sense of virtue. Nazi concentration camps, Gulag Archipelagos, Japanese prisoner of war camps, have all provided such inspirational accounts.[52] If the human being can adhere to virtue in these circumstances, then it begs the question as to what we free and autonomous individuals are doing with our time.

FINAL THOUGHTS

Virtues do not need to be a forgotten concept. We have the autonomy to live our lives in the ways we choose. Our actions then are a manifestation of our internally held qualities. We must therefore ask ourselves 'what virtues do we hold dear and deem necessary?' How willing and robust are we in the face of that which would dissuade us from demonstrating these virtues? From the danger of telling the truth in difficult situations, to the allure of potential recognition and superiority, there are many things that can get in the way of moralistic action. But even in the darkest of moments, honesty, modesty, selflessness, and the courage to remain consistent are all within our power. Our only choice is whether to embrace them or not.

*"**Pepper Potts**: Is this about the Avengers? Which I know nothing about.*
***Tony Stark**: The Avengers initiative was scrapped, I thought. And I didn't even qualify.*
***Potts**: I didn't know that either.*
***Stark**: Apparently I'm volatile, self-obsessed, and don't play well with others.*
***Potts**: That I did know."*
***From the movie 'Avengers Assemble'**[53]*

CHAPTER 13

THE TREATMENT OF OTHERS

PART A: UNIVERSAL LAWS, RESPECT AND KINDNESS

"Never respect men merely for their riches, but rather for their philanthropy; we do not value the sun for its height, but for its use."
Gamaliel Bailey[1]

"I speak to everyone in the same way, whether he is the garbage man or the president of the university."
Albert Einstein[2]

How we treat others is a very clear sign of who are as individuals. Our choice of action in relation to our fellow kin reveals what virtues we really hold to be valuable. Our treatment of others can also shine a torch on how we feel about ourselves. Our outward displays of contempt may indeed show deep-rooted contempt for ourselves and our need to be superior may in turn show our fear of being inferior. Our actions are thus a reflection of what we contain inside. As we will see, much of society's reactions are reciprocal in nature. Our actions start or contribute to the never-ending cycle.

Understanding our motives for actions towards others and their subsequent impact is the first step towards changing our behaviour. If we can appreciate their origin, we can accept our faults and move towards changing them for the better. We can set our minds to virtues that benefit the cycle of existence and social exchange, improving both the lives of others and our own. No one tires of receiving kindness, respect, and fair treatment. These things are universally and fundamentally appreciated. What then prevents us from taking more benevolent approaches to our neighbours? What challenges must be faced in order to initiate change for the better? What is required in order for us to do more of what we know to be good and less of what we know to be bad?

UNIVERSAL RULES?

Fundamentally, there are generally accepted norms for how we should treat other people. In virtually every religion or philosophy that deals with ethics, the ideas of basic goodness and reciprocity are a core tenet or even rule. This is generally seen as the 'golden rule' dictating that we treat people as we would have them treat ourselves. Some may instantly think of religious passages found in Judaeo-Christian texts of Leviticus or Matthew, however Confucian, Buddhist, Hindu and other religions extolled this virtue long before those teachings. The golden rule is also subject to a wide amount of interpretation and critique, given the fact that it is often difficult to apply a rule like this universally to all people and all situations.

Depending on the context, we should probably not treat everyone as we wish to be treated. It could incur many a problem if we use this law about specific situations, as it could cause a level of expectation that is not appropriate. Speaking to someone from another country in your own native tongue because you would like them to do the same may be unreasonable if that person has no idea what you are saying and has no experience of your language. Asking that the patient provide medical advice to the doctor may again be another example of this inaccurate expectation. Ultimately, we can arrive at the conclusion that the specifics of the context are not as important as the intent. As described in the last chapter, Immanuel Kant provided an excellent way of articulating this in his Categorical Imperative, suggesting that we should act only in ways that we believe to be ethically sound for everyone to follow.

"Act only according to that maxim whereby you can, at the same time, will that it should become a universal law."
Immanuel Kant[3]

"Thou shalt not avenge, nor bear any grudge against the children of thy people, but thou shalt love thy neighbour as thyself..."
Leviticus 19:18[4]

Some may even go a step further and recommend the intention of additional kindness, without the requirement for exact reciprocation, to make up for any potential unintended transgressions. As we see here:

"I have something that I call my Golden Rule. It goes something like this: "Do unto others twenty-five percent better than you expect them to do unto you.' ... The twenty-five percent is for error."
Linus Pauling[5]

Regardless of how you package the golden rule, the underlying theme is one of universal love, kindness, and respect, which will hopefully be reciprocated. Interestingly, the idea of universal love is found again in those previous religions and philosophies as a mark of benevolence and something to aspire towards for all our interactions in society. The Buddhists have the term *maitri* or *metta*, which means just that and is practised as a form of focused meditation. Reciprocity is one of the fundamental building blocks for functioning societies and is the cornerstone of the collaboration spoken about previously that has led to our success as a race. Reciprocation insists that we respond in kind to the actions of others. When both parties are acting in the best interest of progression and mutual benefit (collaboration), reciprocity provides the catalyst for positive social relations, productive processes, and outcomes. As discussed earlier, in order to ensure our success over our Neanderthal cousins, reciprocity, and thus collaboration, was a prerequisite.

"... but they [our ancestors] shared their goods and services through an economy of favours and obligations. A piece of meat given for free would carry with it the assumption of reciprocity – say, free medical assistance."

Yuval Noah Harari[6]

"Reciprocity is a deep instinct; it is the basic currency of social life."

Jonathan Haidt[7]

If reciprocity is as deep an instinct as we believe, then acting in accordance with Kant's Categorical Imperative would provide the impetus for others to follow, thus ensuring that we receive our actions in return. As Mencius describes, our actions dictate the responses we receive as reciprocation takes effect. This is somewhat different to supposed laws of attraction, however, it must be said to be similar in nature. Positivity may attract positivity, as negativity may attract negativity, in a perpetual cycle of reciprocation in which we are all participants.

"He who loves others is constantly loved by them. He who respects others is constantly respected by them."
Mencius[8]

RESPECT

Working on the assumption of 'treating thy neighbour as we would treat ourselves', we can begin to highlight some of the key qualities and behaviours that make up our outward-facing virtues. Part of the 'universal love' approach is to make qualities like respect and kindness our default setting for action. By doing so, we start the 'reciprocity ball' rolling in a favourable direction. To do so, it means valuing each individual as worthy of our respect and kindness, something that we may all struggle with at times. The quote from Einstein at the beginning of the chapter phrases this well, describing his interaction as being no different (in terms of respect), regardless of with whom he is interacting. Consider at this point the amount of times you have witnessed, received, or have subjected someone to the alternative. How many times have we seen someone treated in a differentiated way based on their social or professional status? How do people talk to their boss versus how they talk to their 'subordinate'? How do people talk to the younger generation versus how they would speak to their elders? In theory, it should never matter as to someone's level in a hierarchy, perceived importance, value or function in society. No matter what our role, we are a human being first and an employee, child, or even Prime Minister second.

"We learned about gratitude and humility – that so many people had a hand in our success, from the teachers who inspired us to the janitor who kept our school clean. And we were taught to value everyone's contribution and treat everyone with respect."

Michelle Obama[9]

What can unfortunately happen is that people become guilty of giving respect to those they believe 'deserve' respect. This is often out of admiration, fear, or ulterior motive. Many an individual can be found to act rather 'differently' around certain people, particularly if they are 'of note' within certain circles. Kant would refer to this type of behaviour as treating people as a 'means' rather than as an 'end'. Treating people as a means is to judge the utility of that person as to their potential benefit for you, whether that be socially or professionally. Treating someone as an end is to value each person for who they are, regardless of their potential to benefit you.

"So act that you treat humanity, whether in your own person or in the person of any other, always at the same time as an end, never merely as a means."

Immanuel Kant[10]

"This is the final test of a gentleman: his respect for those who can be of no possible value to him."

William Lyon Phelps[11]

"You can easily judge the character of a man by how he treats those who can do nothing for him."

Malcolm Forbes[12]

The law of reciprocity would suggest that our ubiquitous respect would be met with respect returned. As mentioned in the opening paragraph however, we may often find that the first person we need to address is ourselves. We may not be able to give or receive respect until we can respect ourselves.

"If you want to be respected by others, the great thing is to respect yourself. Only by that, only by self-respect will you compel others to respect you."
Fyodor Dostoyevsky[13]

KINDNESS

Kindness may well be the most universally understood of all virtues. No matter what the language spoken, the conditions faced, or the previous circumstances experienced, kindness can penetrate any darkness and can be felt by any one person. Even the worst of enemies can show kindness and have it reciprocated. It is a choice and course of action based upon our interpretation of the golden law.

"Kindness is the language which the deaf can hear and the blind can see."
Anonymous[14]

"The best portion of a good man's life is his little, nameless, unremembered acts of kindness and of love."
William Wordsworth[15]

Yet kindness, much like anything else, should not be conducted in the expectation of its return. Perhaps Pauling said it best that we should either not assume it will be returned, or at least do more than we expect to have returned. Our acts of kindness then are best when they are unsolicited or, again, when considered as an end in themselves. We may even question whether kindness should be seen as a one-way street, as an independent act, and separate from the cycle of reciprocity. Is it really kindness if we expect reciprocity? Or are we just initiating an expected exchange of metaphorical goods?

"Volunteering is for suckers. Did you know that volunteers don't even get paid for the stuff they do?"
Homer Simpson[16]

Kindness is therefore more beneficial when it is altruistic in nature. Scientifically, there is overwhelming evidence to support that just being kind to people benefits our psychological, social, and physical well-being. Not only do acts of kindness improve trust and solidify social bonds, but they also reduce negative emotions, improve our sense of happiness, and even reduce symptoms of serious psychological disorders.[17] In turn, receiving kindness also causes an array of positive affect, regardless from whom they receive them.[18] Much like all other virtues, kindness can be learned as is being increasingly taught in schools around the world. All of this may sound a little silly or obvious, but being kind to those who don't necessarily have something to give you in return is not exactly a common occurrence. Maybe it is worth considering the last time that you did something nice for someone else, just because you wanted to improve their day, their mood, or their life?

If giving and receiving kindness is so obviously beneficial to all those involved, why then do we sometimes struggle to give or even receive it on a regular basis? What are the barriers that prevent us from engaging as we know we should? Well, there are many potential issues surrounding kindness. In *A Year of Living Kindly* by Donna Cameron, she lists nine barriers to being kind, including fear, indifference, apathy, and fatigue.[19] 'Compassion fatigue' is actually gaining more attention in the scientific literature, explaining reductions in the prevalence of compassion in nursing staff.[20] Compassion fatigue has been shown to occur through the emotionally draining act of giving compassion and the environments (less compassionate) in which we give it.[21] Interestingly, self-compassion mediates this (being kind to yourself helps prevent/reduce it) as well as the promotion of environments that also promote ubiquitous compassion for all. Whatever the issues, it is up to us to choose the promotion of kindness over a lack thereof, especially since we know of the benefit it yields for both giver and receiver.

KINDNESS AS ANTIDOTE

Virtues like kindness can be contagious and generative. It is the proverbial antidote of negative reciprocity, breaking the cycle of indifference. Aurelius puts it:

> *"As an antidote to battle unkindness we were given kindness."*
>
> ***Marcus Aurelius***[22]

Kindness can prevent the continuation of a downward spiral of negative actions. Take for example the harsh words traded in 'keyboard warrior' fashion, so abundant in today's technological world. Much like the reduction in empathy mentioned by Sherry Turkle, the 'distance' created by social media platforms offers an element of impunity and anonymity that face-to-face conversations would not provide.[23] Couple that with the research that shows how our brain's reward processes are stimulated by acting on 'moral outrage' and we have some powerful impetus for keeping the negative train moving, and potentially not being as kind as we could be.[23] There are of course positive elements to this platform in that the 'less heard' of our communities can have a voice, however the common trend appears to be of wars raging between people in more of a tribal fashion.[23] Fortunately, acts of kindness (including more cooperative words) appear to change the narrative and foster greater togetherness.

Perhaps it is the simplest and most effective of all philosophies and the easiest to adopt into our lives. For once again, what better do we have to do with our time than cultivate such a beautiful and ever-giving virtue? Our acts of kindness, whilst making a significant immediate contribution to the world, will rarely be forgotten or go unappreciated. Even if they are, you still receive the benefit of their execution, especially if you were truly altruistic with your intent.

"This is my simple religion. There is no need for temples; no need for complicated philosophy. Our own brain, our own heart is our temple; the philosophy is kindness."

Dalai Lama[24]

FINAL THOUGHTS

The treatment of others is something that is largely under our control. Regardless of how you define your golden rule in relation to those discussed, the way in which you treat people reflects your ideas of virtue and reciprocity. We can either contribute positively or negatively, but must be aware of and take responsibility for the choices we make. In a long list of possible virtues, perhaps none are so valuable as respect and kindness. These have the power to break the downward spiral of human relations and human suffering. What's more is that they can also bring just as much value to the giver as the receiver. What better motivation could we have for adopting a more compassionate disposition?

"Forget injuries, never forget kindnesses."

Confucius[25]

PART B: ANGER, REVENGE AND THE USE OF POWER

"Anger and intolerance are the enemies of correct understanding."
Mahatma Gandhi[26]

How am I to remain virtuous when all those around me are not? How can I prevent negative reciprocation when people go out of their way to wrong me? In turn, how can we swap retribution for kindness? Unfortunately, there are no easy answers to these questions. The all-too-familiar feeling of anger is all too quick to rear its ugly head. In the blink of an eye, anger and frustration can result in acts or plots of revenge. In one fell swoop, our virtuous nature is betrayed by a hate-fuelled reaction. Therein lies the beauty of the situation, however. We can choose our response and we can select our process. Processes that help us maintain virtue, cool the flames, and bring about positive change in a situation. If we give thought as to how we react, we can do the same for how we act. Rather than just consider what the world does to us, we can consider what we do to others. Whilst some of us may have some form of power and superiority over others, we all have power and superiority over ourselves.

ANGER, RESENTMENT, AND HATRED

Many circumstances in life would have us practising something other than love and kindness. Our personal and professional lives are fraught with situations causing reactions that sit at the opposite side of the benevolent continuum. It is not always as easy as saying 'just be kind' in order to overcome the unkindness of others. Whilst our intentions may generally be virtuous, our actions may not always support this. When we have been wronged, it may feel impossible to 'turn that frown upside down' and take the higher moral ground or lead by example.

As previously stated, to live a more virtuous existence is not always the most profitable of choices. It may appear to some that the less-than-genuine path is the path of least resistance. The maltreatment of others can come all too easily to those who allow themselves to be taken in by it. Unfortunately, our businesses are often ruled in this manner (ruled being the operative word), where the persecution, victimisation or rudeness exhibited becomes commonplace, expected or even respected. Harm then becomes the first thought in many a brain, especially if they are subject to harm themselves (the downside of reciprocity, it would seem).

"Any man may easily do harm, but not every man can do good to another."

Plato[27]

Again, Aurelius would argue that causing harm to others is only causing harm to ourselves by way of degradation of our nature and of our character. Many would not see it that way, as it takes a level of introspection to observe our failings as clearly as we observe their opposites. It would also take a removal of ego from the situation, whereby we refrain from placing ourselves at the centre of the world.

"To do harm is to do yourself harm. To do an injustice is to do yourself an injustice. It degrades you. You can also commit injustice by doing nothing."

Marcus Aurelius[22]

Perhaps the most significant problem arises when we have been subjected to some sort of wrongdoing ourselves. The anger, resentment, or hatred that follows makes it all the more difficult to maintain our sense of virtue or be consistently kind. Having perceived ourselves to have been wronged, our emotional responses can dictate our responses and manifest themselves as aggressive, spiteful, and malicious actions. Dealing with anger, for example, has attracted a great deal of philosophical and psychological attention, producing a narrative that has changed somewhat over time (particularly in a clinical sense).

From Eastern to Western philosophy, the management of anger sees some similarities in analysis. From Buddhist teachings of anger acceptance to Aristotelian appreciation for 'appropriate anger', anger is seen as something that can easily occur. The important aspect is to manage anger in a way befitting a wise and rational being. Part of which is derived from an understanding as to the motives for other people's behaviour, what it really means to you as an individual, and what is an appropriate course of action in response.

In terms of motive, Aristotle would suggest any one of three potentials for another's unkindly action: insolence, spite, or contempt. All of which are thought to show a lack of worthiness for better treatment by the individual in question. Aristotle also suggests that our anger can be mediated by a number of things, including our current emotional or physical state, the level of intent from the perpetrator, subsequent apologies, and the quality of previous interactions, to name a few. Regardless of its antecedents, anger can be seen as a necessary or beneficial response.

Neel Burton, a clinical psychiatrist, suggests that anger can help end suffering or threats, maintain commitment to certain causes, and incur important emotional responses in others.[28] He also suggests that having a healthy expression and management of anger can lead to personal optimism, confidence, and self-control. That being said, the ability to exercise our anger in healthy ways is hardly an easy one to come by. On the whole, Burton describes anger leading to bad judgement, destructive behaviour, and an absence of rational thought. Perhaps it is these qualities to which we can all better relate.

"Anybody can become angry — that is easy, but to be angry with the right person and to the right degree and at the right time and for the right purpose, and in the right way — that is not within everybody's power and is not easy."

Aristotle[29]

"Anger is a short madness."

Horace[30]

AN EASTERN PERSPECTIVE

Eastern philosophy would see the potentially subjective 'benefits' of anger completely outweighed by the negatives. Anger is, after all, a removal of better judgement and a more volatile behavioural reaction. Hence why Horace described it as a temporary madness, disassociating one from their better and rational judgement. Anger has the ability to cloud the mind, finding malicious intent in otherwise honest mistakes, or unjustly assuming character deficiencies where situational variances are to blame. Anger, then, is a poisonous element that warps our sense of reality and prevents us from seeing the world as it really is, or the real intent behind another's action. Hanlon's Razor, a proverbial maxim for viewing the behaviour and intentions of those around us, does a wonderful job of shedding light on these tendencies:

"Never attribute to malice that which can be adequately explained by stupidity."

Hanlon's Razor, exact origin unknown[31]

Unfortunately, the intoxication associated with anger does a marvellous job of convincing us that our judgement of something is correct, or that whatever violation has occurred is completely unjust. Think again about the cognitive biases discussed earlier, which anger can fuel or strengthen in the mind. If the cognitive dissonance experienced by a potential situation wasn't enough, then the addition of some anger into the melting pot will surely conjure greater feelings of contempt, compounding our existing biases. With that in mind, anger could be thought of as imprisoning the mind in its potentially limbic-system-driven reactions and its self-serving mental confines.

"There was never an angry man that thought his anger unjust."
Saint Francis de Sales[32]

VENTING AND SUPPRESSING ANGER

If we can agree that to act under the influence of anger is to possibly act against our better judgement, then it may be worth considering what impact this may have. From a philosophical and psychological perspective, the opinion seems clear. Many great thinkers have viewed anger as a toxic entity and one that should be addressed as quickly and healthily as possible. There is a tendency to view anger as a prelude to initiating action against or towards something or someone else. However, this fails to acknowledge that anger itself is harboured and built firstly within us. As a result, this potentially destructive force that would see so much change externally resides in our own minds for as long as necessary before being unveiled (if it actually ever is unveiled).

Depending on circumstances, anger is often then either vented through some form or manifestation, or supressed and locked away to be built upon once again. Venting was historically viewed as a cathartic process used to reduce anger. In more recent years, however, there has been a significant lack of evidence to support this, showing that venting actually makes people angrier and more liable to repeat their anger-based reactions.[33] As a result, clinical psychiatrists have moved away from this option in favour of more meditative, distraction-orientated, or acceptance-related techniques.[34] In simple terms, both harbouring and venting anger is just as philosophers previously suggested; damaging and contagious at best. With regard to the latter, one only need observe mob mentality to see how outward displays of anger can incur similar effects in others. In essence, anger does damage to both the purveyor and the receiver.

"Holding on to anger is like grasping a hot coal with the intent of throwing it at someone else; you are the one who gets burned."
Buddhaghosa[35]

"Anger is an acid that can do more harm to the vessel in which it is stored than to anything on which it is poured."
Mark Twain[36]

There is ample evidence to suggest that anger vented has only one appearance and that is of offence to your own sense of self. The betrayal I mentioned previously is to allow anger and frustration to overcome your sense of control and normal behaviour. People seldom act better under the influence of anger and seldom prosper from inviting its presence. I am sure we have all experienced the detrimental effects of words spoken in anger and of actions driven by temporary hate. Sometimes their impact cannot be overcome or overturned, providing an unwanted and unwavering lasting effect.

"Whatever is begun in anger ends in shame."
Benjamin Franklin[37]

"Years of love have been forgot, In the hatred of a minute."
Edgar Allan Poe[38]

The other common trait is that of the suppression of anger. People often fail to deal with their anger appropriately (we'll discuss this shortly), relying on ignoring the problem or person. Much like venting, ignoring our anger and pushing it deep inside is also pernicious in nature. Deep-rooted anger left to fester may come back stronger to bite us in the proverbial 'behind'.

"A man who has not passed through the inferno of his passions has never overcome them."
Carl Jung[39]

"Anger clouds the mind. Turned inward, it is an unconquerable enemy."
Splinter, from the movie 'Teenage Mutant Ninja Turtles'[40]

REVENGE – BETRAYING OURSELVES

Anger is not always so simply described as the direct result of another's wrongdoing, however. Metaphorically, our anger can also derive from our misguided perception of failure, potential or actual loss, and a lack of control or ability to convert the ubiquitous chaos to order. Whatever its form, the previously cited evidence now supports the philosophical in that exercising or feeding our anger is to convert any wrongdoing, loss, or damage into further internal damage. That may especially be the case if that anger were to manifest as something unbecoming our character, betraying our moral code.

"To be angry, is to revenge the fault of others upon ourselves."
Alexander Pope[41]

"The sinner sins against himself: the wrongdoer wrongs himself, by making himself morally bad."
Marcus Aurelius[22]

Anger not dealt with in more constructive ways has a nasty habit of transforming into revenge, or at least the desire for it. This may be in the form of immediate reaction, or a longer-lasting and more deeply rooted resentment that spells the ruination of those within our gaze.

"Anger ventilated often hurries toward forgiveness; and concealed often hardens into revenge."
Edward G. Bulwer-Lytton[42]

In the words above, the ventilation of anger is not to be confused with venting anger. Ventilation of anger is akin to discussing or examining it, rather than remonstrating. In order to 'cool the flames' as Thich Nhat Hanh would say, we need to take care of our anger and acknowledge it, expressing our suffering to both ourselves and appropriate others. The idea that we deal with our anger is in accordance with the self-knowing content of chapter 2. We do not overcome it by force, but rather by understanding. If not, we risk being contaminated, dominated, and defeated by its presence. Ventilating is about a reluctance to let your feelings fester and compound, nurturing a path back to balance.

However, even in light of the evidence, some people would deem revenge as a natural repercussion of wrongdoing, as old a human tradition as anything else. In the world of collaborative reciprocation, for some, vengeance is seen as no different. I imagine that most of us would be familiar with the 'eye for an eye' saying. This phrase actually originates from the Mesopotamian era and is more accurately described as part of the code of Hammurabi, a famous king from that time. In this period of civilisation, punishments, retribution, and revenge were conducted in accordance with the crime, so to speak, relevant to the social status of the individuals in question.

"If a man has destroyed the eye of a man of the gentleman class, they shall destroy his eye..."
Code of Hammurabi[43]

This code then also found its way into many other subsequent religions, namely Judaism, Christianity, and Islam. Biblical references can be found in Deuteronomy, Leviticus, and Exodus, all of which discuss the premise of an 'eye for an eye; a tooth for a tooth' and so on.[44,45,46] Once again though, the realisation that this release of anger or comparative justice may not be as constructive as it may seem, is found in the words of Jesus where he suggests that we 'turn the other cheek'.[47] Jesus is touching on the idea that the act of avenging our perceived maltreatment does not actually fix or heal the situation, it rather just compounds the issue.

The previous evidence for the negative effects of venting would suggest that Jesus was probably onto something. Much like Aurelius said earlier, the "wrongdoer wrongs themselves" by their actions alone. He goes on to say in a different passage of his *Meditations* that "You should leave another's wrong where it lies", turning the proverbial cheek and refraining from further reactive responses.[20] Interestingly, many have gone on to also question the code of Hammurabi, suggesting that our hasty and equally weighted responses leave everyone involved worse for wear.

"The old law about an eye for an eye leaves everybody blind."
Martin Luther King Jr[48]

"Before you embark on a journey of revenge, dig two graves."
Japanese proverb (often attributed to Confucius)[49]

Here, the proverb is again confirming the thoughts of Aurelius in that nothing good may come from revenge, only the degradation of self, dissolution of character, or even the eventual demise of life. Now of course, this is not to say that we cannot react to situations in life, but that reaction should be in accordance with rational responses and healthy pursuits. Rather than our responses being in accordance with our perception of how we have been wronged, we may instead change our perception of what has actually happened and why we feel the need to respond in a certain manner. We may find that our usual response is born solely of anger and solely of our imagined slights and loss of ego or status.

"Is it your reputation that is bothering you? But look at how soon we're all forgotten. The abyss of endless time that swallows all. The emptiness of all those applauding hands."
Marcus Aurelius[50]

Understanding what is really bothering you about your recent mistreatment may provide extra insight. As Aurelius again says, what has really come to pass through this altercation? What has really happened that has you foaming at the mouth? Have you been hurt, or has your ego been hurt? If so, what does that say about the perpetrator and what do your responses say about you?

*"**Lenny:** There's nothing like revenge for getting back at people.*
***Carl:** I don't know, vengeance is pretty good."*
***From 'The Simpsons'**[51]*

"I've learned that life is one crushing defeat after another until you just wish Flanders was dead."
***Homer Simpson**[52]*

Healthy approaches towards anger and revenge can also form that of more rational judgements of the behaviours of others. What are their motives and their intentions, and from what state of mind are they acting? In reference to previous chapters, a person's worldview, level of knowledge, and cognitive bias may be largely to blame for their behaviour. Should we be angry with them for this? Are we angry at them, or their state of mind? If the latter, perhaps we should provide assistance instead of punishment. If the former, then how can we nurture or ventilate our anger with them?

"A physician is not angry at the intemperance of a mad patient, nor does he take it ill to be railed at by a man in fever. Just so should a wise man treat all mankind, as a physician does his patient, and look upon them only as sick and extravagant."
***Seneca**[53]*

Another potential option is to manage our own expectations of the behaviour of others. Remember the work of Steve Peters where he suggests changing the narrative from how people 'should' behave, to how people 'could' behave. The removal of concrete expectation provides a different perspective through which to view the daily interactions we all participate in. If someone acts in a way that does not conform to social norms or acceptable standards, this is less of a surprise to the 'could' driven individual. As a result, our emotional response is dialled down accordingly. 'Could' entails a multitude of possibilities, whereas 'should' expects only one. When people do not conform to our expectations, it generally causes a negative, emotional, or aggressive response. Changing our default level of expectation from 'should' to 'could' is a powerful way of keeping our emotions in check.

> *"All men are liable to error; and most men are, in many points, by passion or interest, under temptation to it."*
> ***John Locke***[54]

The meditative control mentioned earlier is the process of staying mindful (see chapter 3), whereby we view the situation as needless energy, reaction to provocation, and removal of awareness of our breath or attachment to the present moment. Keeping all these things in mind has been shown to reduce instances of anger, even in those with little experience of practising meditation.[55]

FORGIVENESS

If venting, reaction, and revenge are not the answer, then perhaps ultimately forgiveness is the answer. Forgiveness has long been viewed as the healthiest and most appropriate response to someone's wrongdoing and forms a large basis of people's ability to 'move on' from tragic life occurrences and major mistakes. Balancing other people's mentality, intention, and 'stupidity' with the unhealthy repercussions of anger in us and we realise that very little, if not nothing, is worth becoming angry about or taking revenge for. Perhaps our ability to endure the mistakes and missteps of others is of greater testament to our virtue than is our outward display of more obvious attributes?

"To err is human, to forgive divine."
Alexander Pope[41]

'SUPERIORITY' AND THE USE OF POWER

So far we have focused on the need for kindness and the reluctance to succumb to anger, hatred, and revenge. One of the issues regarding our treatment of others, though, is our desire for and use of power or superiority. It is one thing to treat others with kindness when they are perceived as peers or even superiors, but it is another to do the same when we perceive ourselves as being superior. Plato believed that a more accurate measure of an individual than just common perception is 'what they do with power', suggesting that the real essence of the individual comes to the fore upon receiving the capacity for influence over others. Perhaps the most disheartening thing is that we have probably all been mistreated through the abuse of superiority and the intoxicating drug of power. As always though, our job is to turn the spotlight back around and consider our own actions and fight back any urge to follow suit.

"There is nothing noble in being superior to your fellow man; true nobility is being superior to your former self."
W. L. Sheldon (often attributed to Hemingway)[56]

Superiority is an interesting phenomenon. Essentially, it actually means nothing at all. It is a perception of status based upon hierarchical structures that exist in society (across many species). At this stage, I will not dispute either the socially constructed or biologically constructed arguments, but rather leave that to the modern political patriarchy debates that populate our daily news. Regardless of their origin and effectiveness, hierarchies do exist. However, an agreement as to the behaviour associated with those hierarchies does not. For many, superiority is a chance to show this on a regular basis, put down those 'below' you, and selectively dangle the appropriate carrot or stick when required. This is hardly what would qualify as virtue or benevolence, yet somehow the use of power and superiority seems to exist on a different cognitive plane in many a person's eye. Philosophically at least, the idea of superiority seems to be the opposite. There are a multitude of examples wherein superiority is actually downplayed in order to favour the treatment of the masses over the reverence of the leader.

"A good commander is benevolent and unconcerned with fame."
Sun Tzu[57]

"A leader is best when people barely know he exists, when his work is done, his aim fulfilled, they will say: we did it ourselves."
Lao Tzu[58]

Both of these great figures extol the virtue of compassion and a reluctance to seek fame for their work. This sounds very similar to the benefits of modesty and humility discussed in the previous chapter. Sun Tzu goes on to suggest that:

"Regard your soldiers as your children, and they will follow you into the deepest valleys; look on them as your own beloved sons, and they will stand by you even unto death."
Sun Tzu[57]

His comments raise the notion of caring and compassionate treatment, rather than dictatorships based on fear and punishment.

The latter is the 'measure of a man' described by Plato earlier. Those outward displays reflect our deeper beliefs, intent, and internal struggles. Unfortunately, a choice of action that is driven by insecurity may appear no different to one born of spite and malice when it comes to the perceptions of those who are subjected to it.

"Nothing more despicable than respect based on fear."
Albert Camus[59]

"Distrust all in whom the impulse to punish is powerful."
Friedrich Nietzsche[60]

Instead of using our position as a chance to exercise power, we could instead see it as an opportunity to be even more virtuous than before. Consider the content of chapter 4 and the need for autonomy and you will find an abundance of support for not letting your superiority drive the need for controlling others. If we remove their autonomy, we deprive someone of their ability to obtain self-actualisation, an action that is hardly virtuous by any stretch of the imagination.

"Even though you try to put people under control, it is impossible. You cannot do it. The best way to control people is to encourage them to be mischievous. Then they will be in control in a wider sense. To give your sheep or cow a large spacious meadow is the way to control him. So it is with people: first let them do what they want, and watch them. This is the best policy. To ignore them is not good. That is the worst policy. The second worst is trying to control them. The best one is to watch them, just to watch them, without trying to control them."
Shunryu Suzuki[61]

Instead of controlling others, encourage and nurture them. Demonstrating your power does little more than reveal your desire to control and therefore shows your own weakness. How you behave when you have the choice of how to behave is what shows your true self. Even the tendency to correct the fault of others could be seen as a window into your own soul. What is the motive for doing so? Genuine correction for purpose of combined achievement, or the display of superior knowledge and intellect?

"...To which, if there be added, as is usual, a correcting of any mistake, or a contradiction of what has been said, it is a mark of yet greater pride and self-conceitedness, when we thus intrude ourselves for teachers, and take upon us either to set another right in his story, or shew the mistakes of his judgement."

John Locke[62]

With that in mind, we may want to consider who we are once again, and what we desire to be. Why do we gravitate to exerting our authority? What is dominating our thought processes? Are we using the golden rule, or are we making our own? You may even consider how good you are at being 'inferior' before you start considering what it is to be 'superior'. Either way, our capacity to exert power does not mean we automatically should do so. If the great minds of the past are to be believed, it does very little for our relationships and does equally little to cultivate our virtues.

FINAL THOUGHTS

Respect, kindness, compassion, and encouragement may all form part of the necessary behaviours that make us a more virtuous person. But the inevitable chaos, entropy, and unexpected or malicious actions of others can easily prevent these sensibilities from taking form. Our anger at loss of perceived status and damaged egos, or our emotional drive to take an 'eye for an eye' in the event of wrongdoing can result in our choosing a less-than-gracious course of action. To still choose the right path is therefore a perilous journey, but one that speaks to our true quality as a human being. Can we quieten our angry minds, nurture the flames within, and treat the actions of others as just that? To 'leave the wrongs of others where they lie' is to separate ourselves from the unnecessary and from the ugly.

What's more is that if we can refrain from abusing our position in society, whether that be of perceived or even real superiority, we can set the tone for future benevolence in others. Our need for reciprocation can therefore kick-start a movement towards more beneficial action and the cultivation of better qualities. The mark of true virtue is to focus and rely upon the only one we can ever really control, or should want to; for if not in us, then who? If not now, then when?

"No one is useless in this world who lightens the burdens of another."
Charles Dickens[63]

"Wisdom, compassion, and courage are the three universally recognized moral qualities of men."
Confucius[64]

CHAPTER 14

A FINAL MESSAGE

"He who knows others is clever,
He who knows himself has discernment.
He who overcomes others has force,
He who overcomes himself is strong.
He who knows contentment is rich.
He who perseveres is a man of purpose,
He who does not lose his station will endure.
He who lives out his days has had a long life."
Lao Tzu[1]

This final chapter serves as a conclusion of everything we have discussed and some final words for how you can begin to live a better life. I have summarised the content in terms of the key messages to take away from the wisdom given to us, but stress that this is far from a complete guide. It is up to all of us as students of life to further our knowledge and further our experience to really maximise the content contained within these chapters.

PART 1 – THE SELF

In *Flow*, Csikzentmihalyi discusses an important element that relates to the balance of chaos and order. He mentions that psychic entropy (disturbances of thought) has done nothing but increase since the dawn of Homo sapiens' reflective consciousness. From what was a simple existence driven by primal urges, we now have many things that add fuel to an already burning fire of psychic entropy. Social anxiety, frustration, inferiority, and missed dreams are more akin to the modern world than the prehistoric. They are things we can now only comprehend due to our improved cognitive function. As Csikzentmihalyi states "[the mind]… as it has increased its power to handle information, the potential for inner conflict has increased as well…The psychic entropy peculiar to the human condition involves seeing more to do than one can actually accomplish and feeling able to accomplish more than what conditions allow".[2]

I show you this not as a last-minute contradiction, but as final reminder of how balance is possibly the most important concept to take away. We cannot escape entropy of either our psyche or of the physical world around us. Instead, what we have to do is manage the chaos as best we can and appreciate the order where we can. In doing so, we can manufacture 'flow' in our lives and cherish those moments where we produce order. You are here anyway – so you might as well make the best of your experiences. But remember to keep it all in perspective. There is after all, more to be done than can actually be done.

Moving into the unknown is not about jumping into the abyss, headfirst. It is shining a torch just in front of you. Just past where the light of your order can no longer illuminate the way ahead. It is the conscious initiation of a task, where your skill set and challenges faced are optimally pitted against one another. It is the place where the most growth occurs and where you become what you could be, rather than just what you are. Walking the line is therefore an exploration of possibility, not a perilous journey into destruction.

In order to move forward into darkness, well prepared, we must know where the light finishes. Knowing thyself is then more than just taking stock of what you are; it is arming yourself with the tools to build and move forward. You 'know thyself' in order to better yourself, not to use it as an excuse to excuse yourself. It is its own battle with chaos, where we can all too easily be drawn into the darkness and find a familiar friend in rumination. But if we are to remember that the 'what' is more commonly advantageous than the 'why', we can avoid the deluge and keep our head above water. If we are to seek the 'why', we should do so with detachment. A detachment that comes from a separation of thoughts and the self.

We are not our thoughts and are thoughts are not us. When we see them as images on a screen, we can allow them to leave as easily as they appeared. We can choose to turn off the screen and revisit them later. We can see them for exactly what they are and nothing more – images that do not encapsulate us as human beings.

Living in the now is an active choice. It is being present in exactly what you are doing whilst you are doing it. When you are playing, just play. When reading, just read. See, feel, and hear your way to a more tranquil present and immersed experience. But remember, this does not mean that you cannot reflect, plan, and remember. For in those moments, *that* is exactly what you are doing. When planning for the future, you are doing 'planning for the future'. Living in the now is more about removing the tendency to be doing more than one thing at a time, rather than doing a particular thing over another. Just be sure to limit the time you spend on those things that fall outside of 'now'. Then pour yourself into what you are doing, who you are with, and what is going on.

Take the wheel. Determine your position and then determine your direction. There is no one else that can do this for you. To do anything other is to deprive yourself of the main thing that facilitates self-actualisation and human flourishing—autonomy. We can of course enjoy the ride in the passenger seat. The idea of being chauffeured is one that many would appreciate. However, no journey is as exhilarating as the one you pilot for yourself. You may have people with you along for the ride, but you need to be the one at the helm, initiating your movement. Remember, 'never confuse movement with action'.

> *"Better a diamond with a flaw than a pebble without."*
> ***Confucius***[3]

> *"The goal of practice is always to keep our beginner's mind."*
> ***Shunryu Suzuki***[4]

PART 2 – KNOWLEDGE AND PERCEPTION

Success in life is more about failure and our response to that failure than anything else. The fantastic work of Dweck, Ericsson, and Brailsford shows us that it is our habits, perspectives, and work ethics that make the greatest differences in our outcomes. With the right strategies, not only can we achieve incredible things, but we can also narrow the interpersonal gaps in performance attributed to IQ. Not only that, but we may even be able to increase our IQ, depending on with whom you speak. Success is therefore in our own hands. We are both teacher and student.

We don't just fail at something, we fail at a specific task that we were not completely capable of performing successfully. But therein lay the key. The more attention we give to the selection of those tasks and our subsequent reaction, the more we are inclined to 'fail better'. What's more is that providing opportunity for continual success is to deceive ourselves. Much like the balance of chaos and order, we need to be peering into failure in order to progress. Repeatedly selecting the right tasks is at the very heart of 'deliberate practice'. You can learn pretty much anything, if you go about it the right way.

The idea of perspective is almost ubiquitous in this book. Our perceptions of the unknown, ourselves, living, choosing, failing, and cultivating are but a few of the things that we can potentially see differently than our current viewpoint. Seeing something differently has as much to do with understanding it as it does some socialisation or genetics. Yes, we may have a fairly natural or socialised outlook on life, but that does not stop us from growing and changing. After all, our exploration into the unknown is likely to throw up many situations that make us re-evaluate our original position.

We all have ideas as to 'what this means' or 'what that means' based on our current ideology or worldview. From the philosophical to the practical, the lens that is used can clarify or distort that which is in front of us. Our opinions and assumptions are intertwined with our perspectives. Whether you believe one to cause the other or vice versa, it is up to us to seek greater clarity on whatever is under the microscope. How many assumptions do you hold? How many opinions are you yet to investigate and how many things do you simply 'not know enough about'? What's more is asking yourself what impact these views may have on you and the rest of society.

"The strength of a person's spirit would then be measured by how much 'truth' he could tolerate, or more precisely, to what extent he needs to have it diluted, disguised, sweetened, muted, falsified."

Nietzsche[5]

PART 3 – THE JOURNEY

Our lives will surely be made of many ups and downs. That is both the beauty and tragedy of life. But knowing that presents us with the opportunity to view things in a way that provides solace, comfort, and meaning. We can interpret our hardships as challenges, beneficial learning experiences, and even as something happening to our body and not our soul. From Stoicism to Buddhism, suffering is captured and dealt with in different ways. Yet, the similarity is in that of readiness to take on the next situation, whether through resilience or detachment. What happens to us does not define us.

Likewise, our positive experiences can be viewed in the same way. They do not define us and are also subject to interpretation. There will likely be things in your life that were painful at the time, but are now viewed as 'beneficial' for your character or personal circumstance. By relishing challenge, we may be incidentally volunteering ourselves for even more heartbreak and let-down. But it is our willingness to embrace challenge that provides some of the necessary resilience.

Remembering the deathbed reflections of others should teach us something. If not, then the hard-won lessons of our elders are wasted. If we do not embrace this wisdom, we are more of a fool than we had first thought. Risks not taken, in whatever guise, seem to be far more painful to realise than dealing with the ones that went wrong. Staying 'in the bud' is painful. Although that pain may not be felt immediately, it can echo through all eternity. We may lose if we try, but we definitely lose if we do not.

Much like the risks we do or do not take, our level of fulfilment is dictated by how we spend our time, either doing or not doing that which we are passionate about. We cannot be fulfilled unless we do fulfilling things. What fulfils us is obviously particular to each person, so no real universal guide can be given. Within our autonomy is the need to identify what it is that allows for the expression of our creativity and what brings us a sense of intrinsic achievement and meaning. By doing so, we create a life that is in line with our internal desires and one that is therefore reflective of who we truly are. Not only do we create a 'truer self', but we also alleviate the stresses of life, find flow, and discover purpose. We do not have to make a living from it; for that is rarely the case. But we do have to engage with it.

"A happy life is one that is in accordance with its own nature."
Diogenes Laertius[6]

"The secret of success is learning how to use pain and pleasure instead of having pain and pleasure use you. If you do that, you're in control of your life. If you don't, life controls you."
Tony Robbins[7]

"The three grand essentials of happiness are: Something to do, someone to love, something to hope for."
George Washington Burnap[8]

PART 4 – CULTIVATING VIRTUE

What you want and what you need are two separate things. The 'wants' or 'desires' that the great philosophers speak of are the distractions that cloud our minds, preventing genuine experience in life. Understanding that you need very few of these in order to live a full and content life is to free yourself from an otherwise materialistic existence. But a monk-like existence with no material possessions is hardly the target for even the most humble and content of us. In some respect, it does not matter how many or how much, but rather how attached we are to the more superficial in nature. Yes, there are things we can buy that make us happier – but these will never have the same transcendent effect as realigning our perspective to one of contentment.

The 'magic number' of income that brings with it greater life satisfaction and well-being is predicated on the notion of averages. It is worked out by how society *is*, rather than how it could be.

Granted, flexibility, opportunity, and comfort are indeed helped by money. Yet, our perception of what will make us happy, mixed with the conditions and mentality that comes with the acquisition of those things, is what makes the difference (and why more and more doesn't incur more and more happiness). The need to possess should not be confused with the desire to possess in excess.

What we can indeed possess is a more virtuous disposition. One that embodies everything we believe makes for a better *us* and a better *we*. Our virtues say more about us than anything else we could ever possess or acquire. Real wealth, it seems, is what we can cultivate inside ourselves, rather than inside our houses. I may have only touched on a few virtues that focus internally, yet there are many more you can explore. The important thing is that we take the time to consider those that we have and to what extent we exercise them, and those we are yet to take on board.

How we treat each other is a mark of those virtues and how willing we are to compromise them, or not. In a complex world, we may not always be able to maintain our principles as rigidly as we would like. But could we maintain them more than we do currently? Can you be braver in the face of social pressure? More honest in your actions and conversations? More consistent in your approach towards benevolence? Of course, we may have many an obstacle to overcome in that regard. The way others treat us is something that we cannot completely control. Reciprocity is a strong part of human behaviour. But we can choose to start or end that cycle accordingly. Beginning or ending negative reciprocity may require a fresh outlook on what you do with anger and frustration. But much like the use of power and superiority, we each have a choice to make about what we do with our own power of virtue. We can do some amazing things for each other. We can also do the opposite.

A CALL TO ACTION – WHERE DO YOU GO FROM HERE?

Writing this book, for me, was about providing people with the foundations to grow their selves into what they could be. But even if this information causes little to no cognitive dissonance in you, awareness of an appropriate alternative does not automatically generate a readiness to exercise it. Changing your actions in light of experience gained and knowledge sought takes more than just intelligence and absorbing the information. It takes a willingness to expose ourselves to the uncertain, to fight the contradiction of our actions, and to cease accepting the habits of old. Breaking behaviour patterns and escaping misguided beliefs means destroying a part of yourself that is no longer necessary, no matter how ingrained it may be within your psyche. For many, this is a frightening task and one that drives people to not only maintain their actions, but even justify why change is unnecessary.

"Just because it's what's done, doesn't mean it's what should be done."
Cinderella, from the movie 'Cinderella'[9]

"To think is easy. To act is hard. But the hardest thing in the world is to act in accordance with your thinking."
Goethe[10]

As Goethe states, the thinking is the easy bit. Keeping in mind how difficult that may be in the first place, we get an idea as to how truly monumental is the task of 'acting in accordance with our thinking'. We are often great advice givers, but rarely great advice takers.

"I give myself very good advice, but I very seldom follow it."
Alice, from 'Alice in Wonderland'[11]

"We are who we choose to be."
From the movie 'Spider Man'[12]

What then would it take for us to act accordingly? What do we need in order to spark the initiation of our advised changes? Therein lies the question – and with no easy answer. Perhaps the only things of any real importance are time and control. Our time in life is limited (well, this life at least). As such, we have precious little opportunity for manufacturing the best version possible. Our only real element of control in this world is over ourselves, reflecting the depths of our soul more than any possession, achievement, or material ambition ever could. If we are not to engage with this, then who or what are we really? To busy ourselves with the superficial and the superfluous, whilst ignoring the truly meaningful, may be the greatest internal crime of all.

"...O, I have ta'en
Too little care of this! Take physic, pomp;
Expose thyself to feel what wretches feel,
That thou mayst shake the superflux to them,
And show the heavens more just."
William Shakespeare[13]

"In the pursuit of learning, everyday
something is acquired,
In the pursuit of the way, everyday something
is dropped."
Lao Tzu[14]

Engaging with life in a thoughtful manner is perhaps the only thing that really matters. To that end, neither the hand we have been dealt, nor the eventual outcome should change the willingness to play the game. To believe the opposite is to place oneself at the mercy of circumstance and to become the plaything of fate. Do not blame the 'soil', as Pope would say. Instead, pay attention to what has been developed and nurtured by your own consciousness, either rightly or wrongly.

"O happiness! Our being's end and aim!
Good, pleasure, ease, content! Whete'er thy name:
That something still which prompts th' eternal sigh,
For which we bear to live, or dare to die...
...Where grows? – where grows it not? If vain our toil,
We ought to blame the culture, not the soil."
Alexander Pope[15]

Choosing a life of careful thought and action provides the necessary direction for 'living properly', as Jordan Peterson would say. Not a proper 'life', in the sense of the noun, but rather proper 'living' in the sense of the verb. This way we see life as a process, much more akin to that of 'doing living', like Zen practitioners might suggest. This again shifts our focus from outcomes to processes, from attachment and thoughts of future and past, to present-moment action.

"For modes of faith let graceless zealots fight;
His can't be wrong whose life is in the right."
Alexander Pope[15]

Csikzentmihalyi sums this all up well when he describes the difference between 'vita active' or a life of action, and 'vita contemplative' or the path of reflection.[16] A life of action helps us to obtain flow and happiness by focusing on our goals with great intensity. Yet, without the balance of appropriate reflection, the life of action alone would be at the cost of greater awareness and the realisation of experiences along the way. Once again, the key to this mystery is balance. The Yin and Yang of action and reflection, doing and contemplating.

Make no mistake, though. Life is a game that we can never really dominate. We have to accept that fact in order to keep our minds within the realms of appropriate expectation. We probably need to also accept that losing is par for the course (that annoying entropy again), but how we lose is what is important. Like Buzz Lightyear would say—"that's falling, with style".[17]

"We are all apprentices in a craft where no one ever becomes master."

Ernest Hemingway[18]

We are all a work in progress. What's more is that progress may move at many different speeds and reach many different heights. Believing we have reached the pinnacle is perhaps the only true mistake we can make. The minute we assume victory is the minute we stop trying. An alternative would be to consider ourselves the eternally 'unfinished piece' or the cup that is never full. That is not to say that we consider ourselves empty in the sense of fulfilment, but that we never believe ourselves to be the finished article, or beyond reproach. If we can do that, we can keep seeing challenges where others find threat; we can keep moving forward where others likely stop.

It is never too late to start living a better life and never too early to let go of your current one.

NOTES

INTRODUCTION

1. Matsuo Basho, The Narrow Road to the Deep North and Other Travel Stories (1966) Penguin, London.
2. 1975 (Copyright 1932), Have His Carcase by Dorothy L. Sayers, Series: A Lord Peter Wimsey Novel, Quote Page 52 and 53, Avon Books: A Division of The Hearst Corporation, New York. (Verified with scans)
3. John Wooden, Year Unknown.
4. *Ecclesiastes 1:18. King James Version*
5. Attributed to Carl Jung. Retrieved from https://www.goodreads.com/quotes/44379-until-you-make-the-unconscious-conscious-it-will-direct-your
6. Aristotle Nicomachean Ethics, revised edition (2004) Penguin Books, London.
7. Young, David C., "*Mens Sana in Corpore Sano*? Body and Mind in Ancient Greece", *The International Journal of the History of Sport*, Vol.22, No.1, (January 2005), pp.22–41.
8. John Locke *Some Thoughts Concerning Education (1 ed.). London: A.and J. Churchill at the Black Swan in Paternoster-row. 1693. Retrieved 28 July 2016 – via Internet Archive.*

CHAPTER 1 – IN A WORLD OF CHAOS, CREATE A LITTLE ORDER

1. Terry Pratchett, Discworld. Retrieved from https://goodizen.com/it-was-amazing-this-mystic-business-terry-pratchett/

2. "*THE NEVER ENDING STORY* (U)». *British Board of Film Classification.* 26 June 1984.
3. Stephen Hawking, A Brief History of Time (2016) Penguin: London.
4. Charles Addams – Uknown
5. Henry Adams The Education of Henry Adams (1995). Penguin Classics. ISBN 0-14-044557-9
6. Yiddish Proverb, Author Unknown
7. Lao Tzu, Tao Te Ching Page 6 (1963) Penguin, London
8. Lao Tzu, Tao Te Ching Page 84 (1963) Penguin, London
9. *Genesis 12:1 King James Version*
10. Wachowski, A., Wachowski, L., Reeves, K., Fishburne, L., Moss, C.-A., Warner Bros., Village Roadshow Pictures., ... Silver Pictures. (1999). *The matrix*. Burbank, CA: Warner Home Video.
11. Adapted from 'Flow: The classic work on how to achieve happiness' Mihalyi Csikszentmihalyi. Page 74. Ryder: The Random House Group
12. Turner, M.J., et al., Cardiovascular indices of challenge and threat states predict competitive performance, Int. J. Psychophysiol. (2012), http://dx.doi.org/10.1016/j.ijpsycho.2012.08.004
13. Hardy, L., Beattie, S. & Woodman, T. (2007) Anxiety-induced performance catastrophes: Investigating effort required as an asymmetry factor. *British Journal of Psychology, 98*, 15-31.
14. Helgeland, B., Van, R. T., Black, T., Ledger, H., Addy, M., Sewell, R., Bettany, P., ... Columbia TriStar Home Entertainment (Firm),. (2001). *A knight's tale.*
15. Pierre De Coubertin As quoted in *The Olympian* (1984) by Peter L. Dixon, p. 210
16. From '$E=mc^2$', in Science Illustrated (1946). In Albert Einstein, The Einstein reader (2006), 99.
17. Attributed to Eleanor Roosevelt – Year Unknown
18. Frost, R., Untermeyer, L., & Frost, R. (1991). *The road not taken: A selection of Robert Frost's poems*. New York: H. Holt and Co.
19. Stephen Pinker 2017 What Scientific Term or Concept Ought to be More Widely Known. https://www.edge.org/response-detail/27023

20. Naval Admiral William McRaven, University of Texas, Austin, May 17th (2014) https://news.utexas.edu/2014/05/16/mcraven-urges-graduates-to-find-courage-to-change-the-world/
21. Jordan Peterson, February 2017, University of Toronto. Retrieved from https://www.youtube.com/watch?v=68tFnjkIZ1Q
22. Feng Shui and removing clutter. Tchi, Rodika. 2019. Retrieved from https://www.thespruce.com/feng-shui-house-areas-to-keep-clutter-free-1275242
23. Hygge – Decluttering, the Danish Way. Tanner, K. 2016. Retrieved from https://hellohygge.com/2016/12/28/decluttering-the-danish-way/
24. Ferrari, J.R., Roster, C.A. Delaying Disposing: Examining the Relationship between Procrastination and Clutter across Generations. *Curr Psychol* 37, 426–431 (2018). https://doi.org/10.1007/s12144-017-9679-4
25. Pauls, D. L., Alsobrook, J. P., Goodman, W., Rasmussen, S., & Leckman, J. F. (1995). A family study of obsessive-compulsive disorder. *The American Journal of Psychiatry, 152*(1), 76–84. https://doi.org/10.1176/ajp.152.1.76
26. Marcus Aurelius, Meditations, Book 7:67 (2006). Penguin: London
27. Alexander Pope, An Essay on Man in 'The Rape of the Lock and Other Major Writings (2011), Line 95, Page 100.
28. Csikszentmihalyi, M. 'Flow: The classic work on how to achieve happiness' Page 224. Ryder: The Random House Group
29. Clear, J. (2018). *Atomic habits: Tiny changes, remarkable results : an easy & proven way to build good habits & break bad ones*.
30. Will Durant, 'What is Civilization?', *Ladies' Home Journal*, LXIII, Jan. 1946,

CHAPTER 2 – KNOW THYSELF; OVERCOME THYSELF

1. Pythagoras. As quoted in Fragments of Reality: Daily Entries of Lived Life (2006) by Peter Cajander, p. 109

2. The Simpsons, Groening, M., Brooks, J. L., Simon, S., Clausen, A., Castellaneta, D., Kavner, J., Cartwright, N., ... Twentieth Century Fox Home Entertainment, Inc.,. (2007). *The Simpsons.*
3. Kerr, G. (2019) A Short Introduction to Religion. P. 24 Old Castle Books: Hearts
4. Csikszentmihalyi, M. 'Flow: The classic work on how to achieve happiness' Page 225. Ryder: The Random House Group
5. Marcus Aurelius, Meditations P. 39 (2006). Penguin: London
6. Jung, C, G. 1971. Psychological Types (R. F. C. Hull, Trans) (H. Read et al., Eds.) The Collected Works of C. G. Jung (Vol. 6.) Princeton, NJ: Princeton University Press. (Original work published in 1921).
7. Jung, C. (1977) The Structure of the Unconscious CW 7, Par.399
8. Pope, A. (2011) An Essay on Man. P. 106. Penguin:London
9. Eurich, T. (2017) The right way to be introspective (yes, there's a wrong way). Retrieved from https://ideas.ted.com/the-right-way-to-be-introspective-yes-theres-a-wrong-way/
10. Lieberman, M. D., Eisenberger, N. I., Crockett, M. J., Tom, S. M., Pfeifer, J. H., & Way, B. M. (2007). Putting feelings into words: affect labeling disrupts amygdala activity in response to affective stimuli. *Psychological science*, *18*(5), 421–428. https://doi.org/10.1111/j.1467-9280.2007.01916.x
11. Kross, E., Ayduk, O. & Mischel, W. 2005. When asking 'why' does not hurt. Psychological Science. Retrieved from http://selfcontrol.psych.lsa.umich.edu/wp-content/uploads/2013/09/Kross-When-Asking-Why-Does-Not-Hurt-2005.pdf
12. Baer, D. 2016 The right way to do introspection. Retrieved from https://www.thecut.com/2016/09/the-right-way-s-to-do-introspection.html
13. Lew, M.D.N., Schmidt, H.G. Self-reflection and academic performance: is there a relationship?. *Adv in Health Sci Educ* 16, 529 (2011). https://doi.org/10.1007/s10459-011-9298-z
14. Csikszentmihalyi, M. 'Flow: The classic work on how to achieve happiness' Page 226. Ryder: The Random House Group

15. Eckhart, M. Year unknown.
16. Cameron, J., Landau, J., Fiore, M., Wilson, C., Kalogridis, L., Worthington, S., Saldana, Z., ... Lightstorm Entertainment (Firm). (2010). *Avatar*.
17. Aristotle, ., & Ross, W. D. (1981). Aristotle's Metaphysics. Book 1 Chapter 2. Oxford [England: Clarendon Press.
18. Wilde, O. The Critic as Artist (1891). The Nineteenth Century.
19. Jacques Rigaut (1993). "Lord Patchogue & Other Texts"
20. Marcus Aurelius, Meditations 7:71 (2006). Penguin: London
21. Marcus Aurelius, Meditations 10:37 (2006). Penguin: London
22. Krueger, J. 2012. Psychology Today Blog. Retrieved from https://www.psychologytoday.com/us/blog/one-among-many/201209/do-others-know-you-better-you-know-yourself
23. Ann Landers, Year unknown.
24. *Williamson, M. Mother Jones Magazine, Volume 22, No. 6, November - December 1997.*
25. Dwayne 'The Rock' Johnson. Year unknown.
26. Haslam, A., Reicher, S. & Platow, M. (2011). *The New Psychology of Leadership*. Psychology Press: New York
27. Marcus Aurelius, Meditations (2006). Penguin: London
28. *Little, J. (1997). Jeet Kune Do. Charles E. Tuttle Co., Inc. p. 1. ISBN 0-8048-3132-7.*
29. Hwang, K & Chang, J. 2009 Self-Cultivation: Culturally Sensitive Psychotherapies in Confucian Societies. The Counseling Psychologist 37(7):1010-1032
30. Seneca. Seneca: Letters from a Stoic. Letter 101. (1969) Lexicos Publishing
31. Nietzsche, F. 2003. Beyond Good and Evil: Prelude to a Philosophy of the Future. Chapter IV. Penguin: London.
32. Aurelius, M. Meditations (2006). Penguin: London
33. Lao Tzu, Tao Te Ching Page 38 (1963) Penguin, London
34. Sun Tzu (2009). The Art of War. Boston: Shambhala.
35. Aristotle. Origin unknown.

36. *The Project Gutenberg EBook of Laws, by Plato. 2008 E-book.* https://www.gutenberg.org/files/1750/1750-h/1750-h.htm
37. Baruch, B. Year unknown.
38. Gibbs reflective cycle. Taken from https://sites.marjon.ac.uk/handbook/study-skills/ Cole, M. (2000) Learning through reflective practice: a professional approach to effective continuing professional development among healthcare professionals, Research in Post-Compulsory Education, 5:1, 23-38, DOI: 10.1080/13596740000200067
39. Dixon, M., Lee, S. & Ghaye, T. (2015). Strengths-based reflective practices for the management of change: applications from sport and positive psychology, *Journal of Change Management,*
40. Von Goethe, J. Year unknown.
41. "*THE NEVER ENDING STORY* (U)». *British Board of Film Classification*. 26 June 1984.
42. Krishnamurti, J. (1975). *Freedom from the known*. New York: Harper & Row.
43. Confucius. (1979). The analects (Lun yü). Harmondsworth ; New York :Penguin Books,
44. Hemingway, E. (1954). *The sun also rises*. Chapter 2. New York: Scribner.

CHAPTER 3 – IN THE MOMENT

1. Anonymous. Often attributed to Lao Tzu.
2. *Milne, A. A. (Alan Alexander), 1882-1956. (2003). Winnie-the-Pooh. [New York] :Harper Children's Audio,*
3. Seneca. Seneca: Letters from a Stoic. Letter 101. (1969) Lexicos Publishing
4. Marcus Aurelius, Meditations, (2006). Penguin: London
5. Seneca. Seneca: Letters from a Stoic. (1969) Lexicos Publishing
6. As in. Vaporis, C, N. An encycolpedia of Japan's Cultured Warriors. Page 36 (2019) ABC-CLIO:Santa Barbara. CA.

7. A. L. Sadler, tr., *The Beginner's Book of Bushido.* Tokyo: Kokusai Bunka Shinkokai, the Society for International Cultural Relations, 1941, pp. 3-5, 50-53, 74-79.
8. Vail, Kenneth E., Juhl, Jacob, Arndt, Jamie, Vess, Matthew, Routledge, Clay and Rutjens, Bastiaan T. (2012) When death is good for life: considering the positive trajectories of terror management. *Personality and Social Psychology Review*, 16 (4), 303-329. (doi:10.1177/108886 8312440046). (PMID:22490977)
9. Tolle, E., & OverDrive Inc. (2010). The power of now: A guide to spiritual enlightenment. Novato, CA: New World Library.
10. Williams, P. (2004) Page 5. Quotable Michael Jordan : words of wit, wisdom, and inspiration by and about Michael Jordan, basketball's greatest superstar.
11. *Aristotle (1998). "The Politics", p.428, OUP Oxford*
12. Stephen Hawking, A Brief History of Time (2016) Penguin: London.
13. Hanh, T. The Miracle of Mindfulness, p.3. (2008) Rider: Random House Publishing
14. Suzuki, S., & Dixon, T. (2010). *Zen mind, beginner's mind.* P. 49 Boston: Shambhala.
15. Hanh, T. The Miracle of Mindfulness (2008) Rider: Random House Publishing
16. Ernest Hemingway, letter of advice to a young writer, reported in Malcolm Cowley, "Mister Papa", *LIFE* magazine (January 10, 1949), Volume 26, No. 2, p. 90.
17. Suzuki, S., & Dixon, T. (2010). *Zen mind, beginner's mind.* Boston: Shambhala.
18. 'Load Rage' https://www.independent.co.uk/life-style/millennials-load-rage-slow-download-speed-content-anger-a9035281.html
19. The Simpsons, Groening, M., Brooks, J. L., Simon, S., Clausen, A., Castellaneta, D., Kavner, J., Cartwright, N., ... Twentieth Century Fox Home Entertainment, Inc.,. (2007). *The Simpsons*. Season 7, episode 4. Bart Sells his Soul.
20. Kersemaekers W, Rupprecht S, Wittmann M, Tamdjidi C, Falke P,

Donders R, Speckens A and Kohls N (2018) A Workplace Mindfulness Intervention May Be Associated With Improved Psychological Well-Being and Productivity. A Preliminary Field Study in a Company Setting. Front. Psychol. 9:195

21. Hülsheger, U. R., Alberts, H. J. E. M., Feinholdt, A., & Lang, J. W. B. (2012, December 31). Benefits of Mindfulness at Work: The Role of Mindfulness in Emotion Regulation, Emotional Exhaustion, and Job Satisfaction. Journal of Applied Psychology. Advance online publication. doi: 10.1037/a0031313
22. Hecker, Jeffrey E. and Kaczor, Linda M., "Application of Imagery Theory to Sport Psychology: Some Preliminary Findings" (1988). Psychology Faculty Scholarship. 11. https://digitalcommons.library.umaine.edu/psy_facpub/11
23. *The last samurai*. (2003). Burbank, CA: Warner Home Video.
24. Chien, H. C., Chung, Y. C., Yeh, M. L., & Lee, J. F. (2015). Breathing exercise combined with cognitive behavioural intervention improves sleep quality and heart rate variability in major depression. *Journal of clinical nursing, 24*(21-22), 3206–3214.
25. Tang, Y., Holzel, B. & Posner, M. 2015. The Neuroscience of Mindfulness Meditation. Nature reviews Neuroscience. doi:10.1038/nrn3916
26. Van Wilder (2002) *National Lampoon's Van Wilder. [United States] :Artisan Entertainment,*
27. *Walt Whitman, Sculley Bradley, Harold W. Blodgett (2008). "Leaves of Grass: A Textual Variorum of the Printed Poems, 1855-1856", p.97, NYU Press*
28. *"Carrey: 'Life Is Too Beautiful'". www.cbsnews.com. November 18, 2004.*

CHAPTER 4 – BE THE DRIVER NOT THE PASSENGER

1. Boyd, B. 2000. Drive (recorded by Incubus) from Make Yourself.
2. Nietzsche, F. 1965. Schopenhauer as Eduator. Chicago: Regenery.

3. Hotchner, A, E. (1966 edition) *Papa Hemingway. New York: Random House*
4. Rounders. 1998. Spanky Pictures: Miramax Films.
5. Klint, K. A., & Weiss, M. R. (1987). Perceived competence and motives for participating in youth sports: A test of Harter's competence motivation theory. *Journal of Sport Psychology, 9*(1), 55–65.
6. King, S. 2000. On Writing: A Memoir of the Craft. New York: Scribner
7. Considered to be coined by LaTisha Cotto, although history unknown.
8. The Simpsons, Groening, M., Brooks, J. L., Simon, S., Clausen, A., Castellaneta, D., Kavner, J., Cartwright, N., ... Twentieth Century Fox Home Entertainment, Inc.,. (2007). *The Simpsons*. Season 3, episode 1. Stark Raving Dad.
9. Haslam, A., Reicher, S. & Platow, M. (2011). *The New Psychology of Leadership*. Psychology Press: New York
10. Deci, E. L., & Ryan, R. M. (2012). *Self-determination theory.* In P. A. M. Van Lange, A. W. Kruglanski, & E. T. Higgins (Eds.), *Handbook of theories of social psychology* (p. 416–436). Sage Publications Ltd. https://doi.org/10.4135/9781446249215.n21
11. Meyer, J., & Gagnè, M. (2008). Employee Engagement From a Self-Determination Theory Perspective. *Industrial and Organizational Psychology, 1*(1), 60-62. doi:10.1111/j.1754-9434.2007.00010.x
12. Retrieved from https://www.simplypsychology.org/maslow.html
13. Epicurus. 2019. On Happiness. Arcturus Publishing.
14. Aurelius, M. Meditations. P. 19 (2006). Penguin: London
15. Suzuki, S., & Dixon, T. (2010). *Zen mind, beginner's mind.* Boston: Shambhala.
16. Steve Jobs (Co-founder of Apple Inc.) in his commencement address at Stanford University in 2005.
17. Epicurus. Translated by Peter Saint-Andre (2010) Vatican Sayings. Retrieved from http://monadnock.net/epicurus/vatican-sayings.html
18. Hadot, P. Year Unknown. Retrieved from https://modernstoicism.com/hadots-active-stoic-exercises-by-anitra-russell/
19. Jordan, M. Attributed to Michael Jordan. Year unknown.

20. Dweck, Carol S.. (2008) *Mindset :the new psychology of success* New York : Ballantine Books
21. Seibert, S. E., Wang, G., & Courtright, S. H. (2011). Antecedents and consequences of psychological and team empowerment in organizations: A meta-analytic review. *Journal of Applied Psychology, 96*(5), 981–1003. https://doi.org/10.1037/a0022676
22. Jobs, S. Retrieved from https://www.inc.com/marcel-schwantes/this-classic-quote-from-steve-jobs-about-hiring-employees-describes-what-great-leadership-looks-like.html
23. Mageau, G. A., & Vallerand, R. J. (2003). The coach-athlete relationship: A motivational model. Journal of Sports Sciences, 21, 883-904.
24. Sinek, S. 2012 retrieved from Twitter. https://twitter.com/simonsinek/status/174469085726375936
25. Attributed to Mark Zuckerberg. Year Unknown.
26. Kant. I. 1784. An Answer to the Question: What is Enlightenment. Retrieved from http://web.mnstate.edu/gracyk/courses/web%20publishing/KantOnElightenment.htm
27. Botwinick, J. (1973). *Aging and behavior: A comprehensive integration of research findings.* Springer.
28. Survey of computer game playing across generations. Retrieved from https://www.alistdaily.com/strategy/different-generations-play-video-games-platforms-genres/
29. Von Goethe, J. 2015 Faust in Plain and Simple English: First Part of the Tragedy: (A Modern Translation and the Original Version). CreateSpace Independent Publishing Platform; Translation edition
30. *Epicurus (1964). "Letters: Principles Doctrines, and Vatican Sayings Translated, with an Introd. and Notes, by Russel M. Geor. Indianapolis Merrill"*
31. Bay, M., Orci, R., Kurtzman, A., Di, B. L., DeSanto, T., Murphy, D., Bryce, I., ... DreamWorks Home Entertainment (Firm),. (2007). *Transformers.*
32. Whitman, Walt. *Leaves of Grass.* Philadelphia: David McKay, [c1900]; Bartleby.com, 1999. www.bartleby.com/142/.

33. Csikszentmihalyi, M. 'Flow: The classic work on how to achieve happiness' Page 225. Ryder: The Random House Group

CHAPTER 5 – LEARNING TO LEARN

PART A – WHY WE NEED TO FAIL

1. Nietzsche, F. W., & Kaufmann, W. (1995). *Thus spoke Zarathustra: A book for all and none*. New York: Modern Library.
2. The Simpsons, Groening, M., Brooks, J. L., Simon, S., Clausen, A., Castellaneta, D., Kavner, J., Cartwright, N., ... Twentieth Century Fox Home Entertainment, Inc.,. (2007). *The Simpsons*. Season 5, Episode 18 – Burn's Heir.
3. Bajtelsmit, J. & Gershman, L. 1976. Covert Positive Reinforcement: Efficacy and Conceptualisation. Journal of Behaviour Therapy and Experimental Psychiatry. 7:3.
4. Alanazi, A. 2016. A Critical Review of Constructivist Theory and the Emergence of Constructionism. American Research Journal of Humanities and Social Sciences, 2: 8.
5. Rogers, CR, Lyon, Harold C. Jr, and Tausch: (2013) *On Becoming an Effective Teacher- On–Person-centered Teaching, Psychology, Philosophy, and Dialogues with Carl R. Rogers and HaroldLyon*. London Routledge
6. Attributed to Bertrand Russell . A paraphrase of Bertrand Russell's 'On Education, especially in early childhood'. 1926. Retrieved from https://russell-j.com/beginner/ON_EDU-TEXT.HTM
7. Sir Ken Robinson - Changing Paradigms RSA •4 Feb 2010
8. Attributed to Albert Einstein, a paraphrase of Grant Allen. 1894, Post-Prandial Philosophy by Grant Allen, XV: Eye versus Ear, Page 129, Chatto & Windus, London.
9. Cameron, J., Landau, J., Fiore, M., Wilson, C., Kalogridis, L., Worthington, S., Saldana, Z., ... Lightstorm Entertainment (Firm). (2010). *Avatar*.

10. Suzuki, S., & Dixon, T. (2010). *Zen mind, beginner's mind.* P. 49 Boston: Shambhala.
11. Marshik, T. TEDx presentation (2015). Retrieved from https://singjupost.com/tesia-marshik-learning-styles-the-importance-of-critical-self-reflection-at-tedxuwlacrosse-transcript/
12. Attributed to Confucius, Xunzi anwd many others. Retrieved from https://www.academia.edu/39742237/_The_Master_Said_-_Confucius_as_a_Quote
13. Aristotle Nicomachean Ethics, revised edition. Book II (2004) Penguin Books, London.
14. Symeonidis, V., & Schwarz, J. F. (2016). Phenomenon-Based Teaching and Learning through the Pedagogical Lenses of Phenomenology: The Recent Curriculum Reform in Finland. Forum Oświatowe, 28(2), 31–47. Retrieved from http://forumoswiatowe.pl/ index.php/czasopismo/article/view/458
15. Aeschylus. (1848). The Agamemnon of Aeschylus. *Agamemnon*, verse 177. London :J. W. Parker.
16. Alexander Pope, An Essay on Man in 'The Rape of the Lock and Other Major Writings (2011). Penguin: London.
17. Nhất, H., Ho, M., & Vo-Dinh, M. (1987). *The miracle of mindfulness: An introduction to the practice of meditation*. Boston: Beacon Press.
18. Flood, A. J K Rowling says she receveied 'loads' of rejections before Harry Potter success. The Guardian – online. Retrieved from https://www.theguardian.com/books/2015/mar/24/jk-rowling-tells-fans-twitter-loads-rejections-before-harry-potter-success
19. 1762, The Citizen of the World: or, Letters from a Chinese Philosopher, Residing in London, to His Friends in the East by Lien Chi Altangi (Oliver Goldsmith), Letter VII and Letter XXII, Printed for George and Alex. Ewing, Dublin, Ireland. (ECCO TCP: Eighteenth Century Collections Online, Text Creation Partnership)
20. As quoted in *Nike Culture : The Sign of the Swoosh* (1998), by Robert Goldman and Stephen Papson, p. 49
21. Ellison, J. W. (2000). *Finding Forrester: A novel.* New York:

Newmarket Press.

22. Russell, B. 1950. Unpopular Essays. P.106. Retrieved from https://en.wikiquote.org/wiki/Unpopular_Essays#Chapter_7:_An_Outline_of_Intellectual_Rubbish
23. Haier R. J. (2014). Increased intelligence is a myth (so far). *Frontiers in systems neuroscience*, *8*, 34. https://doi.org/10.3389/fnsys.2014.00034
24. Cox, L. 2013. 5 Experts Answer: Can Your IQ Change? Retrieved from https://www.livescience.com/36143-iq-change-time.html
25. Flynn, J. R. (2012). *Are we getting smarter? Rising IQ in the twenty-first century.* Cambridge University Press. https://doi.org/10.1017/CBO9781139235679
26. Brownstein, J. 2011. First Foods Seem to Affect a Child's Brain Power. Retrieved from https://www.livescience.com/12813-foods-affect-child-brain-power.html

PART B - IT'S ALL IN THE MINDSET

27. Coyle, D. (2009). *The talent code: Greatness isn't born : it's grown, here's how*. New York: Bantam Books.
28. Dweck, Carol S.. (2008) *Mindset :the new psychology of success* New York : Ballantine Books,
29. Cyrus K. Foroughi, Samuel S. Monfort, Martin Paczynski, Patrick E. McKnight, P. M. Greenwood. Proceedings of the National Academy of Sciences Jun 2016, 201601243; DOI: 10.1073/pnas.1601243113
30. Cherry, K. 2020. How Average IQ Scores are Measured. Retrieved from https://www.verywellmind.com/what-is-the-average-iq-2795284
31. Dweck, C. 2008. Mindsets and Maths / Science Achievement. Stanford University, CA. Retrieved from http://www.growthmindsetmaths.com/uploads/2/3/7/7/23776169/mindset_and_math_science_achievement_-_nov_2013.pdf
32. Marcus Aurelius, Meditations. (2006). Penguin: London
33. Attributed to Bill Joe Armstrong. Green Day.
Retrieved from https://www.goodreads.com/

quotes/351328-to-do-something-that-you-feel-in-your-heart-that-s

34. Syed, M. (2015). *Black box thinking: The surprising truth about success (and why some people never learn from their mistakes).*
35. Attributed to Confucius. Retrieved from https://oll.libertyfund.org/titles/confucius-the-ethics-of-confucius/simple
36. Goethe, J. Translated by John Anster, Faustus: The Second Part, Notes (p. 476), Longman, Green, Longman, Roberts & Green. 1864
37. Ramsden, K. 2018. Success Hangover: Ignite Your Next Act. Screw Your Status Quo. Feel Alive Again. Lioncrest publishing.
38. Kierkegaard, S., & In Bretall, R. W. (1946). *A Kierkegaard anthology*. P.194.
39. Ericsson, A. Prietula, M & Cokely, E. The Making of an Expert. 2007. The Harvard Business Review. July – August Issues. Retrieved from https://hbr.org/2007/07/the-making-of-an-expert
40. Gladwell, M. (2011) Outliers: The Story of Success. First Back Bay paperback edition. New York: Back Bay Books.
41. Syed, M. (2010). *Bounce: Mozart, Federer, Picasso, Beckham, and the science of success*. New York: HarperCollins e-books.
42. Clear, J. (2018). *Atomic habits: Tiny changes, remarkable results : an easy & proven way to build good habits & break bad ones.*
43. Attributed to Aristotle. Year Unknown.
44. Yamamoto, T. (1979). *Hagakure: The book of the samurai*. Tokyo: Kodansha International.
45. Paraphrase of Thomas Eddison. Retrieved from https://quoteinvestigator.com/2012/12/14/genius-ratio/#note-5018-6
46. Jordan, M., & Vancil, M. (1998). *For the love of the game: My story by Michael Jordan*. Ringwood, Vic: Viking.
47. Attributed to Lao Tzu. Year Unknown.
48. Brod, G., Breitwieser, J. Lighting the wick in the candle of learning: generating a prediction stimulates curiosity. *npj Sci. Learn.* 4, 17 (2019). https://doi.org/10.1038/s41539-019-0056-y
49. Harford, T. 2018. Stephen Hawking's Restless Curiosity Pulled US All In. Financial Times. Retrieved from https://www.ft.com/content/

fdb990f8-27a3-11e8-b27e-cc62a39d57a0

50. Quotes from Christopher Nolan. Taken from https://screencraft.org/2019/12/16/screenwriting-wisdom-from-christopher-nolan/
51. Beckett, S. (1983). *Worstward ho*. New York: Grove Press.
52. The Simpsons, Groening, M., Brooks, J. L., Simon, S., Clausen, A., Castellaneta, D., Kavner, J., Cartwright, N., ... Twentieth Century Fox Home Entertainment, Inc.,. (2007). *The Simpsons*. Realty Bites.

CHAPTER 6 – GET SOME PERSPECTIVE

1. 1961 copyright, Seduction of the Minotaur by Anaïs Nin, Quote Page 124, The Swallow Press, Chicago, Illinois. (Afterword added in 1969; sixth printing in 1972) (Verified on paper in sixth printing 1972)
2. Lorre, C., Prady, B., Aronsohn, L., Collier, M., Belyeu, F. O., Cohen, R., Goetsch, D., ... Warner Home Video (Firm),. (2008). *The big bang theory: Season 2, Episode 20 The* Hofstader Isotope.
3. Jung, C. G. (1969). The structure of the psyche. In Read, H., Fordham, M., Adler, G., & McGuire, W. (Eds.) (R. F. C. Hull, Trans.), The collected works of C. G. Jung: Vol. 8. The structure and dynamics of the psyche (2nd ed., pp. 139-158). Princeton, NJ: Princeton University Press. (Original work published 1931)
4. Nilsson, A. (2013). The Psychology of Worldviews: Toward a Non-Reductive Science of Personality. Lund University.
5. Funk, K. 2001. What is a worldview. Retreived from: http://web.engr.oregonstate.edu/~funkk/Personal/worldview.html
6. Tyson, N. Beyond Belief. November 7th 2006. A Final Sermon on Cosmonic Perspective.
7. Pope, A. (2011) An Essay on Man. Penguin:London
8. Ogle, C. quoting Siri Hustvedt. https://www.miamiherald.com/entertainment/books/article3931325.html
9. Van Vliet, V. (2010). *Peter Senge*. Retrieved from ToolsHero: https://www.toolshero.com/toolshero.com/toolsheroes/peter-senge/

10. Ryan Holiday Quotes. (n.d.). Jar of Quotes. Retrieved 2020-05-03, from JarofQuotes.com Web site: https://www.jarofquotes.com/view.php?id=what-ive-found-in-my-research-is-that-realism-self-honesty-are-antidote-to-ego-hubris-delusion
11. Sinek, S. 2011. Pragmatism (Twitter Post) Retrieved from https://twitter.com/simonsinek/status/100631117488599040?lang=en
12. Kierkegaard, S., Hong, H. V., & Hong, E. H. (1983). *The sickness unto death: A Christian psychological exposition for upbuilding and awakening*. Princeton, N.J: Princeton University Press.
13. Loder, K. Rolling Stone Magazine. The Rolling Stone Interview: Bruce Springsteen 'Born in the USA'. https://www.rollingstone.com/music/music-news/the-rolling-stone-interview-bruce-springsteen-on-born-in-the-u-s-a-184690/
14. Epicurus. Translated by Peter Saint-Andre (2010) Vatican Sayings. Retrieved from http://monadnock.net/epicurus/vatican-sayings.html
15. Turkle, S., & Potter, K. (2015) *Reclaiming Conversation: The Power of Talk in a Digital Age. Unabridged. New York, NY: Penguin.*
16. Lee, Harper. (2006). To kill a mockingbird. P.39. New York :Harper Perennial Modern Classics
17. Birnbaum, D & Ryan. M. People v. O.J. Simpson' Star Sterling K. Brown on Playing Chris Darden and How His View of the Verdict Changed. Retrieved from https://variety.com/2016/tv/features/people-v-o-j-simpson-sterling-k-brown-chris-darden-1201692561/
18. Abraham H. Maslow (1966). *The Psychology of Science*. p. 15. ISBN 9780976040231.
19. Pope, A. (2011) An Essay on Criticism. Line 558. Penguin:London
20. Fontenelle, B. 1777, Pensées Nouvelles et Philosophiques, Statement Number 264 (CCLXIV), Quote Page 75, Published by Marc-Michel Rey, Amsterdam. (Google Books Full View).
21. 2011. Chemistry's Understated Majesty. MacMillan Publishers Ltd. 469:5. http://www.uco.es/quimica2011/uploads/1/0/3/0/10304/nature1.pdf
22. Attributed to Michael Jordan. Year unknown.

23. Nietzsche, F. W., & Large, D. (1998). Twilight of the idols, or, How to philosophize with a hammer. Oxford: Oxford University Press.
24. Popular paraphrase of Schopenhauer from 2012, The World as Will and Representation by Arthur Schopenhauer, Translation from German to English by E. F. J. Payne, Volume 1 of 2, Section: Preface to the first edition, Quote Page xvii, Dover Publications, Inc., New York. (Translation originally published in 1958 by The Falcon's Wing Press, Indian Hills, Colorado)(Google Books Preview; accessed Nov 18, 2016)
25. Directed by Joss Whedon ; story by Zak Penn and Joss Whedon ; screenplay by Joss Whedon ; produced by Kevin Feige ; Marvel Studios presents ; association with Paramount Pictures ; a Marvel Studios production ; a Joss Wheden film. (2012). Marvel's The Avengers. Burbank, Calif. :Distributed by Buena Vista Home Entertainment,
26. The Simpsons, Groening, M., Brooks, J. L., Simon, S., Clausen, A., Castellaneta, D., Kavner, J., Cartwright, N., ... Twentieth Century Fox Home Entertainment, Inc.,. (2007). *The Simpsons*. Three Men and a Comic Book.
27. Herodotus Book 7: Polymnia, 226 (trans. Macaulay 1890).
28. Almar Haflidason (9 October 2001). "BBC - Films - Review - Bruce Lee A Warrior's Journey". BBC. Retrieved 6 January 2011
29. Pope, A. (2011) Rape of the Lock. *canto 1, l. 1.* Penguin:London
30. Carey, J. 2018. On the soul. Retrieved from https://twitter.com/jimcarrey/status/979588063155245056?lang=en
31. Gervais, R. 2014. On Life. Retrieved from https://www.facebook.com/rickygervais/posts/290112454446448
32. Ron Shelton & Bennie Wallace. (1992) White Men Can't Jump. USA

CHAPTER 7 – A TENDENCY TOWARDS NARROWMINDEDNESS

PART A – ASSUMPTIONS, CONVICTIONS AND OPINIONS

1. Russell, B. 1933. "The Triumph of Stupidity". P. 203–204. New York American.
2. The Simpsons, Groening, M., Brooks, J. L., Simon, S., Clausen, A., Castellaneta, D., Kavner, J., Cartwright, N., ... Twentieth Century Fox Home Entertainment, Inc.,. (2007). *The Simpsons*. Season 5, episode 3. Homer Goes to College.
3. "Books: The Great Gadfly", Time magazine, 8 October 1965 (review of The Age of Voltaire by Will and Ariel Durant)
4. Le Guin, U.K. Lao Tzu: "Tao Te Ching – A Book About the Wat and the Power of the Way. Shambala Publications, Boston (1997).
5. Broadwell, Martin M. (20 February 1969). "Teaching for learning (XVI)". *wordsfitlyspoken.org*. The Gospel Guardian. Retrieved 11 May 2018.
6. Competence Hierarchy adapted from Noel Burch by Igor Kokcharov. Retrieved from https://en.wikipedia.org/wiki/Four_stages_of_competence
7. Prochaska, J. O., & DiClemente, C. C. (1982). Transtheoretical therapy: Toward a more integrative model of change. *Psychotherapy: Theory, Research & Practice, 19*(3), 276–288
8. Nietzsche, F. W., & Hollingdale, R. J. (1986). *Human, all too human: A book for free spirits*. Cambridge [Cambridgeshire: Cambridge University Press.
9. Pratchett, T. 1992. The Reaper Man. P.230. BCA Hardback Edition. London.
10. Plato, . (1955). *The Republic*. Baltimore, Md: Penguin Books.
11. Pope, A. (2011) An Essay on Criticism. Line 215-218. Penguin:London
12. *Durant, W. (2011). "The Age of Faith: The Story of Civilization", p.1077, Simon and Schuster*
13. Attributed to Aristotle. Year Unknown.

PART B – HOW BIAS ARE YOU?

14. Kahneman, D. (2011). Thinking, fast and slow. New York: Farrar, Straus and Giroux.
15. Kruger, J., & Dunning, D. (1999). Unskilled and unaware of it: How difficulties in recognizing one's own incompetence lead to inflated self-assessments. *Journal of Personality and Social Psychology, 77*(6), 1121–1134
16. Proverbs 26:12 New King James Version
17. Syed, M. (2015). *Black box thinking: The surprising truth about success (and why some people never learn from their mistakes).*
18. The Simpsons, Groening, M., Brooks, J. L., Simon, S., Clausen, A., Castellaneta, D., Kavner, J., Cartwright, N., ... Twentieth Century Fox Home Entertainment, Inc.,. (2007). *The Simpsons.* Season 9, episode 8. Lisa the Skeptic.
19. Plato. Plato in Twelve Volumes, Vols. 5 & 6 Book 7 of the *Republic* translated by Paul Shorey. Cambridge, MA, Harvard University Press; London, William Heinemann Ltd. 1969. Book 7 of the *Republic*
20. Locke, J. An Essay Concerning Human Understanding (1689) Book IV, Ch. 7
21. Lao Tzu. Tao Te Ching. Chapter 56.
22. Attributed to Aristotle. Year unknown.
23. Ehrlinger, Joyce; Johnson, Kerri; Banner, Matthew; Dunning, David; Kruger, Justin (2008). «Why the unskilled are unaware: Further explorations of (absent) self-insight among the incompetent». *Organizational Behavior and Human Decision Processes.* 105 (1): 98–121.
24. Pope, A. *Miscellanies* (1727) vol. 2 'Thoughts on Various Subjects'.
25. Locke, J. An Essay Concerning Human Understanding (1689)

PART C – AN ANSWER TO IGNORANCE

26. Bostock, D., 1988, *Plato's Theaetetus.* 187a–200d, Oxford: Oxford

University Press.

27. Locke, J. An Essay Concerning Human Understanding (1689) Book IV, Ch. 19 : Of Enthusiasm (Chapter added in the fourth edition)
28. Attributed to Confucius. Year unknown.
29. Aristotle Nicomachean Ethics, revised edition (2004) Penguin Books, London.
30. Aurelius, M. Meditations (2006). Penguin: London
31. Russell, B. 1928. The Recrudescence of Puritanism, in Sceptical Essays.
32. Pope, A. (2011) An Essay on Criticism. Line 46-49. Penguin:London
33. Cameron, J., Landau, J., Worthington, S., Saldana, Z., Ribisi, G., Rodriguez, M., Lang, S., ... Twentieth Century-Fox Film Corporation. (2010). *Avatar*. Beverly Hills, Calif: 20th Century Fox.
34. Kishimi, I., & Koga, F. (2018). *The courage to be disliked: The Japanese phenomenon that shows you how to change your life and achieve real happiness.*
35. Siegel, E. 2016. Forbes Magazine online. Retrieved from https://www.forbes.com/sites/startswithabang/2016/12/29/the-four-biggest-mistakes-of-einsteins-scientific-life/#3dde04c98db4
36. Lao Tzu. Tao Te Ching. Chapter VII.
37. Pope, A. *Miscellanies* (1727) vol. 2 'Thoughts on Various Subjects'.
38. Aurelius, M. Meditations. *(Book VI, Chapter 21)* (2006). Penguin: London
39. Csikszentmihalyi, M. 'Flow: The classic work on how to achieve happiness' Page 226. Ryder: The Random House Group
40. Tetlock, P. E., & Gardner, D. (2015). *Superforecasting: The art and science of prediction.* P. 213-216.
41. Words of Paul Samuelson. 1978 October 13, Wall Street Journal, U.S. Monetary Troubles by Lindley H. Clark Jr., Page 22, New York.
42. Yamamoto, T. (1979). *Hagakure: The book of the samurai.* Tokyo: Kodansha International.
43. Lyons, L. 1964 New York Post, Section: Post Daily Magazine, The Lyons Den by Leonard Lyons, Quote Page 27 (Magazine Page 3),

Column 3, New York.

44. *Monty Python (Comedy troupe). (1979). Monty Python's The life of Brian (of Nazareth). London :Eyre Methuen,*

CHAPTER 8 - OVERCOMING ADVERSITY AND RELISHING CHALLENGE

1. *Rugrats: Decade in diapers*. (2001). Hollywood, CA: Paramount.
2. Carpenter, J. Big Trouble in Little China. 1986. Hollywood, CA.
3. Epictetus. 2008. Discourses and Selected Writings. Penguin: London.
4. Shakespeare, W. (1992). The tragedy of Hamlet, prince of Denmark (New Folger's ed.). New York: Washington Square Press/Pocket Books.
5. Ginott, H. 1972, Teacher and Child: A Book for Parents and Teachers by Dr. Haim G. Ginott, Chapter: Preface, Quote Page 15, The Macmillan Company, New York.
6. Aurelius, M. Meditations (2006). IV, 42. Penguin: London
7. Sullivan, A. & Gilbert, W. S. (1889) An entirely original comic opera in two acts, entitled The Goldoliers, or, The King of Barataria. (Published by the John Church Co., 74 W. Fourth St., Cincinnati, monographic. Retrieved from the Library of Congress, https://www.loc.gov/item/2010656873/.
8. Chinese Proverb. Year Unknown.
9. Lao Tzu. Tao Te Ching. Chapter 15.
10. Confucius. (1979). The analects (Lun yü). Harmondsworth ; New York :Penguin Books,
11. Attributed to Michael Jordan. Year Unknown.
12. Suzuki, S., & Dixon, T. (2010). *Zen mind, beginner's mind.* P. 49 Boston: Shambhala.
13. Attributed to Tiger Woods. Year Unknown.
14. Turner, M. Jones, M. Sheffield, D. Barker, J. & Coffee, P. 2014. Manipulating cardiovascular indices of challenge and threat using resource appraisals. International Journal of Psychophysiology. 94, 9-18.

15. Kahneman, D. 2011. Thinking: Fast and Slow. P. 241 Farrar, Straus and Giroux. New York, USA.
16. Haidt, J. (2006). The happiness hypothesis: Finding modern truth in ancient wisdom. New York: Basic Books.
17. Baumeister, R. F., Bratslavsky, E., Finkenauer, C., & Vohs, K. D. (2001). Bad is stronger than good. Review of General Psychology, 5, 323–370.
18. Hardy, L. 2012. Interview for the BPS. Retrieved from https://www.youtube.com/watch?v=UiA00Om_gXc
19. Attributed to Tiger Woods. Year Unknown.
20. Robbins, T. 2015. On thoughts. Retrieved from https://twitter.com/tonyrobbins/status/637266065391681536?lang=en
21. Wallis, G. (2004). *The Dhammapada: Verses on the Way : a new translation of the teachings of the Buddha, with a guide to reading the text*. New York: Modern Library.
22. Hemingway, E., & Herman Finkelstein Collection (Library of Congress). (1952). *The old man and the sea.*
23. Attributed to Aristotle. Year Unknown.
24. Aurelius, M. Meditations. P. 33 (2006). Penguin: London
25. Attributed to von Goethe. Year Unknown.
26. Lao Tzu. Tao Te Ching. Chapter 7.
27. Lao Tzu. Tao Te Ching. Chapter 1.
28. Peters, S. (2012). *The chimp paradox*. London: Random House Audio.
29. Carey, J. 2014. Maharishi University Graduation Speech. Retrieved from https://www.graduationwisdom.com/speeches/0150-Jim-Carrey-Graduation-Speech-2014.htm
30. Lao Tzu. Tao Te Ching. Chapter 48
31. Attributed to Tony Robbins. Year Unknown.
32. Attributed to Greg Norman, Year Unknown.
33. Attributed to Confucius. Year Unknown.
34. Seneca. Seneca: Letters from a Stoic. Letter 101. (1969) Lexicos Publishing
35. (2002). Cast away. Beverly Hills, CA: 20th Century Fox Home

Entertainment.

36. Stanton, A., Unkrich, L., Peterson, B., Reynolds, D., Brooks, A., DeGeneres, E., Gould, A., & Newman, T. (2003). *Finding Nemo*. Collector's ed., widescreen and fullscreen, Burbank, CA: Distributed by Buena Vista Home Entertainment.
37. Attributed to Cicero. Year Unknown.
38. Henley, W. retrieved from https://www.poetryfoundation.org/poems/51642/invictus
39. Gervais, R. 2018. On adversity. Retrieved from https://twitter.com/rickygervais/status/976052726726627329?lang=en
40. Hemingway, E. (1957). A farewell to arms. New York: Scribner.
41. Rowling, J. K., author. (2002). Harry Potter and the goblet of fire. New York :Scholastic,
42. Allers, R., Minkoff, R., Hahn, D., Mecchi, I., Roberts, J., Woolverton, L., Thomas, J. T., ... Buena Vista Home Entertainment (Firm),. (2003). *The lion king*.
43. Pope, A. (2011) The Rape of the Lock and Other Major Writings. Penguin:London
44. Attributed to Epircurus. Year Unknown.
45. Seneca. Seneca: Letters from a Stoic. Letter 101. (1969) Lexicos Publishing
46. Marcus Aurelius, Meditations. (2006). Penguin: London
47. Homer, ., & Fitzgerald, R. (1990). The Odyssey. New York: Vintage Books.
48. Cook, B., Bancroft, T., Coats, P., Hsiao, R., Sanders, C., LaZebnik, P., Singer, R., ... Buena Vista Home Entertainment (Firm). (2004). *Mulan*. United States: Walt Disney Home Entertainment.

CHAPTER 9 – RISKING IT ALL

1. From Elizabeth Appell but wrongly attributed to Anais Nin. Retreived from http://anaisninblog.skybluepress.com/2013/03/

who-wrote-risk-is-the-mystery-solved/

2. The Simpsons, Groening, M., Brooks, J. L., Simon, S., Clausen, A., Castellaneta, D., Kavner, J., Cartwright, N., ... Twentieth Century Fox Home Entertainment, Inc.,. (2007). *The Simpsons*. Season 9, episode 24. Bart Sells his Soul.
3. Retrieved from https://rarediseases.info.nih.gov/diseases/6840/kluver-bucy-syndrome
4. Risk of dying through driving. Retrieved from http://www.bandolier.org.uk/booth/Risk/trasnsportpop.html
5. Ware, B. (2012). *The top five regrets of the dying: A life transformed by the dearly departing*. Carlsbad, Calif.: Hay House.
6. Wilde, O., & Elfenbein, A. (2007). *Oscar Wilde's The picture of Dorian Gray*. Chapter 3. New York: Pearson Longman.
7. Attributed to George Adair. Year Unknown.
8. Attributed to Will Durant. Year unknown.
9. Lawrence, T. E., Wilson, J., & Wilson, N. (2004). *Seven pillars of wisdom: The complete 1922 text*. Fordingbridge, Hampshire: J. and N. Wilson.
10. Figner, Bernd & Weber, Elke. (2011). Who Takes Risks When and Why?: Determinants of Risk Taking. Current Directions in Psychological Science - CURR DIRECTIONS PSYCHOL SCI. 20. 211-216. 10.1177/0963721411415790.
11. https://www.livescience.com/33471-people-take-risks.html
12. Josef, A. K., Richter, D., Samanez-Larkin, G. R., Wagner, G. G., Hertwig, R., & Mata, R. (2016). Stability and change in risk-taking propensity across the adult life span. *Journal of personality and social psychology*, *111*(3), 430–450. https://doi.org/10.1037/pspp0000090
13. Johnson, S. (1998). *Who moved my cheese?: An amazing way to deal with change in your work and in your life*. New York: Putnam.
14. Aurelius, M. Meditations. (2006). Penguin: London
15. Carey, J. 2014. Maharishi University Graduation Speech. Retrieved from https://www.graduationwisdom.com/speeches/0150-Jim-Carrey-Graduation-Speech-2014.htm

16. Fitzgerald, F. S., & Brown, C. (2008). *The curious case of Benjamin Button*. New York: Collins Design.
17. DeGeneres, E. (2013). *Seriously--I'm kidding*. Philadelphia: Running Press.
18. The Simpsons, Groening, M., Brooks, J. L., Simon, S., Clausen, A., Castellaneta, D., Kavner, J., Cartwright, N., ... Twentieth Century Fox Home Entertainment, Inc.,. (2007). *The Simpsons*. Season 8, episode 6.
19. Tolkien, J.R.R. (1954). *Lord of the Rings*. (2nd Ed.). England: Houghton Mifflin.
20. Shapiro, F. 2006, The Yale Book of Quotations Section: John A. Shedd, Page 705, Yale University Press, New Haven.
21. *Milne, A. A. (Alan Alexander), 1882-1956. (2003). Winnie-the-Pooh. [New York] :Harper Children's Audio,*
22. Zuckerberg, M. 2011. Interview at Palo Alto, California. https://www.cbsnews.com/news/facebooks-mark-zuckerberg-insights-for-entrepreneurs/
23. Attributed to Wolfgang von Goethe. Year unknown.
24. Shorr, F. 2018. The discomfort zone: How to get what you want by living fearlessly. Piatkus.
25. Attributed to Marlo Morgan. https://quotefancy.com/quote/1588307/Marlo-Morgan-The-only-way-to-pass-any-test-is-to-take-the-test-All-tests-on-every-level
26. Matthew 7:7. *King James Version*
27. Carey, J. 2014. Maharishi University Graduation Speech. Retrieved from https://www.graduationwisdom.com/speeches/0150-Jim-Carrey-Graduation-Speech-2014.htm
28. Byrne, R., & Byrne, R. (2006). *The secret*. New York: Atria Books.
29. Attributed to Michael Jordan, Year Unknown.
30. Hemingway, E. (2003). *The complete short stories of Ernest Hemingway*. New York: Scribner
31. Kurtz, G., Brackett, L., Kasdan, L., Kershner, I., Lucas, G., Hamill, M., Ford, H., ... Twentieth Century Fox Home Entertainment, Inc. (2004). *Star wars: Episode V*. United States: 20th Century Fox.

32. Plato, . (1955). *The Republic*. Book 1. 377. Baltimore, Md: Penguin Books.
33. Goethe, J. W., & In Hecker, M. F. (1907). *Goethe. Maximen und Reflexionen*. Weimar: Goethe-Gesellschaft.
34. Bansal, A., Garg, C., Pakhare, A., & Gupta, S. (2018). Selfies: A boon or bane?. *Journal of family medicine and primary care*, *7*(4), 828–831. https://doi.org/10.4103/jfmpc.jfmpc_109_18
35. Bay, M., Orci, R., Kurtzman, A., Di, B. L., DeSanto, T., Murphy, D., Bryce, I., ... DreamWorks Home Entertainment (Firm),. (2007). *Transformers*.
36. Jones, J, P. As cited in https://www.theguardian.com/voluntary-sector-network/2013/jul/17/young-people-risks-volunteering
37. 1977 April 14, Fort Lauderdale News, Ali, Louis: The Spectre of Greatness Past (Continuation title: More Lincicome) by Bernie Lincicome (Sports Editor), Start Page 1D, Quote Page 6D, Column 1, Fort Lauderdale, Florida.
38. Attributed to Johan Wolfgang von Goethe. Year unknown.
39. Alexander Pope, An Essay on Criticism 'The Rape of the Lock and Other Major Writings (2011), Line 625.
40. Shakespeare, W., Raffel, B., & Bloom, H. (2006). *Julius Caesar*. Act II, scene ii New Haven: Yale University Press.
41. Hemingway, E. (1957). *A farewell to arms*. P. 178. New York: Scribner.
42. Attributed to Swami Vivekananda. Year unknown.
43. Steve Jobs (Co-founder of Apple Inc.) in his commencement address at Stanford University in 2005.
44. Canfield, J. 2015. Twitter post retrieved from https://twitter.com/JackCanfield/status/652170836032401408
45. Attributed to Gena Davis. Year unknown.

CHAPTER 10 – CREATIVITY AND PASSION

PART A – THE HUMAN NEED FOR CREATIVITY

1. Von Goethe, J. 1835. 1835. Faustus, A Dramatic Mystery; The Bride of Corinth; The First Walpurgis Night, Translated from the German of Goethe, and Illustrated with Notes by John Anster, Section: Prelude at the Theatre, (Spoken by Manager), Quote Page 15, Printed for Longman, Rees, Orme, Brown, Green, & Longman, London.
2. Epicurus. Translated by Peter Saint-Andre (2010) Vatican Sayings. Retrieved from http://monadnock.net/epicurus/vatican-sayings.html
3. *Matthew 5:16, King James Version.*
4. Harari, Y. N. (2014). *Sapiens: A brief history of humankind.* [Toronto]: Signal.
5. Kim, Z. 2008. Meta-analyses of the relationship of creative achievement to both IQ and Divergent Thinking Test Scores. The Journal of Creative Behaviour. 42.
6. October 4, 1976, Periodical: Time, Article: Modern Living: Ozmosis in Central Park, Note: The quotation appears as an epigraph at the beginning of the article.
7. *Le Guin, U, K. (2017). "No Time to Spare: Thinking about what Matters", p.120, Houghton Mifflin Harcourt*
8. Kim, K. Can only intelligent people be creative? A meta-analysis. 2005.. *Journal of Secondary Gifted Education,* Volume: 16 issue: 2-3, page(s): 57-66 Issue published: February 1,
9. Jauk, E., Benedek, M., Dunst, B., & Neubauer, A. C. (2013). The relationship between intelligence and creativity: New support for the threshold hypothesis by means of empirical breakpoint detection. *Intelligence, 41*(4), 212–221. https://doi.org/10.1016/j.intell.2013.03.003
10. Aljoscha C. Neubauer, Khatuna Martskvishvili. Creativity and intelligence: A link to different levels of human needs hierarchy?. Heliyon 4 (2018) e00623.
11. Runco, M. A., Ebersole, P., & Mraz, W. (1991). Creativity and

self-actualization. *Journal of Social Behavior & Personality, 6*(5), 161–167.

12. Maslow, A. H. (1970). *Motivation and personality*. New York: Harper & Row.
13. *Leo Burnett (1961). "Communications of an Advertising Man: Selections from the Speeches, Articles, Memoranda, and Miscellaneous Writings of Leo Burnett"*
14. Conner, T. S., DeYoung C. G., & Silvia P. J. (2017). Everyday creative activity as a path to flourishing. *Journal of Positive Psychology.* http://dx.doi.org/10.1080/17439760.2016.1257049
15. Buck, P. The Joy of Children. Retrieved from https://en.wikipedia.org/wiki/Pearl_S._Buck
16. Attributed to Earl Nightingale. Year unknown.
17. Seuss, D. (1975). *Oh, the thinks you can think!*. New York, Beginner's Books.
18. Attributed to Bernard Shaw. Year unknown.
19. Attributed to Jim Carey. Year unknown.
20. Attributed to Aristotle. Year unknown.
21. Gabor, D. 1964. Inventing the future. Page 207, Alfred A, Knopf, New York.
22. Carey, J. 2014. Maharishi University Graduation Speech. Retrieved from https://www.graduationwisdom.com/speeches/0150-Jim-Carrey-Graduation-Speech-2014.htm
23. Attributed to Bill Gates. Year unknown.
24. Attributed to Mark Twain. Year unknown.

PART B – FINDING YOUR CALLING

25. *Hemingway, E. (2014). "The Hemingway Collection", p.3159. E-book. Simon and Schuster, Scribner*
26. A popular paraphrase of Confucius. Paraphrase kept for ease of understanding - 1861, The Chinese Classics with a Translation, Critical and Exegetical Notes, Prolegomena, and Copious Indexes by James Legge

(London Missionary Society), Volume 1 of 7, Section: Confucian Analects, Quote Page 216 and 217, Printed at the London Missionary Society's Printing Office in Hong Kong, China; also published by Trubner and Company, Paternoster Row, London

27. Locke, J., & Laslett, P. (1988). *Two treatises of government.* Cambridge [England: Cambridge University Press.
28. Retrieved from https://www.forbes.com/sites/amitchowdhry/2013/10/05/lessons-learned-from-4-steve-jobs-quotes/#51cd4ab84f69
29. Buffett, W. Retrieved from https://www.businessinsider.com/warren-buffett-on-resume-building-2015-11?r=US&IR=T
30. García, H., Miralles, F., Cleary, H., & García, H. (2017). *Ikigai: The Japanese secret to a long and happy life.*
31. Whitehorn, K. 1975. "The Ten-Hour Week is Here to Stay," from *The Observer*. London.
32. Sir Ken Robinson - Changing Paradigms RSA •4 Feb 2010
33. Attributed to Ella Fitzgerald. Retrieved from http://www.ellafitzgerald.com/about/quotes
34. Attributed to Rumi. Year Unknown.
35. Luther King, M. 1967. A speech at a school in Philadelphia, USA. Retrieved from https://www.americanmanufacturing.org/blog/entry/mlk-on-work-here-lived-a-great-street-sweeper-who-swept-his-job-well
36. Anonymous -1978 March 15, The Surrey Leader, Classified Ads: Help Wanted, Quote Page 10, Column 5, Surrey, British Columbia, Canada. Retrieved from https://quoteinvestigator.com/2018/02/10/beauty-dreams/
37. Locke, J. An Essay Concerning Human Understanding (1689) Retrieved from - Dedicatory epistle, as quoted in *Fred R Shapiro (2006). The Yale Book of Quotations. Yale University Press. p. 468.* ISBN 0-300-10798-6.
38. Attributed to Pablo Picasso. Retrieved from https://www.pablopicasso.org/quotes.jsp

39. Attributed to Matt Groening. Year unknown.
40. Seneca, L. A., Hurst, J. F., & In Whiting, H. C. (1877). *Treatises: On providence, On tranquility of mind, On shortness of life, On happy life*. New York: Harper & Brothers.
41. Schopenhauer, A. Retrieved from 1851, Title: Parerga und Paralipomena: Kleine Philosophische Schriften, Author: Arthur Schopenhauer, Volume 2, Section: 76, Quote Page 93, Publisher: A. W. Hayn, Berlin
42. Cleese, J. As quoted in *"Best New Games" by Dale N. LeFevre, (p. 9), 2002.*
43. Bradbury, R. (1990). *Zen in the art of writing*. Santa Barbara, Calif: Joshua Odell Editions.
44. 1984 March-April, Harvard Magazine, Volume 86, Number 4, The Browser: Mindplay by George Scialabba, (Book Review of Howard Gardner's "Frames of Mind: The Theory of Multiple Intelligences"), Start Page 16, Quote Page 19, Published by Harvard Magazine Inc., Cambridge, Massachusetts. Retrieved from https://quoteinvestigator.com/2017/03/02/fun/#note-15588-2
45. Angelou, M. 2009. Facebook post retrieved from https://www.politico.com/story/2014/05/getting-there-maya-angelou-107195
46. Keats, J. 1818. Endymion. Retrieved from https://www.poetryfoundation.org/poems/44469/endymion-56d2239287ca5

CHAPTER 11 – LIMITING DESIRES AND BEING CONTENT

PART A – NEEDS VS WANTS

1. The Simpsons, Groening, M., Brooks, J. L., Simon, S., Clausen, A., Castellaneta, D., Kavner, J., Cartwright, N., ... Twentieth Century Fox Home Entertainment, Inc.,. (2007). *The Simpsons*. Season 5, episode 13. Bart gets an elephant.
2. Lao Tzu, Tao Te Ching Chapter 44 (1963) Penguin, London

3. Epictetus. 2008. Discourses and Selected Writings. 4.1.175. Penguin: London.
4. Epicurus. Translated by Peter Saint-Andre (2010) Vatican Sayings. Retrieved from http://monadnock.net/epicurus/vatican-sayings.html
5. Attributed to Immanuel Kant. Year unknown. Retrieved from https://en.wikiquote.org/wiki/Talk:Immanuel_Kant
6. Alexander Pope, An Essay on Man in 'The Rape of the Lock and Other Major Writings (2011). Penguin: London.
7. Frost, R. Fire and Ice. Retrieved from https://www.poetryfoundation.org/poems/44263/fire-and-ice
8. Boven, L. & Gilovich, T. 2003. To Do or To Have: That is the Question. Journal of Personality and Social Psychology, Vol. 85, No. 6, 1193–1202
9. Sachan, D. 2016. Scientific Proof that Buying Things Can Lead to Happiness (Sometimes). Retrieved from https://www.fastcompany.com/3061516/scientific-proof-that-buying-things-can-actually-buy-happiness-sometimes
10. Matz, S., Gladstone, J,. & Stillwell. 2016. Money Buys Happiness When Spending Matches Our Personality. Psychological Science, 1-11. http://foxfellowship.yale.edu/sites/default/files/files/Money%20Buys%20Happiness%20When%20Spending%20Fits%20Our%20Personality%20(1).pdf
11. Guevarra, D.A., & Howell, R.T., To have in order to do: Exploring the effects of consuming experiential products on well-being, Journal of Consumer Psychology (2014), http://dx.doi.org/10.1016/j.jcps.2014.06.006
12. Weidman, A. C., & Dunn, E. W. (2016). The Unsung Benefits of Material Things: Material Purchases Provide More Frequent Momentary Happiness Than Experiential Purchases. *Social Psychological and Personality Science*, *7*(4), 390–399. https://doi.org/10.1177/1948550615619761
13. The Simpsons, Groening, M., Brooks, J. L., Simon, S., Clausen, A., Castellaneta, D., Kavner, J., Cartwright, N., ... Twentieth Century Fox

Home Entertainment, Inc.,. (2007). *The Simpsons*. Season 3. Brother, Can you Spare Two Dimes?

14. https://ourworldindata.org/happiness-and-life-satisfaction
15. Jebb, A. Tay, L., Diener, E. & Oishi, S. 2018. Happiness, Income Satiation and Turning Points Around the World. Nature Human Behaviour. VOL 2, 33–38, www.nature.com/nathumbehav
16. https://www.express.co.uk/life-style/life/918900/Money-buy-happiness-annual-salary-income-life-study
17. https://www.cnbc.com/2017/11/20/how-much-money-you-need-to-be-happy-according-to-wealth-experts.html
18. Carey, J. 2014. Maharishi University Graduation Speech. Retrieved from https://www.graduationwisdom.com/speeches/0150-Jim-Carrey-Graduation-Speech-2014.htm
19. https://www.independent.co.uk/voices/top-five-percent-salary-uk-wealth-tax-rich-average-a9213406.html
20. Zhuangzi, ., & Merton, T. (1965). *The way of Chuang-Tzŭ*. New York: New Directions.
21. Guthrie, T.1865. Man and the Gospel. Retrieved from https://en.wikiquote.org/wiki/Dorothy_Parker

PART B – LETTING GO OF ATTACHMENT

22. Lao Tzu, Tao Te Ching P. 69, 105. (1963) Penguin, London
23. TOLLE, E. (2018). *ONENESS WITH ALL LIFE: Inspirational selections from a new earth*. Place of publication not identified: MICHAEL JOSEPH LTD.
24. Haynes, T. 2018. Harvard University Blog. Retrieved from http://sitn.hms.harvard.edu/flash/2018/dopamine-smartphones-battle-time/
25. Pope, A. (2011) An Essay on Criticism. Line 215-218. Penguin:London
26. Ackerman, T., Robertson, S., Russell, D. O., Apatow, J., Ferrell, W., McKay, A., Applegate, C., ... DreamWorks Home Entertainment (Firm). (2004). *Anchorman: The legend of Ron Burgundy*. United States: DreamWorks Home Entertainment.

27. Epicurus. Translated by Peter Saint Andre. 2010. Vatican Sayings. Retrieved from http://monadnock.net/epicurus/vatican-sayings.html
28. Attributed to Aristotle. Year unknown. Retrieved from https://www.goodreads.com/quotes/95206-the-high-minded-man-must-care-more-for-the-truth-than
29. Attributed to Immanuel Kant. Year Unknown. Retrieved from https://en.wikiquote.org/wiki/Talk:Immanuel_Kant
30. Lyubomirsky, S. (2008). *The how of happiness: A new approach to getting the life you want*. New York, N.Y: Penguin Books.
31. TNS Global Survey. Retrieved from https://www.businesswire.com/news/home/20130402005600/en/Ebates-Survey-51.8-Americans-Engage-Retail-Therapy%E2%80%94
32. Russell, B. 1917. *"Principles of Social Reconstruction". Retrieved from* https://www.azquotes.com/quote/254931
33. Herlihy, T. 1998. The Wedding Singer. New Line Cinema. United States.
34. Shaddix, J. & Esperance, T. 2001. Between Angels and Insects. Dreamworks. United States.
35. Epicurus. Translated by Peter Saint-Andre (2010) Vatican Sayings. Retrieved from http://monadnock.net/epicurus/vatican-sayings.html
36. Suzuki, S., & Dixon, T. (2010). *Zen mind, beginner's mind*. P. 49 Boston: Shambhala.
37. Attributed to Plato. Year Unknown. Retrieved from https://www.goodreads.com/quotes/420410-the-greatest-wealth-is-to-live-content-with-little
38. Seneca. Seneca: Letters from a Stoic. Letter 101. (1969) Lexicos Publishing
39. Waldinger, R. Ongoing study at Harvard University. Retrieved from https://news.harvard.edu/gazette/story/2017/04/over-nearly-80-years-harvard-study-has-been-showing-how-to-live-a-healthy-and-happy-life/
40. Lao Tzu, Tao Te Ching Page 6 (1963) Penguin, London
41. Attributed to Lao Tzu. Year Unknown.

42. Buddhist saying. Retrieved from https://philosiblog.com/2014/03/10/in-the-end-only-three-things-matter-how-much-you-loved-how-gently-you-lived-and-how-gracefully-you-let-go-of-the-things-not-meant-for-you/
43. Pope, A. (2011) An Essay on Man. Penguin:London

CHAPTER 12 – A PATH TOWARD VIRTUE

PART A: THE ORIGIN OF VIRTUE

1. Alexander Pope, An Essay on Criticism. 'The Rape of the Lock and Other Major Writings (2011), part 3. Penguin: London.
2. Rowling, J. K. (2000). *Harry Potter and the chamber of secrets.* Vancouver: Raincoast Books.
3. Locke, J. An Essay Concerning Human Understanding (1689).
4. Matthew 7:20. King James Version.
5. Lingard, R.1670, Title: A Letter of Advice to a Young Gentleman Leaveing the University Concerning His Behaviour and Conversation in the World, Author: R. L. (Richard Lingard), Quote Page 50 and 51, Printed by Benjamin Tooke, Dublin, Ireland, Sold by Mary Crook. Retrieved from https://quoteinvestigator.com/2015/07/30/hour-play/#note-11729-1
6. Goethe, J. W., & Saunders, T. B. (1893). *The maxims and reflections of Goethe.* Maxim 39. New York: Macmillan and Co.
7. Matthew 7:17-18, King James Version.
8. Attributed to Marcus Aurelius. Year unknown.
9. Kant, I. 1824. (English translation of original 1784 article) "Idea of a Universal History on a Cosmo-Political Plan" in The London Magazine: pp. 385-393.
10. Rowling, J. K. (1997). *Harry Potter and the philosopher's stone.* London: Bloomsbury Pub.
11. Kant, I. Categorical Imperative. Retrieved from https://www.csus.

edu/indiv/g/gaskilld/ethics/kantian%20ethics.htm

12. Maori proverb. Retrieved from https://teara.govt.nz/en/mountains/page-5
13. Seneca. Seneca: Letters from a Stoic. Letter 101. (1969) Lexicos Publishing.
14. Confucius. (1979). The analects. Lunyu XVII. 6. (453) Harmondsworth ; New York :Penguin Books,
15. Greek proverb, collected by Richard Taverner. Retrieved from https://english.stackexchange.com/questions/320830/a-swallow-does-not-make-a-summer-or-a-spring
16. Robbins, A. (1992). *Awaken the giant within: How to take immediate control of your mental, emotional, physical & financial destiny!*. New York: Simon & Schuster.
17. Lally, P., Van Jaarsveld, C., Potts, H. & Wardle, J. 2009. European Journal of Social Psychology. Vol 40, 6.
18. *Durant, Will, 1885-1981. (1961). The story of philosophy : the lives and opinions of the great philosophers of the western world. New York :Simon and Schuster,*
19. Attributed to Michael Jordan. Retrieved from https://www.goodreads.com/quotes/95287-if-you-quit-once-it-becomes-a-habit-never-quit
20. The Simpsons, Groening, M., Brooks, J. L., Simon, S., Clausen, A., Castellaneta, D., Kavner, J., Cartwright, N., ... Twentieth Century Fox Home Entertainment, Inc.,. (2007). *The Simpsons*. Season 3, episode 1.
21. *Dickens, Charles, 1812-1870. (2000). David Copperfield. New York :Modern Library*
22. Mandela, N. 2008. Long Walk to Freedom: The Autobiography of Nelson Mandela (ed. Little, Brown, 2008) - ISBN: 978075952104
23. Lao Tzu. (1963) Tao Te Ching. Chapter 54. Penguin, London.

PART B: INWARD VIRTUE

24. Locke, J. An Essay Concerning Human Understanding (1689). Book II, Ch. 21, sec. 70 - An Essay Concerning Human Understanding

25. The Simpsons, Groening, M., Brooks, J. L., Simon, S., Clausen, A., Castellaneta, D., Kavner, J., Cartwright, N., ... Twentieth Century Fox Home Entertainment, Inc.,. (2007). *The Simpsons*. The PTA disbands.
26. Confucius, Mencius, Shih ching (Translated by Legge, J.) (1867). “The Chinese Classics: The life and works of Mencius”, p.117
27. Scott, Walter, 1771-1832. (1810). Marmion : a tale of Flodden Field. London :Printed by J. M’Creery ... for Archibald Constable and Co., Edinburgh, and William Miller ... and John Murray, London,
28. Pope, A. (2011) ‘The Rape of the Lock and Other Major Writings. Penguin: London.
29. Aurelius, M. (2006). Meditations. Penguin: London
30. Plato (1955). *The Republic*. Chapter 2. Baltimore, Md: Penguin Books
31. Dunn, P. 2006. Aristotle (384-322 BC): Philosopher and scientist of ancient Greece. Arch Dis Child Fetal Neonatal Ed2006;91:F75–F77.
32. Epicurus. Translated by Peter Saint-Andre (2010) Vatican Sayings. Retrieved from http://monadnock.net/epicurus/vatican-sayings.html
33. *Ernest Hemingway (2008). “The Good Life According to Hemingway”. Retrieved from* https://www.azquotes.com/quote/129384
34. https://www.lexico.com/en/definition/modesty
35. https://johannanalau.com/2019/07/28/how-to-assess-true-competence-vs-confidence/
36. https://hbr.org/2013/08/why-do-so-many-incompetent-men
37. Confucius. (1979). The analects. Harmondsworth ; New York :Penguin Books,
38. Pratchett, T. & Baxter, S. 2012. The Long Earth. Retrieved from https://en.wikipedia.org/wiki/The_Long_Earth
39. *Milne, A. A. (Alan Alexander), 1882-1956. (2003). Winnie-the-Pooh. [New York] :Harper Children's Audio*
40. *Emerson, R, W. (2010). “Compensation and Self-Reliance”, p.23, Cosimo, Inc*
41. Montague, C. 1922. 1922, Disenchantment, Page 260, Brentano’s, New York. Retrieved from https://quoteinvestigator.com/2010/12/21/doing-good-selfless/

42. Austen, J. (2010). *Pride and prejudice*. P. 94. New York: Modern Library
43. *Plato (2008). "Laws", p.126, Cosimo, Inc. retrieved from* https://www.azquotes.com/quote/668199
44. Newton, I. 1675. In a letter to Robert Hooke. Retrieved from https://www.bbc.co.uk/worldservice/learningenglish/movingwords/shortlist/newton.shtml
45. Dickens, C., & Mitchell, C. (2003). *Great expectations*. London: Penguin Books.
46. Attributed to Hemingway. Retrieved from https://1000quotesproject.wordpress.com/2019/02/07/746-the-best-people-possess-a-feeling-for-beauty-the-courage-to-take-risks-the-discipline-to-tell-the-truth-the-capacity-for-sacrifice-ironically-their-virtues-make-them-vulnerable-they-are/
47. Angelou, M. As quoted in *Diversity : Leaders Not Labels* (2006) by Stedman Graham, p. 224
48. Niebuhr, R. As quoted in https://en.wikipedia.org/wiki/Serenity_Prayer#cite_note-FRS-1
49. Russell, B. (1967). *A history of western philosophy*. New York: Simon and Schuster.
50. Attrbiuted to Ernest Hemingway. Retrieved from https://jfk.blogs.archives.gov/2018/07/20/jfk-hemingway/
51. *Lucado, M. (2010). "Chronicles of the Cross Collection", p.205, Harper Collins. Retrieved from* https://www.azquotes.com/quote/180020
52. *Solzhenitsyn, A. 1918-2008. (197478). The Gulag Archipelago, 1918-1956: an experiment in literary investigation. New York :Harper & Row,*
53. Feige, K., Penn, Z., Whedon, J., Downey, R., Johansson, S., Renner, J., Ruffalo, M., ... Buena Vista Home Entertainment (Firm). (2012). *Marvel's the Avengers*. Burbank, CA: Distributed by Buena Vista Home Entertainment.

CHAPTER 13 – THE TREATMENT OF OTHERS

PART A – UNIVERSAL LAWS, RESPECT AND KINDNESS

1. Attributed to Gamaliel Bailey. Retrieved from https://www.azquotes.com/quote/15456
2. Einstein, A. *(2010). "The Ultimate Quotable Einstein", p.480, Princeton University Press. Retrieved from* https://www.azquotes.com/quote/344550
3. *Kant, Immanuel (1993) [1785]. Grounding for the Metaphysics of Morals. Translated by Ellington, James W. (3rd ed.). Hackett. p. 30. ISBN 0-87220-166-X.*. It is standard to also reference the *Akademie Ausgabe* of Kant's works. The *Groundwork* occurs in the fourth volume.
4. Leviticus 9:18. King James Version.
5. Lius, Pauling. Pauling's reply to an audience question about his ethical system, following his lecture circa 1961 at Monterey Peninsula College, in Monterey, California. Retrieved from https://en.wikiquote.org/wiki/Linus_Pauling
6. Harari, Y. N. (2014). *Sapiens: A brief history of humankind.* [Toronto]: Signal.
7. *Haidt, J. (2006). "The Happiness Hypothesis: Finding Modern Truth in Ancient Wisdom", p.47, Basic Books*
8. The Works of Mencius, Volume 2 (Lane, Crawford & Company, 1861), p. 209. Retrieved from https://libquotes.com/mencius/quote/lbn7p2o
9. Obama, M. 2012. Democratic national Convention in Charlotte. Retrieved from https://www.npr.org/2012/09/04/160578836/transcript-michelle-obamas-convention-speech
10. Kant, I. retrieved from https://plato.stanford.edu/entries/persons-means/
11. Phelps, W. 1935 July, Golden Book Magazine, Clues, (One quotation from set of eight), Quote Page 81, The Review of Reviews

Corporation, New York. Retrieved from https://quoteinvestigator.com/2013/12/28/gentleman/#note-7919-1

12. Forbes, M. 1972 August 6, Hartford Courant, Coco Offered Fatty Arbuckle Role by Earl Wilson, Page 10F, Hartford, Connecticut. Retrieved from https://quoteinvestigator.com/2011/10/28/judge-character/
13. Dostoevsky, F. *The Insulted and the Injured* (1861). Retrieved from https://quotes.yourdictionary.com/author/fyodor-dostoevsky/
14. A mixture of references, retrieved from https://quoteinvestigator.com/2013/10/26/kindness-see/#note-7519-11
15. Worsdworth, W. 1798. Tintern Abbey. Retrieved from https://www.prosperosisle.org/spip.php?article223
16. The Simpsons, Groening, M., Brooks, J. L., Simon, S., Clausen, A., Castellaneta, D., Kavner, J., Cartwright, N., ... Twentieth Century Fox Home Entertainment, Inc.,. (2007). *The Simpsons*.
17. Kerr, S. O'Donovan, A. & Pepping, C. 2015. Can gratitude and kindness interventions enhance well-being in a clinical sample? Journal of Happiness Studies, 16:17-36.
18. Baskerville, K. Johnson, K. Monk-Turner, E. Slone, Q. Standley, H. Stansbury, S. Williams, M. & Young, J. Reactions to random acts of kindness. The Social Science Journal. 37:2, 293-298.
19. Cameron, D. Retrieved from https://ayearoflivingkindly.com/2015/10/07/9-barriers-to-kindness/
20. Gallo, Dianne, "Working with compassion : the impact of loving kindness meditation on compassion satisfaction and compassion fatigue among social workers and other mental health workers" (2016). Masters Thesis, Smith College, Northampton, MA.
21. Upton, K.V. An investigation into compassion fatigue and self-compassion in acute medical care hospital nurses: a mixed methods study. *J of Compassionate Health Care* 5, 7 (2018). https://doi.org/10.1186/s40639-018-0050-x
22. Aurelius, M. Meditations (2006). Penguin: London
23. Vince, G. 2018. Retrieved from https://www.bbc.com/future/

article/20180403-why-do-people-become-trolls-online-and-in-social-media

24. Dalai Lama XIV, The Dalai Lama: A Policy of Kindness: An Anthology of Writings By and About the Dalai Lama. Retrieved from https://www.goodreads.com/quotes/59162-this-is-my-simple-religion-there-is-no-need-for
25. Attributed to Confucius. Year unknown. Retreived from https://www.azquotes.com/quote/372687

PART B – ANGER, REVENGE AND THE USE OF POWER

26. Gandhi, M. Year unknown. Retrieved from https://www.azquotes.com/quote/1416953
27. *Plato (2008). "Laws", p.194, Cosimo, Inc. retrieved from* https://www.azquotes.com/quote/670384
28. Burton, N. 2017. Should we get angry? Psychology Today. Retrieved from https://www.psychologytoday.com/gb/blog/hide-and-seek/201203/should-we-get-angry
29. Aristotle. & Freese, J. H. (1926). *The "art" of rhetoric*. London: W. Heinemann.
30. Attributed to Horace. Year unknown. Retrieved from https://www.forbes.com/quotes/4395/
31. *Hanlon's Razor, exact origin unknown. Retrieved from* https://en.wikipedia.org/wiki/Hanlon%27s_razor
32. Wright, W. M. (1993). *Francis de Sales: Introduction to the devout life and Treatise on the love of God*. New York: Crossroad.
33. Bushman, B. J. (2002). Does venting anger feed or extinguish the flame? Catharsis, rumination, distraction, anger and aggressive responding. *Personality and Social Psychology Bulletin, 28*(6), 724–731.
34. Lohr, J. M., Olatunji, B. O., Baumeister, R. F., & Bushman, B. J. (2007). The psychology of anger venting and empirically supported alternatives that do no harm. *The Scientific Review of Mental Health*

Practice: Objective Investigations of Controversial and Unorthodox Claims in Clinical Psychology, Psychiatry, and Social Work, 5(1), 53–64.

35. Buddhaghosa. 1931 (Part III was published in 1931 and Part II was completed before this), The Path of Purity: A Translation of Buddhaghosa's Visuddhimagga by Pe Maung Tin (Professor of Oriental Studies, University of Rangoon), Part II: Of Concentration, Translation Series Number 17, Chapter 9: Exposition of Divine States: Section 1: The Developing of Love, Quote Page 346 and 347, Published for The Pali Text Society by Oxford University Press, London. Retrieved from https://quoteinvestigator.com/2018/06/18/hot/
36. Attributed to Mark Twain. Retrieved from https://www.azquotes.com/quote/298588
37. *Franklin, B. (2008). "The Way to Wealth and Poor Richard's Almanac", p.36, Nayika Publishing. Retrieved from* https://www.azquotes.com/quote/101903
38. Attributed to Edgar Allen Poe. Retrieved from https://en.wikiquote.org/wiki/Edgar_Allan_Poe
39. Attributed to Carl Jung. Retrieved from https://www.azquotes.com/quote/1122653
40. Herbeck, B. 1990. Teenage Mutant Ninja Turtles. New Line Cinema. United States.
41. Pope, A. (2011) The Rape of the Lock and Other Major Writings. Penguin:London
42. Bulwer-Lyton, E. Year unknown. Retrieved from https://www.goodreads.com/quotes/531654-anger-ventilated-often-hurries-toward-forgiveness-and-concealed-often-hardens
43. Code of Hammurabi. Babylonian rule. Year unknown. Retrieved from https://en.wikipedia.org/wiki/Code_of_Hammurabi
44. Leviticus 24:19-21, King James Version.
45. Exodus 21:24, King James Version.
46. Deuteronomy 19:16-21. King James Version.
47. Matthew 5:38-42, King James Version.

48. Luther King, M. 1958, "Stride Toward Freedom: The Montgomery Story". Page 213, Harper & Row, New York
49. Japanese proverb. Griffiths, W. 1876, The Mikado's Empire, Book I: History of Japan From 660 B.C. to 1872 A.D., Book II: Personal Experiences, Observations, and Studies in Japan: 1870-1874 (Late of the Imperial University of Tokio, Japan), Chapter XIV: Japanese Proverbs, Start Page 504, Quote Page 511, Harper & Brothers Publishers, New York.
50. *Aurelius (2002). "Meditations: A New Translation", p.38, Modern Library. Retrieved from* https://www.azquotes.com/author/666-Marcus_Aurelius/tag/reputation
51. The Simpsons, Groening, M., Brooks, J. L., Simon, S., Clausen, A., Castellaneta, D., Kavner, J., Cartwright, N., ... Twentieth Century Fox Home Entertainment, Inc.,. (2007). *The Simpsons*. A Tale of Two Springfields.
52. The Simpsons, Groening, M., Brooks, J. L., Simon, S., Clausen, A., Castellaneta, D., Kavner, J., Cartwright, N., ... Twentieth Century Fox Home Entertainment, Inc.,. (2007). *The Simpsons*. Homer and Apu.
53. Seneca, L. A., & L'Estrange, R. (1882). *Seneca's morals: Of a happy life, benefits, anger and clemency*. Chicago: Cornelius H. Shaver.
54. John Locke, *The Works of John Locke in Nine Volumes,* (London: Rivington, 1824 12th ed.). Vol. 2. https://oll.libertyfund.org/titles/762. Retrieved from https://oll.libertyfund.org/titles/locke-the-works-vol-2-an-essay-concerning-human-understanding-part-2-and-other-writings/simple
55. Fennell, A, B. Benau, E, M. Atchley, R, A. 2016. A single session of meditation reduces physiological indices of anger in both experienced and novice meditators. Conscious Cognition. 40:54-66.
56. Sheldon, W. 1897 April, Ethical Addresses, Series 4, Number 4, What To Believe: An Ethical Creed. (Lecturer of the Ethical Society of St. Louis), Start Page 57, Quote Page 61, S. Burns Weston, Philadelphia, Pennsylvania. Retrieved from https://quoteinvestigator.com/2017/03/11/superior/#note-15653-1

57. Sun Tzu (2009). The Art of War. Boston: Shambhala.
58. Lao Tzu, Tao Te Ching Chapter 17 (1963) Penguin, London
59. *Albert Camus (1963). "Carnets: 1935-1942". Retrieved from* https://www.azquotes.com/quote/46606
60. Nietzsche, F. W., & Kaufmann, W. (1995). *Thus spoke Zarathustra: A book for all and none*. New York: Modern Library.
61. Suzuki, S., & Dixon, T. (2010). *Zen mind, beginner's mind*. P. 49 Boston: Shambhala.
62. John Locke Some Thoughts Concerning Education *(1 ed.). London:* A.and J. Churchill at the Black Swan in Paternoster-row. 1693. Retrieved 28 July 2016 – via Internet Archive.
63. Dickens, C., & Stone, M. (1974). *Our mutual friend*. London: Oxford University Press.
64. Confucius. (1979). The analects (Lun yü). Harmondsworth ; New York :Penguin Books,

CHAPTER 14 A FINAL MESSAGE

1. Lao Tzu, Tao Te Ching Chapter 33 (1963) Penguin, London
2. Csikszentmihalyi, M. 'Flow: The classic work on how to achieve happiness' Page 227. Ryder: The Random House Group
3. Attributed to Confucius. Retrieved from https://www.azquotes.com/quote/62138
4. Suzuki, S., & Dixon, T. (2010). *Zen mind, beginner's mind*. Boston: Shambhala.
5. Nietzsche, F. W., Hollingdale, R. J., & Tanner, M. (1990). *Beyond good and evil: Prelude to a philosophy of the future*. London, England: Penguin Books.
6. Laertius, D. Year unknown. Retrieved from http://penelope.uchicago.edu/Thayer/E/Roman/Texts/Diogenes_Laertius/Lives_of_the_Eminent_Philosophers/7/Chrysippus*.html
7. Robbins, A. Retrieved from https://www.tonyrobbins.com/

mind-meaning/what-drives-your-decisions/

8. Burnap, G, W. (1802–1859), published in Burnap's *The Sphere and Duties of Woman: A Course of Lectures (1848)*, Lecture IV. Retrieved from https://en.wikipedia.org/wiki/Alexander_Chalmers#cite_note-1
9. Branagh, K., Weitz, C., Kinberg, S., Shearmur, A., Barron, D., James, L., Blanchett, C., ... Buena Vista Home Entertainment (Firm),. (2015). *Cinderella.*
10. Attributed to Johann Wolfgang von Goethe. Retrieved from https://www.goodreads.com/quotes/21696-to-think-is-easy-to-act-is-hard-but-the
11. Carroll, L., Haughton, H., & Carroll, L. (2009). *Alice's adventures in Wonderland ; and, Through the looking-glass and What Alice found there*. New York: Penguin Classics.
12. Ziskin, L., Bryce, I., Koepp, D., Raimi, S., Maguire, T., Dafoe, W., Dunst, K., ... Columbia TriStar Home Entertainment (Firm),. (2002). *Spider-Man.*
13. Shakespeare, W., & Orgel, S. (1999). *King Lear*. New York, Act 3, Scene 4. N.Y: Penguin Books.
14. Lao Tzu, Tao Te Ching Chapter 48 (1963) Penguin, London
15. Alexander Pope, An Essay on Man in 'The Rape of the Lock and Other Major Writings (2011), Line 95, Page 100
16. Csikszentmihalyi, M. 'Flow: The classic work on how to achieve happiness' Page 226. Ryder: The Random House Group
17. Guggenheim, R., Arnold, B., Lasseter, J., Whedon, J., Hanks, T., Allen, T., Gordon, R., ... Image Entertainment (Firm). (2000). *Toy story*. Burbank, Calif: Disney/Pixar.
18. Hemingway, E. 1961. *New York Journal-American" Newspaper. Retrieved from* https://www.azquotes.com/quote/129408

Did you enjoy #Life?

As a first time author book reviews are vital for future success. I would hugely appreciate it if you would log back on to Amazon and give it an honest review. I will be reading them and making sure that my next book benefits from this collective wisdom.

Thanks!

Jym Brown

To be among the first to receive special offers like free chapters of upcoming books, blog posts and more, sign up to Jym Brown's mailing list:

www.jymbrown.co.uk

JYM BROWN

Jym Brown is a Lecturer, Writer and Public Speaker. He is a PhD researcher in Philosophy and Psychology and author of the upcoming title 'Clever Enough to be Stupid'. He is passionate about helping people to think differently and question the status quo for the benefit of society.

Printed in Great Britain
by Amazon

16783661R00217